W9-BWH-664

DONALD TRUMP AND
THE NEW AMERICAN POPULISM vs. THE OLD ORDER

SWAMP WARS

JEFFREY LORD

BOMBARDIER
BOOKS

A BOMBARDIER BOOKS BOOK
An Imprint of Post Hill Press
ISBN: 978-1-64293-018-4
ISBN (eBook): 978-1-64293-019-1

Swamp Wars:
Donald Trump and the New American Populism vs. The Old Order
© 2019 by Jeffrey Lord
All Rights Reserved

Post Hill Press, LLC
New York • Nashville
posthillpress.com

Published in the United States of America

In memory of my mother,
Kathleen Rose Jackson Lord. Whose love, energy,
and intelligence was and always will be an inspiration to her son.

CONTENTS

IT'S WAR: THE SWAMP VS. AMERICA

"My nomination was, as I have said, merely one battleground in a long-running war for control of our legal culture, which, in turn, was part of a larger war for control of our general culture."

—Robert Bork in
The Tempting of America:
The Political Seduction of the Law

It's war.

A Swamp War.

Swamp Wars are bitter and increasingly savage conflicts waged by an elitist Old Order for the cultural control—not simply the political control—of America. They have been appearing on occasion since the 1980s. But the pace at which Swamp Wars now regularly explode into public view has rapidly accelerated—and their size, scope, and intensity have increased.

The major Swamp War of today is the titanic clash over President Donald Trump. It began as a covert attempt by corrupt Old Order bureaucrats in the FBI, the CIA, and the Department of Justice to thwart the election of the dreaded politically incorrect Washington outsider by doing two things. First, putting in the fix at the FBI to block prosecution of Hillary Clinton for her misuse of classified information—using a private server to house her government emails—while Clinton herself was defying a congressional subpoena that demanded she preserve them. The Bureau's pro-Hillary agents—including the viscerally anti-Trump FBI Director James Comey—made a point of changing the language describing Clinton's actions from the prosacutable standard of "grossly negligent" to "extremely careless." Second, the bureaucrats artfully manipulated a Clinton-campaign-funded "dossier" on Trump compiled by an ex-British spy to get a Foreign Intelligence Surveillance Act

(FISA) warrant authorizing surveillance of the Trump campaign. In essence, they were using the U.S. government first to spy on Trump—and then to frame him.

Eventually, the mainstream media joined in the attack on Trump. After the election, Harvard's Shorenstein Center on Media, Politics and Public Policy released a study of the media coverage in the 2016 campaign, with Thomas E. Patterson, the Bradlee Professor of Government and the Press at Harvard saying of Trump: "His coverage was negative from the start [of the general election] and never came close to entering positive territory. During his best weeks, the coverage ran 2-to-1 negative over positive. In his worst weeks, the ratio was more than 10-to-1."

When Trump was elected anyway (shocking Old Order insiders), the object of this Old Order Swamp War was then redefined as "The Resistance." Resisting what? At a minimum, what was being resisted was the Trump agenda. At a maximum? The real goal of The Resistance in its anti-Trump Swamp War was a bureaucratic coup d'état using a "special counsel" and federal prosecutors whose real goal—again aided and abetted in various media quarters—was to remove the new duly-elected President Trump from the White House altogether.

Indeed, as I write this, a forty-page sentencing memorandum filed by federal prosecutors from the U.S. Attorney's Office for the Southern District of New York is recommending a "substantial term of imprisonment" for Trump's ex-lawyer Michael Cohen. No observer has missed the point that the filing indicates that there is a move afoot to indict the president himself for campaign finance violations because of "hush money" paid to silence two women who claimed to have had affairs with Trump, alleged affairs that happened well before he was president. Interestingly, the news accounts ignored a recent story that the U.S. Congress had been operating a taxpayer-funded secret slush fund that had paid out $17 million over the years from 1997 to 2017 to silence news of over 260 settlements that were paid out by the slush fund on charges that included sexual harassment. This is a stark difference from the accusations against Trump, which involve what the president himself has described as a "private transaction." The speculation about Trump payments inadvertently backfired, opening members of Congress to far more serious charges of using taxpayer dollars to silence victims. Not to mention, the media also ignored the fact that no less than the Barack Obama presidential campaign of 2008 was fined $375,000 for a violation of campaign finance laws.

Nonetheless, as expected, the news fueled the worst-kept secret in the Swamp—the desire of a number of House Democrats to impeach the president.

The reason for the escalation from the occasional skirmish of years gone by to today's constant explosions of full-blown Swamp Wars, not to mention the headlining Swamp War targeting the Trump presidency, is the iron-fisted, decidedly authoritarian Old Order's obsession with demanding complete obedience of and submission to Old Order orthodoxy. An obedience and a submission that not coincidentally preserves Old Order power and privilege as this group exerts its cultural and political control over the entire country. Anyone—*anyone*—who is seen as standing in the way of Old Order power and privilege, not to mention violating any Old Order sacrament or doctrine, must, in one fashion or another, have his or her reputation damaged, if not having an entire career or a business—or a presidency—destroyed.

Arguably the first Swamp War was the 1987 Senate confirmation battle over President Ronald Reagan's Supreme Court nominee Robert Bork. As a young White House associate political director at the time, I saw close up how the first Swamp War worked. No sooner had President Reagan stepped away from the podium where he announced the nomination than Bork was under assault.

In the ferocious, unprecedented campaign that was suddenly launched against Bork—which eventually acquired the descriptive term "borking"—Massachusetts senator Ted Kennedy began with a now infamous speech on the Senate floor conjuring the imagined horrors of "Robert Bork's America" that summoned wildly false images of racism, sexism, and worse. For the first time in history, there was a television commercial attacking a Supreme Court nominee, replete with narration by the immediately recognizable voice of Hollywood A-list actor Gregory Peck. In declaring war on the Bork nomination, the Old Order of the day effectively instigated the first Swamp War.

In his book *The Tempting of America: The Political Seduction of the Law*, Bork describes his opponents as the "intellectual or knowledge class" and adds:

> *The public campaign, designed to influence senators through pub-*
> *lic opinion polls, consisted of systematic distortion of my academic*
> *writings and my judicial record and, it must be said, employed*
> *racial and gender politics of a most pernicious variety. The ferocity*
> *of the attack, the ideological stance of the assailants, and the tactics*
> *they used all showed that the opposition knew they were fighting*

*over more than one judge. They were fighting for control of the
legal culture....*

*My nomination was...merely one battleground in a
long-running war for control of our legal culture, which, in
turn, was part of a larger war for control of our general culture.*

Bork was right. A Swamp War is exactly about "a larger war for control of our general culture" and what he also calls "a class struggle about social and political values." Since that first Swamp War in 1987, Swamp Wars have become a standard, weaponized feature of the Old Order elites and what Bork calls the "authoritarian character of that movement." And authoritarian it is.

Two other Supreme Court nominations that followed Reagan's nomination of Robert Bork—George H. W. Bush's nomination of Clarence Thomas and Donald Trump's nomination of Brett Kavanaugh—were savaged in their confirmation battles. In the case of Justice Thomas, twenty-five years after his showdown with Anita Hill and the Washington liberal establishment, Hollywood Swamp Warriors in the form of HBO were cranking out a movie to continue smearing Thomas in the culture. Why? Thomas's real offense is that he is both a conservative and a black man. He defied the Old Order sacraments by walking off the Old Order plantation that demands in the most racist of fashions that African Americans must be liberals and toe the Old Order line on cultural, legal, and political issues. Thomas refuses. So, a movie is needed to remind future generations of his alleged cultural sins.

Let it not be forgotten that in his statement to the Senate Judiciary Committee, Thomas specifically called out the Old Order, saying (emphasis mine):

> "And from my standpoint as a black American, *as far as I'm
> concerned, it is a high-tech lynching for uppity blacks who in
> any way deign to think for themselves, to do for themselves, to
> have different ideas, and* it is a message that unless you kow-
> tow to an old order, this is what will happen to you. You will
> be lynched, destroyed, caricatured by a committee of the
> U.S. Senate, rather than hung from a tree."

A measure of the depth of the Old Order obsession with cultural and political control could be seen in the hearings surrounding the Senate confirmation of Trump nominee Judge Brett Kavanaugh for the Supreme Court—a full twenty-five years after the Thomas Swamp War. With the 2018 midterm election only weeks away, Old Order Senate Democrats and the left-wing interest groups that control them had to know that televised hearings that featured shouting protestors disrupting the hearings when not literally storming both the Capitol and Supreme Court buildings or shrieking from the Senate gallery were not an election asset for those Senate Democrats up for re-election. So too did Senate Democrats on the Judiciary Committee have to realize that their own disrupting of the once orderly committee proceedings and badgering of committee chairman Senator Charles Grassley was not helpful to their larger cause. The televised images were anything but flattering.

They had to know as well that Kavanaugh would fight back. Just as Clarence Thomas had fought back in riveting, scathing testimony, so too did Kavanaugh. In the transcript provided by *Time* magazine, Kavanaugh said this:

> *"This confirmation process has become a national disgrace. The constitution gives the Senate an important role in the confirmation process, but you have replaced advice and consent with search and destroy.*
>
> *"Since my nomination in July there's been a frenzy on the left to come up with something, anything to block my confirmation. Shortly after I was nominated, the Democratic Senate leader said he would, quote, 'oppose me with everything he's got.' A Democratic Senator on this committee publicly referred to me as 'evil.' Evil. Think about that word. And said that those who supported me were, quote, 'complicit in evil.' Another Democratic senator on this committee said, quote, 'Judge Kavanaugh is your worst nightmare.' A former head of the Democratic National Committee said, quote, 'Judge Kavanaugh will threaten the lives of millions of Americans for decades to come.'*
>
> *I understand the passions of the moment, but I would say to those senators: Your words have meaning. Millions of Americans listen carefully to you, given comments like those, is it any surprise that people have been willing to do anything, to make any physical threat against my family, to send any violent*

email to my wife, to make any kind of allegation against me, and against my friends, to blow me up and take me down.

You sowed the wind for decades to come. I fear that the whole country will reap the whirlwind.

The behavior of several of the Democratic members of this committee at my hearing a few weeks ago was an embarrassment, but at least it was a good old-fashioned attempt at Borking.

Those efforts didn't work. When I did at least okay enough at the hearings that it looked like I might actually get confirmed a new tactic was needed.

Some of you were lying in wait and had it ready."

When the hearing was finally finished, even South Carolina Republican senator Lindsey Graham, a usually calm and decided Senate bipartisan institutionalist, angrily pushed back against what he was seeing, snapping to his Democratic colleagues as he spoke to Kavanaugh, the latter sitting at the witness table:

"What you want to do is destroy this guy's life, hold this seat open and hope you win in 2020. You've said that, not me. This is the most unethical sham since I've been in politics. Boy, y'all want power. I hope you never get it. I hope the American people can see through this sham. God, I hate to say it, because these have been my friends. But let me tell you, when it comes to this, you're looking for a fair process? You came to the wrong town at the wrong time, my friend."

And there it was. Graham's words echoed the meaning of Bork's point thirty-one years earlier that this Swamp War was really about "fighting over more than one judge." Said Graham: "Boy, y'all want power." Power is indeed exactly what Swamp Wars are all about.

Senate Democrats had to have known that their conduct combined with that of the intemperate protestors would not help them, but they acted as they did anyway, almost as if they simply could not help themselves. Indeed, Senate Republican Leader Mitch McConnell smiled broadly in the aftermath of the hearings, saying: "It's been a great political gift for us....I want to thank the mob, because they've done the one thing we were having trouble doing, which was energizing our base." Sure enough, when the election dust had settled, Republicans had broken the pattern of a presidential party's losing Senate seats in a first midterm election, with four incumbent Democrats losing their re-election bids and Trump's Republicans maintaining their hold on the Senate. When the Senate convened in 2019, Lindsey Graham, who, post-Kavanaugh hearings, is the toast of conservative media for fighting back in the Kavanaugh Swamp War, was the new chairman of the Senate Judiciary Committee.

But Swamp Wars target more than the president and Supreme Court nominees.

Earlier in 2018 there was a Swamp War over Scott Pruitt, the conservative Oklahoma attorney general turned head of the Trump Environmental Protection Agency. Other than abortion, left-wing environmentalism is perhaps the most sacred of Old Order sacraments. Pruitt was drummed out of his job over charges that seemingly had nothing to do with his conservative views on the environment, including flying first class, leasing a town house from a lobbyist, taking a trip abroad, and more. Yet this in reality had everything to do with both Pruitt's conservative views on the environment and his role in executing the Trump conservative environmental agenda. It was Pruitt who used his post as EPA administrator to advise Trump to pull the United States out of the Paris Agreement on climate change. He was instantly seen as a serious threat to the Old Order way of doing business at the EPA—and so a Swamp War was declared, with the use of anything and everything in Pruitt's life being fair game to take him out.

As if to prove the point, Pruitt's resignation brought the news that the EPA was now going to be run by one Andrew Wheeler—then the EPA deputy administrator and, of course, a Trump appointee. Reported the website *The Daily Caller*: "Environmental Protection Agency (EPA) acting administrator Andrew Wheeler has not finished a day as head of the agency before getting attacked for his stance on climate change and history as a coal lobbyist."

But of course. Behold the Old Order at work.

In November 2018, President Trump officially nominated Wheeler for the job as EPA administrator. In a blink, the Swamp War on Wheeler was back in the news, with the Sierra Club's executive director declaring: "Putting a coal lobbyist like Andrew Wheeler in charge of the EPA is like giving a thief the keys to a bank vault." The Swamp War over Wheeler continues.

Conservative media has long been a favorite target of Old Order Swamp Warriors. The goal always is to either shut down an entire network—Fox News specifically—or get various of its conservative hosts off television. Targets in these Swamp Wars have included Fox stars Glenn Beck, Bill O'Reilly, Lou Dobbs, Tucker Carlson, Sean Hannity, and Laura Ingraham. Not to mention that Steve Doocy and Brian Kilmeade, hosts of Fox's morning show *Fox & Friends*, have also been targeted. In Carlson's case, the self-described "anti-fascist" left-wing group Antifa (they are, in fact, seriously fascist, masking their faces Ku Klux Klan-style to boot) showed up outside of the Carlson family home, yelling, pounding on the front door, and spray-painting on the driveway. A terrified Mrs. Carlson, home alone, hid in the pantry to call police.

Conservative talk radio stars have long been subjected to Swamp Wars, as with the Fox hosts. Rush Limbaugh has been repeatedly targeted in attempts to intimidate his sponsors and get him taken off the air. Various conservative journalists such as Kevin Williamson, briefly of *The Atlantic*, Pat Buchanan of MSNBC, and conservative media stars like Monica Crowley, Ann Coulter and Ben Shapiro have all been subjected to attacks from Old Order elites designed to silence them, with Crowley being targeted in a successful political hit job contrived to keep her out of the Trump White House as a deputy national security advisor. And oh yes—this list includes yours truly, with a firing from CNN for mocking and holding out for contempt and condemnation the documented anti-Semitism of the far-left organization Media Matters for America. More on this shortly.

There are others in the media decidedly not seen as conservatives who have been taken out by a Swamp War, including NBC's Megyn Kelly and Fox's Juan Williams when he was at NPR. At the end of 2018, a Swamp War claimed the job of NPR film critic David Edelstein. All three had, in one form or another, violated Old Order doctrine and sacraments on, respectively, race, radical Islam, and sex. Former NBC anchor Tom Brokaw had the audacity to say that "Hispanics should work harder at assimilation" - assimilation in a colorblind America once a pillar of the American civil rights movement, not to mention the Declaration of Independence and its "self-evident" truth that "all men are created equal." The Old Order outcry was immediate, with Brokaw forced to apologize and NBC News issuing a politically correct one-sentence scolding that read: "Tom's comments were inaccurate and inappropriate and we're glad he apologized." Comedian Kevin Hart was forced to step down from hosting the 2019 Oscars because of tweets and remarks about gays made years earlier. As this is written, *The New York Times* reports that comedian and TV host Ellen DeGeneres, whom the paper described as "one of the most prominent gay celebrities working today" had invited Hart on her show and "offered a lengthy defense of Hart and said that she called someone at the Academy of Motion Picture Arts and Sciences to request that he be reinstated as host."

Megyn Kelly was dismissed abruptly from NBC for asking if a Halloween costume featuring blackface was racist. Notably, comedians Jimmy Kimmel and Jimmy Fallon, late-night hosts at, respectively, ABC and NBC, actually have done routines in blackface. Kimmel dressed up in blackface a few years back to impersonate NBA star Karl Malone, while Fallon did his bit to imitate comedian and actor Chris Rock. In Fallon's case, it was done at the 2016 Golden Globes. Unlike Kelly, both Kimmel and Fallon still have their jobs, with Fallon working for the very same network as Kelly had—NBC. Perhaps un-coincidentally, unlike Kelly, neither had previously been a Fox News host.

Pat Buchanan, the conservative ex-aide to Presidents Nixon and Reagan and two-time presidential candidate who had returned to journalism as a columnist, was also, for ten years, a commentator on MSNBC.

Buchanan's offense was writing a book titled *Suicide of a Superpower: Will America Survive to 2025?* In it he discussed race (in a chapter titled "The End of White America") and religion (in a chapter titled "The Death of Christian America"). MSNBC's president, Phil Griffin, said he fired Buchanan in 2012 because: "The ideas he put forth aren't really appropriate for national dialogue, much less the dialogue on MSNBC." I certainly don't agree with Buchanan's take on race, but most assuredly it is ironic to hear Griffin's sentiment when it was he who hired the notoriously racist and anti-Semitic Al Sharpton, giving Sharpton his own MSNBC show.

Ben Shapiro, the editor-in-chief of the website *The Daily Wire*, has his own list. Shapiro, who has been banned from speaking on various college campuses in various Swamp Wars, wrote a *National Review* column on the Swamp War that focused on the firing of Kevin Williamson, the libertarian-leaning Never Trump-movement writer who left the conservative *National Review* for the left-leaning *Atlantic,* only to be fired three days after his start and after writing a solitary column. The Williamson offense was not the column but a four-year-old tweet on abortion and capital punishment—a violation of Old Order sacraments. The headline and subhead of Shapiro's *National Review* column were:

Kevin Williamson and the Twitter Mob

The Left is narrowing the range of acceptable discourse and persons, and there will be a backlash.

The column begins:

Kevin Williamson. Sam Harris. Bret Weinstein. Bari Weiss. Dave Rubin. Jason Riley. Heather Mac Donald. Jordan Peterson. Ayaan Hirsi Ali.

Welcome to the coalition of unpersons.

The people above don't have much in common. They disagree on matters large and small. Ali is a militant atheist; Williamson is a religious Christian. Peterson focuses on the metaphysical import of myths; Harris focuses on verifiable science. Rubin is a gay Jew; Riley is black. Mac Donald is a supporter of stronger policing; Weinstein was a supporter of Occupy Wall Street.

But there is one thing that everyone on this list has in common: We've all been unpersoned by the Left. And that Left is creeping quietly into the mainstream.

What's going on here? The answer was supplied by the conservative Kevin Williamson, who, as he was being fired from the liberal *Atlantic* after a matter of days, reminded his editor at *The Atlantic*, Jeffrey Goldberg, that the late Christopher Hitchens, an *Atlantic* contributor, was often given to writing things that gave offense. In Hitchens's case, this included what Williamson reminded Goldberg were "harshly critical views of Islam," a description of the Jewish scriptures as "evil and mad," and Hitchens's also being a purveyor of "shameful vitriol" about Mother Teresa. Hitchens was a frequent offender.

The response from Goldberg was telling. Said he: "Yes. But Hitchens was in the family. You are not."

And right there, in admission of the junior high school element in all this, is the core issue. Americans who are conservatives, not to mention Trump supporters, or who run afoul of Old Order sacraments, are targeted for Swamp Wars because they are not "in the family" of elites who fervently believe it is their God-given right to run America and the world beyond.

As if to illustrate the point again, at the end of November 2018, *The Daily Caller* ran a story, headlined Exclusive: "Google Employees Debated Burying Conservative Media in Search."

The story focuses on left-wing Google employees (but I repeat myself), stunned by the Trump election and plotting ways to "bury conservative media outlets in the company's search function." Leaked documents also revealed that Google employees were specifically scheming after the 2016 election as to how to shut down the conservative, pro-Trump website *Breitbart*. Which is to say, this was nothing more than a Swamp War, high-tech version.

There are three keys to understanding the American Old Order that runs these Swamp Wars. They are best explained by answering three questions:

1. Who is the Old Order? The Old Order is a club of self-selected elitists who see themselves as intellectually and decidedly morally superior to their fellow Americans—particularly, today, Donald Trump and Trump-supporting Americans. In many ways the Old Order and the targets it chooses to attack in a Swamp War resemble the cliques of junior high school. There is the "in" crowd—the "cool kids," who are popular, attractive, the star athletes, and occasionally, although not always, wealthy and stylish dressers with outgoing personalities. Then there are their opposites, the unfashionable outsiders in junior high who are shy, socially awkward, and not as attractive—the geeks, the nerds, the un-athletic, and the unfashionably dressed, if exasperatingly smart, who aren't invited to sit with the "in" group at lunch in the school cafeteria and who don't get invited to the popular girls' slumber parties. Hillary Clinton would famously label the latter group of Americans in 2016 as a "basket of deplorables" who are "irredeemable." And without doubt, as in junior high school, today's Old Order is all about group virtue signaling. A Swamp War is all about them—with Old Order Swamp Warriors virtue signaling like crazy to their peers inside the Old Order that yes, in the matter of X or Y or Z—a Kavanaugh confirmation or a Trump story or whatever—the people enforcing Old Order conformity share the same narrative. They are, goes the virtue-signaling message, all on the

same page when it comes to protecting whatever sacrament of Old Order doctrine that they perceive as under threat. Really. (The day before he was sworn in as the new Republican senator from Utah, Mitt Romney penned an Op-Ed for the anti-Trump *Washington Post* that attacked the President's character and more. The article was a classic of Old Order virtue signaling to the Swamp.)

2. Where is the Old Order located? While the Swamp—Washington, D.C.—most assuredly is the Old Order capital, it would be a mistake—a huge mistake—to not understand that the Swamp and the Old Order it defends are hardly geographically limited to "inside the Beltway"—the latter being the sixty-four-mile ribbon of concrete surrounding Washington that is Interstate 495, known formally as the Capital Beltway. The Swamp has spread far beyond what Ronald Reagan identified in 1964 as "a little intellectual elite in a far-distant capital [that think they] can plan our lives for us better than we can plan them ourselves."

   In fact, the American Old Order of today rules from Swamp outposts across the country and indeed around the world, not unlike the British Empire once governed its global assets through, as the *Encyclopedia Britannica* describes it, "a worldwide system of dependencies—colonies, protectorates, and other territories." Old Order Swamp outposts in the twenty-first century are not limited to physical locations like the geography of the nation's capital. They include as well more ethereal entities—academia, the media, the judiciary and legal communities, swaths of the Republican and Democratic parties, professional sports, corporations, religion, lobbyists, political consultants, Hollywood, Silicon Valley, European allies, and oh so many more. Twitter and Facebook, with their repeated banning of conservatives and Trump supporters, along with Google and its employees, exploring rigging their search engines against conservative media outlets, have become Swamps unto themselves.

3. How does the Old Order work? Although the Old Order is seemingly on the up-and-up, there is in reality always an Old Order agenda. That agenda is first and foremost about power, privilege, and the protection of Old Order sacraments as diverse as abortion and the environment, not to mention systemic, perpetual racism. In its own

fashion, the Old Order operates not unlike Bendini, Lambert and Locke, the fictional law firm that is the centerpiece of John Grisham's famous novel *The Firm* and the Tom Cruise movie of the book. On the surface all appears on the up-and-up. In fact, the firm is run by the Mafia. Once its young, eager lawyers, who are enticed into joining with all kinds of financial and social incentives, discover whom they are actually working for and try to leave, their mob bosses kill them off.

In the case of the Old Order? First its members invite you in and lavish upon you all manner of goodies: social prestige, money, introductions to all the "right" people. Once you are in and become uneasy with the agenda—illegal immigration and open borders, "social justice," unlimited taxing and spending, systemic racism, abortion, radical environmentalism, bad trade deals, allies who don't pay their financial obligations, courts who legislate from the bench, and more—it is impossible to leave without being flagged as some sort of social or political undesirable. You are, as it were, politically, socially, and possibly financially dead, courtesy of a Swamp War.

As for the "New Populism"? It is without doubt a descendant of Reagan conservatism and Reagan's description of the rebellion from average Americans against "a little intellectual elite in a far-distant capital [that think they] can plan our lives for us better than we can plan them ourselves." That "little intellectual elite" has spread far beyond the Swamp's capital of Washington, and its contempt for the average Americans whose lives these elites seek to control through everything from Supreme Court decisions to globalism has finally generated an enormous backlash in the person of Donald Trump.

It is impossible to look at these Swamp Wars and not notice, as Judge Bork noted years ago, their effect on the larger culture—in schools, Hollywood, workplaces, and internet spaces from Facebook to Twitter to Google and more. Examples:

- It cost the University of California at Berkeley $600,000 just to protect Ben Shapiro when he was invited to give a speech. In 2019, young conservative activist Hayden Williams, also at Berkeley, was abruptly punched in the face merely for manning a table to recruit students for Turning Point USA. I myself was assigned four security guards when

I was invited to appear at my alma mater, Franklin and Marshall College in Lancaster, Pennsylvania. The subject? My opposition to a proposed college speech code. From one college campus after another pour forth stories of speakers, professors, and students being banned, fired, silenced, or even physically assaulted because they have, in some fashion, violated this or that Old Order sacrament.

- In Hollywood, Trump-supporting actor James Woods, a two-time nominee for an Academy Award, got this note from his politically liberal agent: "It's the 4th of July and I'm feeling patriotic. I don't want to represent you anymore. I mean I can go on a rant but you know what I'd say."
- In 2008, Brendan Eich, co-founder of the tech company Mozilla, was forced into resigning because he had contributed $1,000 to Proposition 8, a proposition on California ballots that would have banned gay marriage.
- In 2017, Google software engineer James Damore was fired after writing a memo calling for ideological diversity at the tech giant and arguing that the Google "diversity" policy was in reality discriminating against employees who were not women or people of color.
- In 2016, there were multiple stories of employees losing their jobs at various places around the country, like tech companies, local government agencies, and banks, because they were known to be Trump supporters.

As noted earlier, there have been continual efforts to take down Fox News hosts. But something has happened along the way. While there was success early on in getting first Glenn Beck and later Bill O'Reilly off Fox, eventually the Fox audience caught on to the game. When the Swamp War mob came for Laura Ingraham in 2018 after she had tweeted about the college rejections of Parkland shooting survivor David Hogg—to which Hogg himself had drawn attention and then launched a bid to get her fired—Ingraham's ratings went up. In spite of yet another Media Matters for America campaign to take Sean Hannity off the air, Hannity's ratings too went up. Hannity has consistently been at the very top of cable ratings one month after another ever since.

In discussing this in an interview posted on the website *The Inquisitr, The Hill* media reporter Joe Concha said of the response to Ingraham: "Fox News audiences, and I've been told this by the people at the highest levels at other networks, are the most loyal in television. It's an us-versus-them mentality that is bigger than any one host. And in this case, they weren't got [sic] to sit by and watch another host they like go down over something so silly."

When another Swamp War threatened to take Rush Limbaugh off the air in 2012, his audience also rallied, and *Mediaite* reported Limbaugh noting that his ratings spiked anywhere from 10 to 60 percent.

It is very safe to say that millions of Americans have had enough of Swamp Wars and the Old Order that launches them—and those millions are fighting back. Whether famous or unknown, Americans are fighting back against the iron-fisted, authoritarian-style control over their lives that is central to the Old Order agenda and its endless Swamp Wars.

Exactly as Ben Shapiro predicted in the headline of his piece on the targeting of Kevin Williamson, there has been a backlash to the constant thuggery of authoritarianism in both public and private life—and that fighting back has, most notably of all, taken the form of the election of Donald Trump.

In January 2016, as Old Order journalists were beginning to realize to their astonishment that Donald Trump might actually be able to win at least a few primaries, this headline appeared in *The Washington Post*: "Why Trump may be winning the war on 'political correctness.'"

Among other things, the story, by reporters Karen Tumulty and Jenna Johnson, says:

> *Cathy Cuthbertson once worked at what might be thought of as a command post of political correctness—the campus of a prestigious liberal arts college in Ohio.*
>
> *"You know, I couldn't say 'Merry Christmas.' And when we wrote things, we couldn't even say 'he' or 'she,' because we had transgender. People of color. I mean, we had to watch every word that came out of our mouth, because we were afraid of offending someone, but nobody's afraid of offending me," the former administrator said.*
>
> *All of which helps explain why the 63-year-old grandmother showed up at a recent Donald Trump rally in Hilton Head Island, S.C., where she moved when she retired a year ago.*
>
> *The Republican front-runner is "saying what a lot of Americans are thinking but are afraid to say because they don't think that it's politically correct," she said. "But we're tired of*

just standing back and letting everyone else dictate what we're supposed to think and do."

Donald Trump is the personification of the backlash to what Bork foresaw all the way back in 1987—an attempted authoritarian Old Order takeover of American culture and politics with Swamp Wars.

To my surprise, in 2017, I was about to find myself a target in my very own Swamp War—at CNN.

CHAPTER ONE

FIRED BY CNN

"We must, indeed, all hang together or, most assuredly, we shall all hang separately."

> —*attributed to Benjamin Franklin*
> *on the signing of the Declaration of*
> *Independence, July 1776*

"**I**ndefensible."

With that one word, as I wrote in *The American Spectator* at the time, CNN notified the media that I had been fired from my role as a CNN contributor. A contributor who had become well known for supporting Donald Trump.

The irony is that I was on CNN in the first place because of Donald Trump. On June 3, 2013, in my capacity as a contributing editor and columnist for *The American Spectator*, I had responded to a colleague's blog post that recommended ignoring Trump's latest thoughts on a possible presidential run. Trump had appeared on NBC's *Today Show*, making it plain in response to a question from host Matt Lauer that yes, in fact, he was thinking of running for president in 2016. My column was titled "Never Ignore Donald Trump." In it I quoted from a recent appearance Trump had made on *Fox & Friends* when he said: "People in this country are just desperate for leadership, so whether it's me—or, frankly, let it be somebody—but somebody has to come along and straighten out this country."

Said I in response: "Well...not just yes...but *hell* yes. Somebody, *somebody*...exactly as he says...most assuredly *does* have "to come along and straighten out this country." I concluded: "We use to have a saying in the Reagan White House: Let Reagan be Reagan. Donald Trump, like Ronald Reagan, is an American Original. Let Donald Trump be Donald Trump."

Trump saw the column and wrote me a kind note, and over time there were phone calls, personal meetings, and a growing belief on my part that in fact, not only could Trump indeed win the presidency but more importantly, for the sake of the country, he should.

Unbeknownst to me, after declaring his candidacy in 2015, and following a column I wrote titled "Yes, Trump Can Win," the new candidate sat down for back-to-back interviews with MSNBC's Katy Tur and CNN's Anderson Cooper.

Tur told him there were conservatives in the media who didn't like him. She cited Charles Krauthammer's calling Trump a "rodeo clown." Trump dismissed Krauthammer as "overrated" and more. Then Trump replied, "By the way, are you going to mention the ones who do like Trump? You don't do that, do you?" She didn't, instead going on to mention two more anti-Trump conservatives, *National Review*'s Jonah Goldberg and *Post* columnist and Fox commentator George Will.

When Trump was finished with his CNN interview with Anderson Cooper, while the subject of conservative media support had not arisen, it was still on the candidate's mind. As the story was relayed to me by a CNN staffer, the candidate said that CNN always followed his appearances with "Bush guys who hate me." He was promptly asked whom they could talk to in conservative media who liked him—and he named me.

Shortly afterward, a surprise certainly to me, I received a call from CNN. Then I started getting repeated calls from CNN. There was also a note from Trump himself recommending that if I were asked to go on Anderson Cooper's show, I should say yes. I thought that highly unlikely—and then in fact the call came in. That day I appeared on-air by phone with Brooke Baldwin and from a local PBS studio in Harrisburg, Pennsylvania, with Erin Burnett. The next night I was back in the Harrisburg studio to be on-air with Anderson Cooper. Some version of this went on for two weeks solid. Having been around the block with appearances over the years on Fox with Sean Hannity, Stuart Varney, and John Gibson, not to mention one memorable occasion in 2009 on CNN for what turned out to be Lou Dobbs's last CNN show, I was not a stranger to this media world.

But I was still surprised when, after two weeks of doing this every weeknight, I got an email from Rebecca Kutler of CNN—her responsibilities included CNN contributors—asking me if I would call her. I did. Would I join CNN as a contributor? I said yes.

Fast-forward to my receiving another call from Kutler. Firing me. She was clearly unhappy with her task. I liked and respected Rebecca Kutler enormously, and she regretted having to make the call, which just as clearly she had been instructed to make. The thought occurred to me that if it was ironic that a recommendation from Trump had landed me the job at CNN, it was perhaps inevitable that my defense of Trump would get me fired from CNN as the network lurched increasingly into becoming viscerally anti-Trump. The reason given for my abrupt dismissal? A retweet from a two-day-old column in *The American Spectator*. The title of the column was "Fascist Media Matters Moves to Silence Hannity," and it focused—as I had on occasion over several years—on the effort of the far left-wing Media Matters for America to bully advertisers into withdrawing sponsorship from shows with a conservative host. This time the target was Sean Hannity.

This was not the first time I had taken the group to task. MMFA was the brainchild of David Brock, ironically a one-time *American Spectator* reporter who had long since turned far left and was a close ally of Hillary Clinton. Brock, not unlike both Hillary and Bill Clinton, President Obama, and others on the left, was obsessed with the success of Fox News, conservative talk radio, and the resulting loss of the liberal media monopoly. He had even spent time writing a book trashing Fox, titled *The Fox Effect: How Roger Ailes Turned a Network Into a Propaganda Machine*. Indeed, Hillary Clinton herself has said that she helped to "start and support" Media Matters, and the group has taken money from left-wing billionaire George Soros.

Investigative reporter Sharyl Attkisson, who has worked variously for CBS News, PBS, and CNN, wrote in detail about Brock and Media Matters in her book *The Smear: How Shady Political Operatives and Fake News Control What You See, What You Think, and How You Vote*. Attkisson said Media Matters was central to what she bluntly labeled the far-left "smear machine." She was right.

Working with a like-minded leftist named Angelo Carusone, whose claim to fame was bullying advertisers of conservative media, Media Matters had moved from simply reporting its own version of the news into the business of targeting Fox, various talk radio hosts, and indeed any conservative on television or radio. All in a decidedly anti-free-press jihad designed to force conservatives off the air.

Their earlier targets included MSNBC's Don Imus, Fox's Glenn Beck, and CNN's Lou Dobbs, the latter a staunch on-air opponent of illegal immigration. In Dobbs's case, a 2012 investigation by *The Daily Caller* reported:

> *Lou Dobbs, then of CNN, was a frequent target.*
>
> *"As part of the Drop Dobbs campaign," explains one internal memo prepared for fundraising, "Media Matters produced and was prepared to run an advertisement against Ford Motor Company on Spanish Language stations in Houston, San Antonio, and other cities targeting its top selling product, pick-up trucks, in its top truck buying markets."*
>
> *Ford pulled its advertising from Dobbs's program before the television ad aired, but Media Matters kept up its efforts, working primarily with Alex Nogales of the National Hispanic Media Coalition, and with the League of United Latin American Citizens, the Mexican American Legal Defense and Educational Fund and other self-described civil rights groups.*
>
> *In November of 2009, Dobbs left CNN. "We got him fired," says one staffer flatly.*
>
> *"Certainly Media Matters deserves a lot of credit for the work they did," Nogales said in an interview. "They're very effective."*

These were campaigns designed to remove conservatives from the air by targeting their advertisers. As Rush Limbaugh, a Media Matters target himself, would say, "Advertisers are bullied and harassed into cancellation."

As it happened, in 2009, I had come across this situation without understanding the role of Media Matters. I had written a series of columns for the *Spectator* in which I revealed the alliance of several American religious denominations who had banded together as a group called So We Might See to petition the Federal Communications Commission (FCC) about supposed hate speech by Rush Limbaugh. As noted, also in their sights, among others, was CNN's Lou Dobbs, for his opposition to illegal immigration. This in turn had launched the aforementioned Drop Dobbs campaign directed at CNN.

I investigated and found that there were seven churches involved—including my own United Church of Christ, the UCC. To my astonishment, the UCC was leading this decidedly anti-free-speech, anti-freedom-of-the-press movement. At the time I was both president of my own UCC church council and a director on the UCC's Penn Central Conference board of directors, the board overseeing hundreds of UCC churches in Central Pennsylvania.

I well knew the history of my own UCC denomination, which had long ago been formed when my family's Congregationalist faith, the descendant faith of the Pilgrims, joined with the Evangelical and Reformed Church in 1957. The UCC emerged from a Uniting General Synod held in Cleveland, with my mother present as a delegate. As I knew full well, the UCC boasted correctly of one Congregationalist minister from the 1600s—Thomas Hooker—who, in 1638, delivered a sermon in Hartford, Connecticut, that inspired the Fundamental Orders of Connecticut. As the UCC likes to correctly boast, "Hooker is regarded by many as the father of democracy in America, for many of his ideas were embodied in the United States Constitution." Those ideas specifically included the principles of free speech and a free press, both later adopted in the First Amendment. Alas, the top leadership of the denomination had now led the national church into the morass of liberal politics, and, in what I saw as a repudiation of Thomas Hooker and the denomination's history of support for free speech and a free press, the UCC was leading this collection of faiths in a bid to shut down Rush Limbaugh and others. It was very disturbing.

Also involved in this anti-free-press movement of 2009 were the U.S. Catholic Conference of Bishops, the Islamic Society of North America, the United Methodists, the Presbyterian Church (USA), the Evangelical Lutheran Church in America, and the Christian Church (Disciples of Christ), plus "several other faith groups."

Particularly worrisome to me was that the UCC national leadership had had a private lunch with the Obama-appointed chairman of the FCC, Michael Copps. After that, the petitioning of the FCC by the So We Might See group of churches occurred. My columns were published in the *American Spectator*, an uproar ensued, and the group effectively collapsed as rank-and-file church members, fans of the targets, sharply protested. Lou Dobbs invited me to New York to be on his CNN show to discuss the episode. As he went on-air that night, to my astonishment, Dobbs opened his show by announcing he was quitting his decades-long career at CNN. Then I was ushered into the studio for my first on-air CNN chat. The subject: a free press and free speech.

Video of the show has been preserved on YouTube. Among other things, I spoke about a politically correct "virus" that was infecting the media as well as the government and other institutions in American life. The conversation included this:

> *Lord: You've got to be able to let people go out and write the movies they want, have the talk shows they want, say what they want, let people call in. That's what's important.*
>
> *Dobbs: You're speaking as though you think America is a free country.*
>
> *Lord: I like to think it is.*

I still like to think it is. But the America that has a free press and free speech is seriously under assault from the American Old Order, and it's worse in 2018 than it was in 2009. As I sat there on that CNN set with Lou Dobbs the night he quit CNN—in a CNN studio I have now been in many times as a CNN contributor—I did not yet understand the role of Media Matters. But I would.

In fact, it was not until the Stop Rush campaign in 2012—which Angelo Carusone masterminded—that my attention was drawn to what he and Media Matters were all about.

On top of their trademark bullying and rabidly vitriolic anti-free-press campaigns, the group had been repeatedly flagged for anti-Semitism, I learned through my research. Among other things, Media Matters had published an article titled "Israel Firsters?" The author was not a fan of Israeli prime minister Benjamin Netanyahu. Fair enough. There is a difference between legitimate criticism of a point of view and outright bigotry. But the term "Israel Firsters" is a serious red flag signaling anti-Semitism.

Among other things, "Israel Firster", as noted in the *Jerusalem Post* in a 2012 editorial, is a deliberate slur whose anti-Semitic roots "originated with Holocaust deniers." The slur is a favorite of the likes of infamous anti-Semitic Ku Klux Klansman David Duke, a notorious anti-Semite who proudly supported the far left's Occupy Wall Street (OWS) because, as Duke said on his website, of "Jewish racism that rules us all." Media Matters, like Duke, had gone to one extreme after another to defend Occupy Wall Street, even preparing a "Guide to the Smear Campaign Against Occupy Wall Street." It included repeated defenses of the OWS movement, going after every prominent conservative of the day who had dared to criticize it.

Commentary magazine investigated OWS, and its headline was "Occupy Wall Street Has an Anti-Semitism Problem."

For the unaware, *Commentary* describes itself in part as supporting "the future of the Jews, Judaism, and Jewish culture in Israel"—which is to say, the magazine has an excellent eye for anti-Semitism when it appears.

Among other things, *Commentary's* Abe Greenwald investigated OWS and reported that the "Jew-hatred among [OWS] protestors is diverse and unapologetic. It is, in fact, atmospheric." None of that kept Media Matters from staunchly and repeatedly defending OWS.

There was more.

As was revealed in a column that appeared in the *Jerusalem Post* by *Weekly Standard* editor Daniel Halper, Media Matters also went after the "Israel lobby"—another anti-Semitic term, targeting Democratic members of Congress—all of whom happened to be Jewish. Halper noted as well that the term "Israel Firster" was "popularized by white supremacists."

No less than renowned Harvard law professor Alan Dershowitz, a liberal Democrat and supporter of both the Clintons and President Obama, specifically noted that Media Matters had "crossed the line into anti-Semitism" and "bigotry" for its slurs against American Jews who were supporters of Israel. Dershowitz, who is both Jewish and a staunch defender of Israel, called on then-president Obama to "do to Media Matters what he did to Jeremiah Wright—totally disassociate, (and) rebuke" the group.

In a 2012 interview in *The Daily Caller*, Dershowitz said, startlingly, of Media Matters: "You know where I get their stuff? I read their stuff mostly on a neo-Nazi website that sends it to me.... Somehow I am on their mailing list. I am not on Media Matters's mailing list. But I tend to read Media Matters articles when they're sent to me by a neo-Nazi website."

In a 2012 appearance on Jay Severin's Boston talk show, Dershowitz said Media Matters is "so virulently anti-Israel and anti-supporters of Israel" that it has "gone over the line from anti-Zionism to anti-Semitism." He added that Media Matters uses the term "'Israel Firsters' the way anti-Catholic bigots used to use the term 'Vatican Firsters' or 'Irish Firsters,' as if to suggest Americans who support Israel have dual loyalty. This false charge goes back to the Bible—goes back to the Book of Esther, goes back thousands of years. It was one of Hitler's justifications for killing the Jews: 'Dual loyalty, they're not good Germans, they're not good Americans,' whatever it is." A full six years after this assessment of the far-left Media Matters in 2012, Dershowitz said in November 2018 on *Fox & Friends* in a discussion of Democrats on the extreme left that they were "tolerating anti-Semitism" to appease their base.

The Reverend Jeremiah Wright, Barack Obama's pastor at a UCC church in Chicago, was accused of anti-Semitism in a sermon during the 2008 campaign. For that and other controversial sermons captured on videotape, Obama, who earlier had described Wright as being like an uncle, publicly abandoned his old pastor and "uncle" once the Wright videos became an issue in the campaign. After Obama became president, Wright was unable to contact his former friend and congregant, saying of those surrounding the new president: "Them Jews ain't going to let him talk to me." Dershowitz was suggesting only that Media Matters get the same deep freeze from President Obama as Wright had. Curiously, the rebuke of Media Matters by Obama in the same fashion as he had rebuked Reverend Wright has never happened.

The liberal Professor Dershowitz wasn't alone in discussing Media Matters in such terms.

In 2012, Ben Shapiro, then of *Breitbart News Network*, had written of the Media Matters anti-Semitism problem. Shapiro, an observant Jew, observed that a prominent Media Matters personality had written elsewhere that he, the Media Matters guy

> …*lamented the fate of Professor Sami Al-Arian, former North American head of the Palestinian Islamic Jihad. This is the same Al-Arian who proclaimed, "God cursed those who are sons of Israel.… Those people, God made monkeys and pigs.… Let us damn America, let us damn Israel, let us damn them and their allies until death." When Al-Arian was suspended from his teaching post at Florida Atlantic University, [Media Matters writer Eric] Boehlert defended Al-Arian as an "innocent professor."*

Then there was this: *The Daily Caller*, the influential website cofounded by Fox's Tucker Carlson, investigated blog postings by Media Matters president Carusone. The report on its 2014 investigation bore the headline "Media Matters Executive Wrote Racist, Anti-Semitic, Anti-'Tranny' Blog Posts."

The story, by reporter Patrick Howley, began by saying this of Carusone:

> *A top executive at Media Matters for America and the principal activist in the "Stop Rush" campaign made racist and anti-Semitic comments and disparaged "trannies" on a dormant blog that he wrote just several years prior to his prominent liberal activism career.*
>
> *Blog entries reviewed by The Daily Caller show that Angelo Carusone made derogatory remarks about ethnic groups and used language to insult "trannies" and ugly "gays" that would be considered hate speech by his own organization.*

The controversial posts were rerun verbatim for all to see, making deniability impossible. There, plain as day, was the head of Media Matters referring to a lover as adorable "despite his jewry." There were repeated racist remarks about a Bangladeshi, not to mention multiple attacks on transvestites. As Howley noted, coming from anyone else, all of this would be considered hate speech by Media Matters and, in this day and age, probably even by the Chamber of Commerce.

Now, only days before my firing, Niger Innis of the Congress of Racial Equality (CORE) had launched his own scathing attack on Media Matters and Carusone, saying this in a formal statement:

> *It is appalling that the President of MMFA, Angelo Carusone, uses racial slurs and language that defames individuals. How can someone who claims to champion the cause of those who find themselves the victims of such vitriol use such despicable language? How could George Soros and David Brock have ever selected this individual to be the face of their organization, knowing the comments he made? Carusone's remarks are publicly cited, documented on news sites, and they spit in the face of all that MMFA claims to represent....*
>
> *CORE is in our 75th year of service to our countrymen. Established in 1942, we have always fought for the respect and dignity of men and women of all backgrounds.*

> *There are many examples of racism, anti-Semitism and the "politics of personal destruction," made up of rumors, half-truths and downright lies.*
>
> *As an African-American, and leader of an organization that truly believes in fairness, equality, and mutual respect, this is "beyond the pale."*

In other words, from the liberal Obama/Clinton supporter Alan Dershowitz to the conservative Tucker Carlson's *Daily Caller* to the *Jerusalem Post* to the head of a venerable American civil rights group and more, Media Matters has been repeatedly flagged for anti-Semitism and racism. In the case of CORE, this was a serious civil rights organization that was legendary for its seventy-five-year-old fight against racism from its 1942 founding to the Freedom Rides of the 1960s, the battle to desegregate Chicago's schools, its role in the iconic 1963 March on Washington with Dr. Martin Luther King Jr., and well beyond. Now, it was calling out Media Matters.

There was still more.

Carusone had boasted publicly about starting the Stop Rush campaign to pressure advertisers into dropping Limbaugh's show. Once aware of this, I interviewed a targeted advertiser of Rush Limbaugh's show. Mark Stevens was a decidedly nonpolitical businessman. An accomplished entrepreneur, Stevens is founder of the marketing company MSCO and author of over two dozen best-selling books, including business books and a biography of investor Carl Icahn. Stevens detailed to me and separately to Fox hosts Stuart Varney and Megyn Kelly that because his firm advertised on the Limbaugh show in the New York media market, he had received threats to his personal safety and his business, and had been inundated with hostile emails and phone calls harassing his female employees. The emails had come from around the country even though he had never advertised outside of the New York media market. Particularly infuriating to him, his female employees had been assailed as "sluts" and "women haters." He had angrily dismissed the description of these activities as a "boycott" and said that in fact, having been on the receiving end, he would describe them as "an organized terror campaign." There is one other fact of note: Mark Stevens is Jewish.

As I also knew, the American left in general—Media Matters was not alone in this respect—had been infected in the previous several years with a rising tide of anti-Semitism. I took note of this in a 2015 column in

NewsBusters, in which I focused on talk radio host Mark Levin's quite specific call for a discussion of the rise of anti-Semitism from the American left—an anti-Semitism he saw as being led by then-President Obama. The headline was "Mark Levin: Time for Discussion of Obama's Anti-Semitism, and 'Praetorian Guard' Media."

My column began:

> *"Both on his own eponymous radio show and in an appearance on Sean Hannity's TV show, in discussing President Obama's treatment of Israel's Prime Minister Benjamin Netanyahu Mark specifically and in detail accused the Obama administration of anti-Semitism and liberals in general of flat-out racism, all of this protected by what he called the 'Praetorian guard' media...'"*

I linked to a piece over on the liberal website *The Daily Beast* by Gil Troy, a professor of history at McGill University. Troy had noted the anti-Semitism of the 2012 Democratic National Convention. The headline was "How Many Democrats Booed Jerusalem at the DNC?"

Among other things, Troy wrote:

> *When the Democrats restored the Party's now traditional affirmation of Jerusalem as Israel's capital, there were so many noes that the move required three attempts to be accepted. Eventually, the plank was pushed through, albeit ham-handedly, to boos from a loud minority. That display of hostility in the Democratic lovefest, as well as the initial desire to drop the Jerusalem plank from the Party platform, tells a tale about an internal Democratic debate—and possible shift—that pro-Israel Democrats are desperately trying to cover up....*
>
> *Like it or not, the Democratic Party is becoming the home address of anti-Israel forces as well as Israel skeptics.... I have criticized the Republicans for trying to make supporting Israel a wedge issue through demagoguery. But Democrats should not deny that they are also helping to make Israel a wedge issue by hosting those who are hostile to Israel and then covering it up dishonestly.*

In short, anti-Semitism was in fact on the rise on the left. What was going on with Media Matters was merely symptomatic of the larger problem. And in fact, over a year after I departed CNN, the 2018 elections, as noted by *The New York Times*, brought forth this headline: "A New Wave of Democrats Tests the Party's Blanket Support for Israel."

The story began:

> *WASHINGTON—One Democratic House candidate has pledged that she will vote against bills that include aid to Israel, denouncing what she saw as the "injustice" of Israel's treatment of the Palestinians. Another wrote that "Israel has hypnotized the world" with its "evil doings."*
>
> *Still another helped write a scathing book on relations between the United States and Israel, while Alexandria Ocasio-Cortez, a progressive political star expected to win a House seat in New York, condemned the "occupation of Palestine."*
>
> *A cluster of activist Democrats—most of them young, most of them cruising toward House seats this fall—has dared to breach what has been an almost inviolable orthodoxy in both political parties, strong support for Israel, raising the specter of a crack in the Democratic Party that Republicans could use to attract Jewish supporters.*

The Jewish *Forward* had this headline in 2018 to a piece by journalist Emily Shire, a self-professed "registered Democrat in New York State": "Anti-Semitism Is Flourishing On The Left. Why Does No One Care?"

Apparently, Democrats in Minnesota did not care. In 2018, they would elect one Ilhan Omar to the U.S. Congress. A Somali American and a Muslim, Omar had tweeted this in 2012: "Israel has hypnotized the world, may Allah awaken the people and help them see the evil doings of Israel."

Over in Michigan, Democrats elected Rashida Tlaib to Congress. Within days of her swearing-in, Tlaib was on Twitter pushing the ancient anti-Semitic slur that Senate Republicans who supported what was called the "Strengthening America's Security in the Middle East Act of 2019," were more loyal to Israel than their own country. "They forgot what country they represent," she tweeted—hinting at the same "Israel Firster" slur that had been both run by Media Matters and used by David Duke. In January of

2019, the *Daily Caller News Foundation*'s Peter Hasson headlined a DCNF investigation of Congresswoman Tlaib this way: "RASHIDA TLAIB'S TIES TO ANTI-SEMITISM RUN DEEPER THAN PREVIOUSLY KNOWN."

What followed was a detailed report that included the news that Tlaib belonged to a Facebook group "where members often demonize Jews."

After the 2018 election, David Harsanyi, a senior editor at *The Federalist*, focused on Congresswoman Omar in an article for the *New York Post* with the headline "Here's the anti-Semitism the media doesn't want to mention."

Wrote Harsanyi:

> *Writer David Steinberg identified 105 news stories written in the immediate aftermath of Omar's victory, and not a single one mentioned that she believed Jewry possessed mind-control abilities or that Israel was "evil." No one called on the Democratic Party to distance itself from this rhetoric.*
>
> *No one at the partisan Anti-Defamation League, ostensibly tasked with stopping anti-Jewish libel but in reality busy hyperventilating over every far-flung right-wing bigot with a handful of supporters, paid her any attention....*
>
> *Omar even wants the US to normalize relations with the Holocaust-denying terror-state of Iran. This seems like a fact reporters might have wanted to shoehorn into one their post-election articles.*
>
> *Then again, the media has a track record of tenaciously ignoring the anti-Semitism creeping into Democratic Party politics. The left, recall, has embraced the Women's March and its co-founders, Tamika Mallory and Linda Sarsour, even though they're both supporters of the Nation of Islam, which has peddled anti-Jewish conspiracies about wicked Jewish influence in America.*
>
> *None of the leaders of the Democratic Party has said anything about the activist wing pushing these age-old hatreds. We have not heard a peep from those who see white supremacy behind every border security measure. There are elections to win, after all. And in the contemporary liberal establishment, conceived in identity politics, even many Jews have remained dutifully silent.*

True to form, shortly after being sworn in, Fox News reported that the new Congresswoman Omar was comparing Israel to the American segregated South, writing of her critics that "many of them truly know this, but don't want to accept it. In the same way many Americans knew separate yet equal was immoral but remained silent until brave few were silent no more."

New York Post columnist and *Commentary* editor John Podhoretz also noted what he called in a column "the potential mainstreaming of anti-Semitism in the Democratic Party as represented by the renewed public importance of Louis Farrakhan and the refusal of vanguard figures on the left, like the leaders of the Women's March, to repudiate his noxious filth."

All of which is to say, as anti-Semitism was on the rise on the left, the media was falling silent—effectively acting, as Mark Levin noted, as the Praetorian Guard for anti-Semitism from the left. This did not mean a given media outlet was itself anti-Semitic. But it did mean there was a reflex when it came to protecting various left-wing politicians and activist groups from the charge, no matter how obvious the evidence.

I am not Jewish. But I am the son of a World War II veteran raised to abhor anti-Semitism and racial bigotry, possessed all my life with friends of all faiths and races, and now I knew full well of Media Matters' repeated, menacing anti-free-press campaigns that were combined with repeated allegations of a seemingly visceral anti-Semitic and racial bent that was increasingly characteristic of the left. There was a decided problem that was metastasizing across the left—not to mention I knew that serious people on both the left and right had called attention to Media Matters' pronounced problem of anti-Semitism and outright bigotry. And I had written myself of the left's increasing problems with anti-Semitism. Knowing all of this, I jumped into the fray again.

I took on the group's latest anti-free-press campaign, this one targeting Hannity and his advertisers. Particularly disturbing was an interview Carusone gave to the Associated Press, in which he was quoted as saying: "Advertisers will get burned if they continue to associate with Hannity— plain and simple." The thuggish, menacing tone combined with the imagery, coming from the head of a group flagged now repeatedly for outright anti-Semitism, was appalling.

Quite specifically in my column I zeroed in on the anti-free-press nature of these "boycotts." The Limbaugh advertiser Stevens had called them "an organized terror campaign." I called those behind it what I saw them as actually being—out-and-out fascists. Fascism, as noted Austrian economist Ludwig von Mises had discussed decades earlier in his landmark book *Socialism*, has long opposed "liberty of thought and the press and the right of assembly."

Sean Hannity, in this instance—just like CNN, Fox, MSNBC, ABC, CBS, NBC, *The New York Times*, *The Washington Post*, and countless print, television, radio, and internet entities—was most assuredly the press. He was a one-man exemplar of a free press, without doubt, as were any number of his fellow talk show hosts on TV and radio. But as with opinion editors who run the editorial pages of print outlets like *The New York Times* and others, a stand-up example of a free press at work on radio and television Hannity was and is.

My column began by citing this Associated Press dispatch:

Liberal group urges advertisers to boycott Fox's Hannity

NEW YORK (AP)—A liberal advocacy group that targeted Glenn Beck and Bill O'Reilly for advertiser boycotts in the past now has its sights set on Fox News Channel's Sean Hannity.

Media Matters for America said Friday it will begin asking Hannity's advertisers to shun him and will ask thousands of its members to also contact companies. The group is setting up a stophannity.com website and plans to hire a plane to carry an anti-Hannity banner in the New York area.

His Fox show "really has moved beyond just being a conservative viewpoint to state-aligned disinformation and propaganda," said Angelo Carusone, Media Matters president. "If we don't do it now, Hannity will only get worse."

In response, I wrote this in a column:

Got that? The arbiter of who can say what in America is now going to be not the First Amendment of the Constitution which, a reminder, reads as follows:

"Congress shall make no law respecting an establishment of religion, or prohibiting the free exercise thereof; or abridging the freedom of speech, or of the press; or the right of the people peace-

ably to assemble, and to petition the Government for a redress of grievances."

The objective of Media Matters (and let's stop with the camouflage and from now on call them what they really are, MMF—Media Matters Fascists), clearly, is to re-write the First Amendment so it will now be modeled after Fascist Italy's Ministero della Cultura Popolare—Mussolini's Ministry of Popular Culture. The Ministry was in turn modeled after the Nazi Reich Ministry of Public Enlightenment and Propaganda. Both Mussolini and Hitler's aim was as simple as it was sinister: to control the flow of information whether that meant broadcast, newspapers, books, films and all the rest of any outlets that were vehicles of the day for the free expression of ideas.

In short? In short what Media Matters Fascists are about is effectively re-writing the First Amendment to say a version of this:

"The United States Ministry of Popular Culture shall make all laws respecting the exercise of speech; abridging speech as judged necessary by or in the press. All sponsors of speech-related television and radio shows, Internet sites and publications of any kind must seek approval from the Ministry or lose their right to speak in America."

I included a reference to the group's disgraceful reputation for anti-Semitism, saying:

The American Spectator *has been unable to confirm reports that the original draft of this Media Matters revision ended with the words: "Seig Heil!"*

Let's be plain. This latest from Media Matters Fascists is straight-up fascism. Question? Who died and left Media Matters, George Soros, and MMF honchos David Brock and Angelo Carusone in charge of free speech in America?

To say the least, I saw then—and I see now—nothing wrong in the least with ridiculing, holding in contempt, and outright condemning those repeatedly flagged for anti-Semitism and bigotry, not to mention those who make a career out of bullying advertisers—threatening that those advertisers "will get burned" if they don't toe the Media Matters line. All of this is done as part of a seriously disturbing effort to shut down a free press.

In a brief Twitter exchange with Carusone that he initiated after the column was posted—he was angry that his name had been misspelled in the *Spectator* column headline, something I personally corrected—I tweeted out to him the last two words of that one sentence from my column—the infamous Nazi salute of "*Sieg Heil!*" I believed it expressed exactly the contempt and ridicule that must be shown to those who have not only been flagged repeatedly for anti-Semitism, racism, and bigotry but have proven themselves to be utterly hostile and thuggishly threatening to a free press.

Mere hours later, in the time it had taken a CNN car to drive me from my Pennsylvania home to the outskirts of New York City—I was scheduled to be in New York that evening for an appearance on Anderson Cooper's show—I received a text message from CNN host Jake Tapper, objecting to my tweet from the now two-day-old column. Alas, in my technical incompetence, I answered him and the answer was posted. It was hardly my intention to disagree with Tapper in public, but I had accidentally done so. Next came an email from Rebecca Kutler at CNN asking me to call her. I did. She told me that I was fired. I was incredulous. Had CNN read the column? I asked. Yes, I was answered, indeed they had. Had they read a second blog post in which I said this to Carusone (after printing his objections verbatim)?

> *Noted here? It is not a lie, Angelo, that you and MMF are trying to end Sean Hannity's free speech. You have been playing this fascist game for years with others—Rush Limbaugh, Glenn Beck, Bill O'Reilly, etc., etc. If there is a conservative with an audience of any size your fascist instinct is not to debate honestly but to simply silence the opposition. Period. Threaten their sponsors and bully.*
>
> *This is America, Angelo. Not Fascist Italy, Nazi Germany or Communist Russia.*
>
> *I have no intention of calling for some regulatory God somewhere or some poohbah donor to shut you down or defund you.*
>
> *I really do believe in free speech. And the dirty little secret here?*
>
> *Your attempt to get Sean Hannity—now that the wider world is onto your game—is only going to help him. Just like*

it helped Rush Limbaugh before that. And for that matter? You
are helping President Trump.

Now, I was asking Rebecca Kutler if both my column and the successive blog post had been read at CNN in their entirety. Yes, came the answer. Yes they had.

I was incredulous. Astounded. The notion that making a stand in a column at *The American Spectator* for a free press, even—make that especially even—one for CNN competitor Hannity was not acceptable to CNN was dumbfounding to me. In essence, I was being fired because I refused to abandon Sean Hannity in an outrageous attempt to kill his free speech outright. And mocking, condemning, and holding Media Matters out for contempt because of its record of repeatedly flagged anti-Semitism was not acceptable to CNN. Three times over I had no intention of apologizing. First, I will never in a thousand years refuse to oppose anti-Semitism and outright bigotry. Second, most assuredly hell will freeze over before I desert the principle of a free press. And third, never, ever would I abandon a friend. If I was to be fired for these three things, so be it.

Was a free press only for CNN? The idea that writing a column in a well-known, mainstream, conservative publication to ridicule and publicly condemn a group that had been repeatedly, deservedly, and quite publicly flagged for out-and-out anti-Semitism, racism, and bigotry by other, very different critics on both the left and right would somehow be a firing offense at CNN had literally never crossed my mind. If taking on Media Matters was such a controversial thing to do, why not have Carusone and myself on CNN to debate the issue in the robust style of a free press? Clearly, this would not be happening. When push came to shove, I had the sudden realization that CNN was not as stalwart about a robust free press as it portrays itself. The network is decidedly selective about defending a free press, something that is, in my humble opinion, a tremendous insult to its own journalists, many of whom I have come to know and greatly respect for their quite serious professionalism, a number of them literally putting their lives on the line to report hard news to the American people and the world beyond. I was, naively without doubt, astonished.

As I will detail in a post-2018 analysis at the end of this book, I was left shaking my head in disbelief when CNN sued the Trump White House over pulling the credentials of CNN's White House correspondent Jim Acosta, with the network presenting itself as defending free speech against a supposed

Trump threat to freedom of the press. The harsh reality is that in bowing to demands from Media Matters, when push comes to shove, the network flinched about a free press—and worse, as I will mention later, it also goes out of its way to push the campaigns of those who run these anti-free-press jihads.

For all of the occasionally intense criticism of CNN from President Trump, I had never felt anything but respect and affection for my CNN colleagues and CNN president Jeff Zucker. When the 2016 presidential campaign was over, CNN produced a coffee table-style book titled *Unprecedented: The Election That Changed Everything*. It was a retelling of the campaign by CNN correspondents and contributors, and I had been invited to contribute a piece and had done so. When the book came out, I took my copy and had colleagues sign it, high school-yearbook style. Jeff Zucker wrote: "My Lord, you have been a huge part of our success! You're the best! Jef." I was one loyal CNN guy who respected and liked my colleagues, every last one of them, regardless of political stripe. I had spent so much time on Anderson Cooper's show that my time there had come to seem like time with an adopted family. They had my total respect—and still do.

A word here about Anderson Cooper. And I confess I write reluctantly, because I am so seriously concerned about a free press, and the last thing I want to do is affix some bull's-eye on his back that makes him a target for far left-wing authoritarians like Media Matters. (This in itself says volumes about the threatening nature of the group CNN has aligned itself with.) Anderson Cooper is a journalist's journalist. Yes, indeed, he is left of center on some matters. But he always, from my point of view, was fair to me.

On one occasion as I Skyped in from home, he was trying to get me to agree that Trump was not smart for saying that fired FBI director James Comey was a "nutjob" to a group of visiting Russians. Not surprisingly, I totally disagreed, seeing this as just one more irrelevant Washington dust-up that literally had no meaning regarding the lives of average Americans. It was, I thought, just fodder for the media. The conversation went this way:

> *Lord: I don't care what he says to the Russians.*
>
> *Cooper: Okay.*
>
> *Lord: I mean, he's the president of the United States.*
>
> *Cooper: Right.*

Lord: If he wants to say that, Barack Obama wants to say whatever, if George Bush says, "I looked in his eyes and—"

Cooper: If he took a dump on his desk, you would defend it.

Lord: What?

Cooper: I mean, I don't know what he would do that you would not defend. You're a loyal guy. I think that speaks well of you.

Lord: Anderson, this is offending Eastern media elite sensibilities. Right here in America, they all think, "Yeah, the FBI director was a nutjob."

Since this was Skype, it took a second for me to absorb the "dump on his desk" comment, and the second I understood it, I burst out laughing on camera. It was, after all, funny, and as I knew by then, Anderson has a great sense of humor. Be that as it may, in a sign of the times, shortly thereafter he felt compelled to tweet out an apology, the original text below:

"I regret the crude sentence i spoke earlier tonight and followed it up by apologizing. It was unprofessional. I am genuinely sorry."

I didn't see the tweet until the middle of the night. Awake, what else to do but check Twitter? Finally seeing Anderson's tweet, I quickly replied: "Anderson Cooper is my colleague and a friend for whom I have the highest professional and personal regard. Message America? It's ok 2 laugh!"

The next time I was on Anderson's show, I walked on the set before airtime bringing him a gift: a toy dump truck to which I had taped a sign reading:

A. COOPER

Desk Dump Removal Inc.

"We Jump for Trump Dumps!"

Laughter erupted.

On another occasion he was catching flak for moderating a CNN-sponsored Democratic debate between Bernie Sanders and Hillary Clinton in Las Vegas. *The Weekly Standard* ran a piece with the headline "Debategate: Cooper Member of Clinton Global Initiative."

The essence here is that Anderson had once spoken to the Clinton Global Initiative, his presence a money-raising lure for the Clintons. The story closed by saying: "In a nutshell, Anderson Cooper helped Hillary Clinton raise money, and now he's presented as an impartial moderator for tonight's debate."

What the story did not say was what I knew. Anderson Cooper's mother, Gloria Vanderbilt, was a close friend of Nancy Reagan. And a few years back, Anderson, at Mrs. Reagan's request, spoke at the Reagan Library and, yes indeed, served as the attraction for a Reagan Library fundraiser—just as he had done for Hillary Clinton. The criticism was wildly unfair, and I took to the cyber pages of *The American Spectator* to defend him.

At one point, *The Drudge Report* showed a photograph of Wolf Blitzer supposedly celebrating the nomination of Hillary Clinton at a party at the Democratic National Convention. The headline accompanying the photo of Wolf with wineglass in hand and a video showing him dancing to "Sweet Caroline" was "CNN celebrates Hillary: Blitzer toasts speech, dancing, party!"

It wasn't true. The photo of Wolf was taken at a convention "after-party" for CNNers and their guests, hosted by CNN. I was in attendance, and the party most assuredly had nothing to do with Hillary Clinton. CNN asked me if I would respond to the Drudge photo and defend Wolf. I was happy to do so. It was fake news. Stories that are not true should be called out no matter where they appear.

As CNN quickly learned when I began, in addition to all my media work, I was caring for my then ninety-seven-year-old mom. Kathleen Rose Jackson Lord was an indomitable force of nature in her heyday—she had been the chairwoman of the Hampshire County, Massachusetts Republican Women's group in the late 1950s, was the president of the Massachusetts Conference of Congregational Women in the 1960s, and at one point was asked to run for Congress (she declined). Now she could no longer walk and had begun to cruise in and out of dementia. My absences from home for CNN necessitated using the Visiting Angels, a company of exceptional caregivers who took charge while I was away. After the election, when I, like everyone else at CNN, was traveling nonstop back and forth across the country to cover the campaign, my on-air time settled back into frequent trips to New York or Washington to appear on Anderson's show.

Because routine is so important in taking care of a senior, I asked to be taken home every night after my on-air appearances. My mother passed away in July 2018, and CNN's dutifully picking me up and sending me back to Pennsylvania every night, a six-hour round trip, each day I was on the air, has left me forever personally grateful to the network, as well as to all of its many hosts—that includes every single on-air host—and off-air talent who always made a point of asking after her. Not least am I appreciative of Jeff Zucker, my professional and political criticisms of CNN notwithstanding.

The CNN audience focused on the on-air joustings between Trump supporters and liberal or Never Trump Republican panelists or Anderson and other CNN hosts. As the campaign year evolved I was repeatedly in situations where the anti-Trump panelists could outnumber me greatly—and in fact, I enjoyed the jousting. One night, things were so stacked against me that during a commercial break I looked down to see that Donald Trump had just tweeted about all those CNN panelists ganging up on "that nice Jeffrey Lord." I smiled. On another, similar occasion, I checked my email during a break to see a note from Sean Hannity that read: "I can't bear to watch this." I laughed. My supporters weren't on the panels, but they were out there—and they were good ones to have!

Courtesy of Donald Trump and CNN, I had surprisingly become the momentary subject of considerable media attention in unexpected venues like *The Hollywood Reporter* and *Vanity Fair*. Indeed, *VF*'s Tina Nguyen trekked all the way to my home in suburban Harrisburg—Camp Hill—to follow me around. She met my mom and then came along as I went through the normal activities of grocery shopping, picking up the dry cleaning, and the rest. In fact, the visit to the dry cleaner—Kaplan's Careful Cleaners—resulted in a sit-down interview with the owner for an interesting and educational talk on just how NAFTA had negatively affected the dry cleaning business. Which is to say, Nguyen wanted to see the environment in which I had begun to understand both the nature and the strength of what would become the Trump rebellion.

From time to time on-air, I would shake my head as I listened to my Clinton-supporting *compadres* talk and gently suggest that what they were talking about was nowhere close to the topics discussed in the Summit Diner in my neighboring borough of Lemoyne, Pennsylvania. Nguyen requested a visit to the diner—and so we went. All of this made it into her pre-election article titled (in all caps), "WHAT'S LEFT FOR DONALD TRUMP'S ANGER TRANSLATOR IN A POST-TRUMP WORLD?"

Nguyen was completely fair—saying, accurately, that I "can lay claim to predicting the rise of a movement that practically nobody saw coming." (Although I couldn't help but notice the title's implication that Trump was going to lose!)

Perhaps the success of all those endless discussions on CNN with my colleagues was that there was nothing phony about them. All of us were really about the issues—not playing to the TV cameras. In my case, as a Reagan conservative who had grown up idolizing John and Robert Kennedy and Dr. Martin Luther King, I had gotten to know, admire, and believe in Donald Trump—the man, not the media caricature. While this campaign was wildly eventful and thus produced some particularly vivid on-air discussions, I never for a moment took any of the heat personally. Nor were my words intended to wound or do anything other than make my case in a professional, collegial manner. Many of my on-air colleagues, liberals and conservatives both, became friends, as was true of a number of people who were behind-the-scenes personnel never on camera. Indeed, my friendship with my famously liberal colleague Van Jones was so remarked on that he would later write that we had become the "'Bert and Ernie' of political analysis," the two of us even making a humorous joint appearance on Anderson's New Year's Eve show with Kathy Griffin. It is a friendship I treasure.

What was on display when all of us who were CNN commentators of different political stripes were on the air was free speech and a free press incarnate, with very different and sometimes not so different ideas discussed with a mix of passion and reason. CNN had every reason to be pleased.

In my column on Media Matters, I was defending a free press and holding out for condemnation those who, as I well knew, had been flagged repeatedly for anti-Semitism and out-and-out bigotry. Who, beyond the targets who so richly deserved being called out, could possibly object?

Answer: Incredibly to me, it was Jeff Zucker. Media Matters had flagged to CNN my post mocking it for its anti-Semitism, Twitter lefties were aflame, and, disturbingly to me then and even more so now, instantly CNN jumped to satisfy both Media Matters and the inevitable left-wing Twitter mob. For a brief moment, the Media Matters effort to remove Hannity from the air had shifted—to me. And I was now, abruptly and quite publicly, gone from CNN. In my heated astonishment, I told a sorrowful Rebecca Kutler that I would talk about this to every conservative show that asked. My dismissal call was no sooner finished than it seemed that I was in fact suddenly the subject on media minds as word of my CNN firing spread.

CNN issued this statement: "Nazi salutes are indefensible. Jeffrey Lord is no longer with the network." I believed then and still believe now that anti-Semitism is indefensible. There was not a solitary mention in CNN's statement that the "salute" was part of a posted column that spent some time ridiculing and holding in contempt a group with a decided animus to a free press and that had been flagged repeatedly by responsible critics left and right for anti-Semitism and outright bigotry. Nor was there any acknowledgment that I had long been on record going after anti-Semitism in general. As mentioned, months before I even joined CNN, I had written in *NewsBusters* of Mark Levin's charges that there was a "Praetorian guard media" that was busy ignoring the rise of anti-Semitism on the left. I went on to add that the "hard historical fact is that racism -- and anti-Semitism as 'the oldest hatred' is a very distinct form of racism -- has historically been at the core of the American Left."

Appallingly, a group calling itself the Anne Frank Center for Mutual Respect applauded my firing, disgracefully taking me to task for calling out the anti-Semitism of Media Matters by falsely accusing me of what Media Matters was doing. As I quickly learned, stories about the Anne Frank Center had been featured in the left-leaning *Atlantic,* the conservative *Daily Caller* and *Breitbart.* All the stories said a version of the same thing: the Anne Frank Center was being run by an executive director named Steven Goldstein - and Goldstein was in fact a left-wing "social justice" activist, not any kind of Holocaust expert. In fact, Goldstein had been politicizing the Anne Frank Center to pillory President Trump as an anti-Semite. This was, of course, a disgraceful slur of the President, he who had a Jewish daughter, son-in-law and grandchildren, not to mention a very close relationship with Israel's Prime Minister Benjamin Netanyahu. Here was a group whose self-proclaimed mission was using Anne Frank's considerably prestigious name to educate about "the dangers of intolerance, anti-Semitism, racism and discrimination" - yet when it came to Media Matters and its slurs about "Israel Firsters", the "Israel lobby" and its support for what *Commentary*'s Abe Greenwald had witheringly called the "Jew hatred" of Occupy Wall Street - Goldstein was strangely silent. Jewish historian David Benkof, no Trump fan, wrote in the *Daily Caller* that Goldstein had made the Anne Frank Center "a sham organization."

As I would eventually realize, there was a reason for CNN's bowing to pressure from Media Matters.

Several months later, the veteran journalist Peter Barry Chowka reported at *American Thinker* that CNN was indeed a "prominent and enthusiastic ally" of Media Matters—which is to say, my real sin was not just being an effective critic of Trump critics. My real sin now was having the nerve to write a column attacking a leftist CNN ally, the facts of Media Matters' seriously troubling reputation be damned. As I would later discover, Sharyl Attkisson had covered the CNN–Brock group relationship, writing that one Brock project, American Bridge, had pumped out a report going after the libertarian/conservative Koch brothers and that the report "resulted in 'a high profile CNN story.'" She also noted that an internal American Bridge memo, published by WikiLeaks in October 2016, "boasts that CNN was receptive to its outreach," also gloating that "CNN recently ran a feature story on our use of livestream technology." The group exulted in the fact that it had "placed" negative stories on Florida's ex-governor Jeb Bush "with CNN."

Amazingly, at a later date, CNN's Brian Stelter had Media Matters' Carusone on his *Reliable Sources* show to answer criticisms from Hannity about the bigotry problem that dogged the organization. Along the way, Stelter asked if Hannity had asked Carusone on Hannity's show to discuss charges of bigotry at MMFA—passing over entirely the idea that CNN itself would rather fire me than pair me with Carusone to debate the issues on CNN. Offending Media Matters for CNN was a bridge too far in the fight for the principle of a free press.

That CNN message—that offending Media Matters was a CNN no-no—to say the least, was clearly if belatedly understood by me. CNN would give Media Matters a pass—because the two entities, as illustrated by journalists Chowka and Attkisson, were in fact at the highest level ideological allies. Indeed, at a later time on another issue, CNN anchor Chris Cuomo was involved in a debate with *Breitbart* editor Joel Pollak. When Pollak contended that the issue—rape on college campuses—had been misrepresented by Media Matters, Cuomo replied: "Listen, you can keep saying, 'Media

Matters,' it's not a dog whistle here." I was amazed, if by that point not surprised. I don't know about a "dog whistle," but if an organization that has acquired such a disturbing reputation for being anti-free press, yet is treated like a respectable ally of a major cable television news network, effectively normalizing its bigotry, that should at a minimum raise a red flag with my friend Chris Cuomo.

As I rode along home, my email and cell phone started going crazy. *The New York Times*, *The Washington Post*, CNN media correspondent Brian Stelter, and more were calling, emailing, texting. Stelter was fair to me—making a point of mentioning my column. "I love CNN, but I feel they are caving to bullies here," I told him. He noted in an article that "Media Matters has repeatedly condemned Lord and criticized CNN for employing him as a commentator." Even reading that, I was as yet unaware of the CNN-Media Matters alliance.

Sean Hannity emailed and called. "What the hell happened?" he asked, incredulous if not totally shocked. Shortly thereafter he tweeted: "How sad in America that only conservatives get investigated, fired, boycotted and attacked. Double standard, & liberal silence is repulsive!"

All of a sudden I was hearing from, so it seemed, the entire media world. *Politico* had the headline "Right-wing media figures rally to ousted CNN analyst Lord."

Even *Buzzfeed*'s Ben Smith—*Buzzfeed* being no conservative outlet—tweeted of CNN: "The enforced humorlessness of these situations is absurd." Indeed. This kind of "enforced humorlessness" is in reality nothing more than breast-beating virtue signaling at its worst. Fox's Laura Ingraham would email me later, saying that my firing was a "badge of honor."

This was, all of a sudden, my own personal Swamp War. It was not a pleasant situation to be in, but it was definitely reassuring when all these conservative folks rallied to me and the caller of the moment was a friend. I was humbled by the support and friendship of my conservative friends and colleagues and so many others, specifically including kind, private notes from many of my CNN colleagues. Being at the center of one of these modern-day media feeding frenzies was never some secret ambition of mine. Having seen my fair share of them, particularly when I was a young Reagan White House aide during the Iran-Contra affair, I can say that no one in their right mind can aspire to be in the middle of one of these.

Over the course of the next few days, I appeared on one radio show after another across the country. Minutes after I arrived home and had time to change clothes, Candy Woodall, a reporter for the *Harrisburg Patriot-News* and its online version, Penn Live, was at my front door. I invited her in, and the phone rang as we talked. The caller's name was flashed on the television screen: "Steven K. Bannon." The White House was calling. I excused myself to take the call. Bannon was nothing but supportive, upbeat, and encouraging. I should write for *Breitbart*, he said. When I returned, I told Woodall that this was the first day of my "non-apology tour." Again, to understate, hell would freeze over before I would ever apologize for calling out a group that had quite voluntarily earned itself such a dismal reputation across the board for its anti-Semitism and outright bigotry, not to mention making it its mission to silence a free press. The national media? They were busy running with headlines that I had been fired for a Nazi salute. Like CNN, many turned the story completely upside down, ignoring my column completely. They were posting fake news—about me.

Rush Limbaugh and Sean Hannity spoke up for me both on-air and privately. Not long afterwards, Fox's Tucker Carlson had me on his TV show to discuss the situation. Limbaugh congratulated me on losing my first media job, laughingly saying that another seven times and I would catch up to him. In Hannity's case I would hear from him again over the next few days, as he made it a point to check in and ask if I was alright. I was. Amazed, but okay, even energized. I was almost immediately a guest on my old friend and former Reagan colleague Mark Levin's radio show. A conservative's conservative, with a well-deserved reputation as a serious supporter of the Constitution through his bestselling books, Levin would later tweet that "Media Matters runs CNN" after another pro-Trump contributor hired to replace me—ex-Missouri state GOP chairman Ed Martin—was targeted by Media Matters and then obligingly dumped by CNN.

Limbaugh said of CNN on his show the next day: "They have wanted to get rid of Jeff—my guess—for a long time. I mean, a pro-Trump person, no matter who, just doesn't fit on CNN, and there's no way they can. So this became a convenient excuse."

There was another note—and a telling one at that. For some time I had been doing a once-a-week unpaid interview as the "Trump Defender" on Phoenix radio station KTAR's *Mac & Gaydos* show. The two hosts, Mac

Watson and Larry Gaydos, great guys both, would play the devil's advocates and be the anti-Trump guys, while I would defend. I enjoyed the lighthearted sparring and the hosts. Out of the blue the next day—a Friday when I was scheduled to appear—the station called to say it was ending my appearances at the direction of a station executive. I was startled. Was I being told that standing up to Media Matters, a group repeatedly flagged for anti-Semitism, was somehow a bad thing? I asked. The caller dodged. I asked again and was told that my presence on the air was disturbing to the station's Phoenix listeners, suggesting, doubtless inadvertently, that its Phoenix audience was a bunch of bigoted, anti-Semitic, and anti-free-press nuts. The thinking was scrambled, upside down, but I didn't believe for a second that this was coming from Mac and Gaydos, two thoroughly decent radio hosts. This decision was coming from a frightened Old Order station executive who was saying, in essence, that there was something askew with the station's audience. I didn't believe that for a second. It had to be something else.

As I well recalled, early in his campaign Trump had appeared at a 2015 Phoenix rally attended by thousands, only to have those Arizonans stunningly dismissed by their own Arizona Republican senator John McCain, who said that "what he [Trump] did was he fired up the crazies. Now he galvanized them. He's really got them activated." I was taken aback at the time by McCain's criticism. I had supported him for president, defending him in my column when he was under attack. I did indeed see him as a genuine American hero, even if I was occasionally baffled by his decidedly non-conservative turns on this or that issue. Upon his death in August 2018, he was correctly recalled as a "lion of the Senate." Yet to say the least, the dismissing of one's own constituents as a bunch of fired-up crazies amazed me—but, in its own way, it was telling about the nature of both Trump's growing support and his opposition as well.

The other GOP senator from Arizona, Jeff Flake, was as time went on so out there with off-the-wall Trump criticism that it finally cost him his re-election. Flake simply gave up what should have been a sure-thing race when he successfully conveyed to Arizonans that he didn't have much regard for them either. Trump had carried the state over Hillary Clinton. Apparently, the station executive thought of the station's Phoenix audience in the same fashion as the Republican senator Flake viewed his own constituents, with a seemingly palpable, barely disguised distaste. This was not one of KTAR's finest moments. Yet at the same time, I was beginning to realize it was typical of Trump opponents. McCain and Flake were hardly alone as one Republican establishment figure after another went out of their way to denounce Trump during the 2016 election. This had, I slowly realized, serious political meaning for the country well beyond Arizona.

Amazingly, HBO's Bill Maher, a decided liberal and fierce Trump critic on whose show I had previously appeared, would sit down on my colleague Fareed Zakaria's CNN show and criticize CNN for firing me. Not because Maher agreed with me—far from it—but because he, like myself, was a serious believer in free speech. Said Maher: "This has got to stop, this idea that people have to go away if they've offended me even for one moment. How about just move on, turn the page, go to the next thing in your life?" Later, he would invite me back to his show, where he and his guest, film director and actor Rob Reiner, both staunch Trump critics, told me off-air and on-air that they thought CNN had given me a "bad deal" in firing me. I was as stunned as I was appreciative. While I disagreed with them both on the subject of Donald Trump, Maher and Reiner were the embodiment of principle in action.

I had no idea initially if Rush Limbaugh's point about CNN's seeking an excuse to fire me was true. But later I would learn from a source well inside CNN that this was in fact the case. My presence, as Jeff Zucker himself told me during the 2016 campaign, had been a boon to CNN during the election cycle. Yet my disagreement on-air with Old Order dogma had made me a pariah to some inside CNN and certainly outside in the anti-Trump liberal world. Ex-CNNer Soledad O'Brien zinged me repeatedly if bizarrely and wildly inaccurately. O'Brien is a staunch defender of the Old Order insistence on identity politics, which I had described repeatedly on CNN as the "son of segregation and the grandson of slavery." She was not happy, and decided that my open opposition to racism was, you guessed it, racist.

The pressure to get rid of me, I came to realize, was constant. And for a reason. As events proceeded, I was not simply defending Trump—I was in reality attacking Old Order dogma, and frequently, as with identity politics, those challenges were to standard modern liberal gospel.

In the Old Order, it is just fine to assail this or that (or any!) conservative as a Nazi, neo-Nazi, racist, xenophobe or, these days, homophobe or Islamophobe. This has been going on since at least the days of the late William F. Buckley

Jr. and Barry Goldwater, both of them attacked by opponents in these terms. On the eve of the 1980 Reagan-Carter election race, no less than Coretta Scott King was reported by *The New York Times* as saying, "I am scared that if Ronald Reagan gets into office, we are going to see more of the Ku Klux Klan and a resurgence of the Nazi Party." (And as I was occasionally pointing out in print in *The American Spectator*, observers as renowned as the legendary economists Ludwig von Mises and F. A. Hayek repeatedly documented decades ago in chapter and verse that Nazism was a creature not of the right but rather straight out of the left—a decidedly inconvenient fact for "mainstream media" outlets determined to insist otherwise.)

Ten years after Ronald Reagan's death, the prominent left-wing academic Noam Chomsky was still insisting that a media trope from Reagan's career that "Ronald Reagan was an extreme racist—though he denied it" was true. It was a frequent charge in the day that infuriated Reagan. At the death of former first lady Barbara Bush in 2018, like clockwork there was the predictable story—in this case from another leftist academic—saying that the wife of President George H. W. Bush was an "amazing racist." Eight months later, when President Bush himself passed away, again like clockwork there was the far-left *Salon's* Amanda Marcotte tweeting out that the late president was the very epitome of "blatant racism and toxic masculinity theatrics," a despicable charge against one of the most decent men in American politics. In the 2000 presidential campaign, the NAACP ran a television ad accusing the GOP nominee, Texas governor George W. Bush, of a connection to an unspeakably vicious racist lynching of a black man, James Byrd, by whites. Byrd was beaten with a bat, chained to the back of a truck, and dragged to his death. Two of the three murderers were sentenced to death, a third to life in prison. But because Bush opposed a bill on hate crimes, he was labeled a racist. And of course, to be discussed later, the now celebrated late senator John McCain was similarly and disgustingly attacked as a racist when he ran for president in 2008.

Assailing conservatives in this manner is done all the time and no one blinks. If one is on the left, one can pander to seriously ugly politics and blow a dog whistle to left-wing bigots—and it is just no big deal. Trashing President Trump like this on CNN is never a cause for firing—to the contrary. On one notable occasion, as reported by *The Daily Caller*, there was an interesting CNN story with the headline "CNN Anchor Compares Trump To Hitler While Her Boss Buys Obama Photos."

The story reported on CNNers attending a 2016 awards dinner in Washington by the International Center for Journalists. The report said, in part:

> *In the weeks after Donald Trump won the election, CNN chief Jeff Zucker watched as one of his employees compared the new president to Adolf Hitler....*
>
> *CNN anchor Wolf Blitzer was the emcee of the November 14, 2016 event. Zucker, CNN's Worldwide president, was also there—sitting near the front of the ballroom—where he had the pleasure of witnessing two of his employees receive awards.*
>
> *First up was Clarissa Ward, a war correspondent for the network, who gave a gracious speech about how journalists "have to listen to voices we don't want to hear."*
>
> *Carmen Aristegui, on the other hand—whose popular show airs on CNN en Español—compared Trump to Adolf Hitler.*
>
> *The Mirror requested a comment from Zucker as well as a CNN publicist. Neither answered our questions....*
>
> *Twice during her speech, Aristegui dramatically raised two fingers to her upper lip to emphasize Trump's supposed similarities to Hitler.*

Suffice it to say, Aristegui was not fired by CNN for comparing the new president to Hitler. There was nothing "indefensible" about that.

CNN itself ran a documentary at the end of 2016 on the Obama presidency, hosted by Fareed Zakaria. *The Washington Times* ran this headline: "CNN documentary: Republicans are racists for opposing Obama."

On another occasion, after my departure, CNN's Don Lemon would open a show by saying, "The president of the United States is racist." Later Lemon would defend his charge by saying that it was his "obligation as a journalist" to say it. None of this resulted in firings for "indefensible" comments—because in the world of the Old Order, there was nothing indefensible about them.

My friend and CNN colleague Ana Navarro would later compare the president to a Nazi and a slave owner, as well as calling him an animal—the latter comment being made long before Trump was taken to task for saying the same of MS-13 gangsters. Note well: Ana was not fired either, and in my opinion should decidedly not have been fired. She has a point of view, and it is her job to put it out there. And she does it well, even if I or others disagree. This is called free speech—in a free press.

Only days after my firing for calling attention to the anti-Semitism and racism charges against Media Matters, a violent battle erupted in Charlottesville, Virginia, between neo-Nazis and the far-left Antifa, with one innocent bystander deliberately hit and killed by a man who was found to have expressed pro-Nazi beliefs. Trump issued a statement that spoke of "hatred, bigotry and violence" on "many sides." All hell broke loose, with the media and others going after Trump for not calling out the bigots they saw as being on the right. *The New York Times* wrote it this way:

> *But like several other statements Mr. Trump made on Saturday, the tweet made no mention that the violence in Charlottesville was initiated by white supremacists brandishing anti-Semitic placards…*

CNN would run an article by John Blake, described as an "activist and Fordham professor." The headline: "White supremacists by default': How ordinary people made Charlottesville possible."

There was *The New York Times* saying that Trump was wrong not to go after those at Charlottesville who had been "brandishing anti-Semitic placards." And here was CNN running a piece that favorably quoted an "activist and Fordham professor" as saying, "If you don't speak up when this sort of ideology is being promoted at the highest level, you end up being complicit in the actions taken by its more extreme adherents. Once the demons are unleashed, you've become a co-conspirator."

This was being run by CNN, incredibly, only days after I was fired for calling out a far-left-wing group repeatedly flagged for exactly the anti-Semitism that was both on the rise in the left and that was on vivid display in Charlottesville. I spoke up—just as Blake and CNN and *The New York Times* were saying should be done—but in the world of the liberal Old Order, this was flatly unacceptable. CNN, to be crystal clear, is not anti-Semitic. That is ridiculous. But as David Harsanyi would note over a year later in that *New York Post* column, "the media has a track record of tenaciously ignoring the anti-Semitism creeping into Democratic Party politics" and the American left. And ignoring the anti-Semitism so flagrantly displayed at the far-left Media Matters—a CNN ally—was exactly what was happening at CNN. This was a perfect example of what Mark Levin had earlier termed the Praetorian Guard media.

It was okay at CNN to demand that the president call out anti-Semitism by white nationalists. Yet at CNN, to call out an Old Order left-wing organization flagged time after time for the very same anti-Semitism and outright racism? No can do.

The notion that CNN had suddenly—out of the blue—turned on me with such intellectually disingenuous garbage just floored me. I still have great affection for the network and my former colleagues, and appreciation for the opportunities it provided me to witness history and make friends. Yet what was done was utterly unworthy of the network.

Pointing out the left's horrendous history on racism, not to mention raising the question of whether the culture of racism that had fueled it, and in my view still fueled it, as I had just done with Media Matters by calling attention to its anti-Semitic and bigoted tendencies—this was just not supposed to be done at CNN. Blowing dog whistles at the ugliest of political sentiments on CNN was just fine and dandy—as long as the ultimate target was Donald Trump. Jeff Zucker would leave no doubt on occasion that he protected me. While I certainly appreciated that, I quietly wondered why in fact a legitimate, mainstream Reagan-conservative commentator with an extensive background in government and columns in all manner of seriously reputable journalistic outlets needed "protection" by a network president in the first place. What in the world, I wondered, was so controversial about beliefs based on the Declaration of Independence, the Constitution, and my heroes or bosses in my political life—John and Robert Kennedy, Martin Luther King, Lincoln, Reagan, and Jack Kemp? Answer: a lot. Because I stood up for Trump and challenged Old Order gospel.

I was unhesitating on serious issues of race. And the use of race as a political tool of the left side of the American Old Order will be discussed in this book.

But over time, I eventually realized that all of these passionate discussions on CNN about race and other topics weren't really about race and those other topics at all. Sure, on the surface, yes.

Yet what was increasingly clear as one issue became another and another across a wide spectrum of issues domestic and foreign was that no matter the discussion at hand, the real concern was what so many of my CNN colleagues on the left and some on the right saw as an assault on what I was increasingly thinking of as that American Old Order. An Old Order that saw Donald Trump and the growing millions of "forgotten Americans" (as he called them) who were supporting him as an existential threat to what was, in its own way, a cozy clubhouse of elites. These are elites of the left and right who have long been accustomed to their mutually agreed upon way of doing business—meaning the business of everything from government and public policy to culture, sports, the media, and more. There was an Old Order way—as rapper mogul Kanye West would later discover the hard way when he revealed his support for Trump—and that was *the* way all of America was supposed to think, believe and, most important, behave. Hillary Clinton was the classic Old Order candidate—and her campaign was soundly repudiated. In the world of the Old Order, her defeat by Donald Trump—whom she has called a "creep"—was a five-alarm fire bell.

Not just making the left face its horrendous racial history, but calling attention to the cold fact that leftists not only haven't changed their political culture on race since it was formed at the very beginning of the American political party system in 1800, but are busy using it for political fuel on an almost daily basis today? That is well outside the acceptable for defenders of the Old Order and its left-wing division, dependent as they are on identity politics.

Their Old Order counterparts on the right would not dare suggest such a thing. Their role is to play defense and spend time saying they aren't racist and how they can prove it. Any interruption of this agreed-upon game is going to be met with the kind of fierce blowback designed to shut down anyone who politely points out the reality of serious historical facts—facts past and present. Why? Because those facts pose a serious threat to the Old Order—an Old Order that must be protected at every turn because, among other things, one of those threats is to the systemic racism that is desperately needed to fuel and preserve Old Order power and privilege. And as mentioned, as Robert Bork noted years ago, the real aim is control of American culture and what is and is not acceptable in that culture.

Experience is, as they say, a great teacher. I knew enough to know, as the CNN car was turned around and I had several more hours to retrace my ride home following my notice from Rebecca Kutler, that the best thing to do was calmly answer the calls—and think about my book project.

As was becoming increasingly frequent during these three-hour rides from my home in suburban Harrisburg, Pennsylvania, to midtown Manhattan and the other three hours back at night, I was thinking about this book.

The tentative title and theme were already set. *Lion at the Gate: Donald Trump and America's War Against the Old Order.* But as the CNN car was turned around and redirected from its original destination of Manhattan and the CNN bureau to take me back home to the middle of a Pennsylvania that had voted solidly for Trump—I had a startling realization:

Donald Trump was no longer the "lion" at the gate of the Old Order—he was now inside it. He was right in the middle of what he and his supporters had so often called "The Swamp." Faced with the new Trump reality, the Old Order viewed itself as fighting for its very existence. This was war. And I was now personally a sudden casualty of the very tumultuous Swamp War I was writing about.

In the words of my astonished editor at *The American Spectator*, R. Emmett Tyrrell Jr., CNN had gone about the business of "scandalizing" me. Indeed, if one read the headlines, this was startlingly true. Sean Hannity, furious at my treatment, recommended suing CNN and offered to get me a lawyer. Taking care of my mom had to come first, and going down the legal path was something that I had no appetite for doing. And there was one more supporter out there: the president himself. Speaking at a nationally televised rally in Phoenix a few days later, the president made headlines by saying this, as reported by *The Washington Post*:

> *Speaking at campaign-style rally in Phoenix, the president ridiculed and condemned the national media as "damned dishonest," eliciting boos and jeers from the friendly audience of supporters.*
>
> *"They fired Jeffrey Lord. Poor Jeffrey," Trump said, shaking his head gently and sounding exasperated, his arms outstretched and palms raised, as if in prayer. "Jeffrey Lord. I guess he was getting a little bit fed up, and he was probably fighting back a little too hard."*

> *On Twitter, Lord expressed his appreciation to the presi-*
> *dent, saying: "Thank you @POTUS !!"*

The wholly dishonest headline in the *Post*? "Trump laments 'poor' Jeffrey Lord, the CNN analyst fired for tweeting a Nazi salute."

The article completely ignored that the tweet was from my column going after Media Matters for its anti-free-press attacks and holding it out for contempt because of its anti-Semitism. It did manage to find a tweet from MSNBC's Katy Tur that read: "After extended rant on how he condemned neo nazis/white supremacists…Trump defends Jeffrey Lord who -wait for it- tweeted Sieg Heil."

It was tempting to tweet out a rejoinder asking Tur if she supported a group flagged for anti-Semitism. Then I recalled that in 2012, *The Daily Caller* had done its series investigating Media Matters. Of many revelations was this one:

> *High profile though these victories against conservatives were, Media Matters has perhaps achieved more influence simply by putting its talking points into the willing hands of liberal jour-nalists. "In '08 it became pretty apparent MSNBC was going left," says one source. "They were using our research to write their stories. They were eager to use our stuff." Media Matters staff had the direct line of MSNBC president Phil Griffin, and used it. Griffin took their calls.*
>
> *Stories about Fox News were especially well received by MSNBC anchors and executives: "If we published something about Fox in the morning, they'd have it on the air that night verbatim."*

Ahhh. But of course. MSNBC was taking memos from a group cited repeatedly for anti-Semitism and bigotry. Not to mention hiring Al Sharpton, he whose quite vivid history of blatant anti-Semitism includes lines like this one delivered in the midst of the Crown Heights riot: "If the Jews want to get it on, tell them to pin their yarmulkes back and come over to my house." Memo to Katy Tur? Look in the mirror.

Which is to say, washed away in the *Post* story about the president's sup-port for me was the fact that I had been calling out an Old Order group in my *Spectator* column (and others long before that) for its anti-Semitism, its raw, open bigotry, and what I saw as a decided anti-free-press fascism. Not to mention that over the years I had frequently used my columns to address the anti-Semitism and racism of the American left.

Never mentioned either was that I was decidedly not the first to do so. Now, right there in the *Post*, the facts were turned upside down or simply ignored (who cares about facts?) and the implication was that *I* was the one with the anti-Semitism problem and not the one calling out a prominent left-ist activist group for its flat-out bigotry. It was a sparkling example of what Trump delights in calling "fake news." As an example of a liberal media outlet's being "damned dishonest," to borrow from the president, that *Post* story and Katy Tur's tweet could not have provided a better example. What they implied was—there is no other way to say it—a willful, deliberate untruth. Otherwise known as a lie. A deliberate lie.

Over at *The Daily Beast*, columnist Lloyd Grove crowed about my dismissal, citing CNN sources who were "elated" I was gone. Grove said that both Don Lemon and Chris Cuomo—decided liberals both—made it a point to keep me off their respective shows after a while. In fact, I frequently turned down requests to do Lemon's shows for the simple reason that they are late at night and I had the three-hour trek back to Pennsylvania to relieve the Visiting Angel taking care of my mother. We did have a dust-up over my comparison of the tactics of Trump and Dr. King, which led to Lemon's summarily ending the conversation—more on that later. And I was scheduled to be on Cuomo's *New Day* show the very next morning before I was summarily fired. So I have no reason to believe the story. In my dealings with both, I found them to be good people, and I certainly valued and respected them as colleagues.

Yet there I was, the soul of politeness on-air and off as demanded by my parents since my arrival in this life, called out by some unnamed CNN insider for "getting uglier and more crude, almost as if he had to keep finding a bigger dog whistle." Had I called the president of the United States Hitler? No. Had I called him a racist? No. Had I called the president unhinged, a dictator, a liar, a loudmouthed dick, a bullshit artist, ignorant, an animal, or xenophobic? No. All of that was said about the president on-air by CNN anchors or commentators or guests, in the latter case without pushback. And every word of it got the green light from CNN.

It is a fact that this kind of thing went on with a disturbing regularity not just at CNN but all over the mainstream media—and it goes on still. If one didn't go along with this program—not unlike those young lawyers in Grisham's book *The Firm*—the long knives came out.

Over at *The Washington Post*, media columnist Margaret Sullivan celebrated my firing, revealing, doubtless unconsciously, just how the Old Order media plays the game. While I was attacked—along with fellow Trump-supporting CNN contributor Kayleigh McEnany—for making "bought-and-paid-for defenses of the often indefensible—candidate Trump and then President Trump," there was not a peep about liberal colleagues, similarly paid, who uttered nary a critical syllable about Barack Obama, Hillary Clinton, or indeed anyone or anything favored by the liberal Old Order. In a classic example of the über-far-left political correctness of the day, Sullivan said our "mere appearance on one's screen was triggering." My first reaction was to FedEx Sullivan a thermos of warm milk and a security blanket. There was, of course, zero recognition that by her logic Sullivan herself was a "bought and paid for" defender of the Old Order's liberal state media.

Over at the left-wing *Daily Beast*, I laughed out loud at a piece by the far, far leftist Matt Wilstein who quickly wrote:

> *ABOUT TIME: The 8 Worst Things Jeffrey Lord Said on CNN That Didn't Get Him Fired*
> *He was fired for tweeting 'Sieg Heil.' But Jeffrey Lord has been saying equally 'indefensible' things on CNN for a long time now.*

As with Sullivan, Wilstein is completely unaware of just how zealous and instinctive is his defense of the Old Order ways. Among his list of "indefensible" things said by me on CNN was the perfectly historically accurate description of the Ku Klux Klan's being used as "the military arm, the terrorist arm of the Democratic Party, according to historians." Either Sullivan and Wilstein are utterly ignorant of American history or, more likely, their devotion to the fiction that is modern-day Old Order liberalism is so intense that they just prefer to ignore the harsh and inconvenient facts. Sullivan said that my appearance on the screen was so offensive to her (truth can be offensive) that she had the desire to go "immediately to a bookstore or the public library and find something that nourishes the mind and intellect, something deep or beautiful or classic."

I would have recommended some history books to her. On the subject of the Klan and its use as a military force by the Democratic Party, I would ever-so-helpfully recommend to Sullivan and Wilstein that they read Columbia University historian Eric Foner's *Reconstruction* (page 425, on which Foner correctly states that the Klan "was a military force serving the interests of the Democratic party") and University of North Carolina historian Allen Trelease's *White Terror: The Ku Klux Klan Conspiracy and Southern Reconstruction* (page xlvii, on which Trelease identifies the Klan as "in effect a terrorist arm of the Democratic party"). Why do I think neither Sullivan nor Wilstein will ever crack the covers of books that clearly document the culture of racism that infects the Old Order and the American left then—and now?

Over at Fox, *Media Buzz*'s Howard Kurtz baffled me. I had met him years ago for a minute at some D.C. event or other, and I really have great respect for him. In reading my comments about CNN and the First Amendment, he seemed to think I was saying CNN had no right to fire me. Not so. Of course any network has the right to hire and fire anyone it chooses. My criticism was that CNN fails to stand up for a free press when it caves to the bullies of Media Matters, whether the target of the moment is me or any other conservative or anyone else, period. As I have said, who died and left Media Matters in charge of the American free press?

What is also true in terms of my ferociously negative reception by various anonymous CNNers, not to mention in the larger liberal media with people like Sullivan and Wilstein, is something noted by the late William F. Buckley Jr. years ago when he described what he called the "liberal mania."

Wrote Buckley in his 1959 book *Up from Liberalism*:

> *I think it is fair to generalize that American liberals are reluctant to co-exist with anyone on their Right. Ours, the liberal credo tells us, is an "open society," the rules of which call for a continuing (never terminal) hearing for all ideas. But close observation of the liberal-in-debate gives the impression that he has given conservatism a terminal audience. When a conservative speaks up demandingly, he runs the gravest risk of triggering the liberal mania; and then before you know it, the*

ideologist of openmindedness and toleration is hurtling toward you, lance cocked...

Buckley added of debates with liberals:

Arguments based on fact are especially to be avoided.... In dismissing a conservative's contentions, it is not enough merely to say that the matter under "discussion" is closed; it is usually necessary, for the sake of discipline, to berate the person who brought the matter up.

Which, in sum, was my experience not just with CNN at the very end, but also with liberals in the larger media as well. Note again that Buckley wrote this way back in 1959, a full twenty-one years before CNN was even invented and a full fifty-six years before I was hired as a CNN contributor.

To be clear, I loved my time at CNN. I loved my colleagues and the wonderfully passionate discussions we had. I believe totally that those sometimes very animated discussions were in the spirit of American free speech, a free press, and democracy in action. I didn't take what was happening to me that day of my firing personally. Then and now I feel a great deal of respect and affection for my former CNN colleagues. But I quickly realized this wasn't really about them at all.

The real question to me in the aftermath of my firing? It wasn't simply, "*What* just happened to me?" It was, "*Why* did this happen to me?" What was I really seeing here? There was more to this than just Buckley's "liberal mania." It was really about Bork's point that the Old Order's authoritarianism demands complete, iron-fisted control over American culture and politics. Any deviation from Old Order doctrine and sacraments—like pointing out the left's problem with anti-Semitism and attacks on a free press—has to be silenced immediately and ruthlessly.

This was about an Old Order media operation instinctively rushing to the defense of the larger push for control of the culture of which it was, quite voluntarily, a decided part. CNN was seemingly blithely unaware that the forces of press censorship it was encouraging by its acquiescence/alliance with Media Matters would, if allowed to go unchecked, surely at some point swing around and target a liberal. In fact, in November 2018 that is exactly what happened when the Trump White House wheeled around after that famous

Trump-Acosta showdown and lifted Acosta's White House pass. The White House was doing to CNN a version of what Media Matters repeatedly does to conservatives in the media—and had just done to me.

The famous statement attributed to Benjamin Franklin (accurately or not remains a mystery) was plain in its meaning to his fellow signers of the Declaration of Independence: "We must, indeed, all hang together or, most assuredly, we shall all hang separately."

It might have been me this day in August 2017, and at other times it had been others in conservative media. But not fighting this kind of flat-out anti-free-press zealotry—much less trying to appease it by allying with it—would doubtless at some point swing around to target a liberal media figure. As I said, it did just that with CNNer Jim Acosta—which is the "we shall all hang separately" part of that statement attributed to Ben Franklin. The point of that Franklin remark would reappear over a century later when German pastor Martin Niemöller made his now famous statement that reads like this:

> *First they came for the socialists, and I did not speak out—*
> *because I was not a socialist.*
> *Then they came for the trade unionists, and I did not speak*
> *out—because I was not a trade unionist.*
> *Then they came for the Jews, and I did not speak out—*
> *because I was not a Jew.*
> *Then they came for me—and there was no one left to speak*
> *for me.*

If it's okay to come after a whole list of conservatives in the media… then what? Who will be there to defend liberal media figures when the lynch mob—or even just a White House press office—turns to them?

In between the flood of personal messages and media requests coming in as news of my firing spread, there was time to reflect on the theme for this book as I rode back through the Pennsylvania countryside. (And a number of those personal messages came from CNN colleagues aghast at Jeff Zucker's decision. No names will be mentioned here, because I refuse to make them targets of Media Matters, which in itself is a testament to the power of the group's creepy authoritarianism.) I realized exactly what my firing and so much more that had taken place over the course of the 2016 election really represented.

Decades ago, as Franklin D. Roosevelt prepared to take office amid the devastation of the Great Depression, theologian Reinhold Niebuhr penned an essay in which he noted: "There is nothing in history to support the thesis that a dominant class ever yields its position or its privileges in society because its rule has been convicted of ineptness or injustices."

Niebuhr was correct—and the Old Order of today's America was not and is not prepared to yield to what it sneers at as "Trumpism" without a ferocious battle. The Old Order—the adult version of junior high school's insider "cool kids"—is about control. And it uses these types of battles—I call them "Swamp Wars"—to fight across American society on the fields of modern media, politics, finance, race relations, college campuses, entertainment, the judiciary, and even, of all the unlikely places, the FBI and the NFL.

Now myself a casualty of a Swamp War, I had one thought as the CNN car raced through the growing darkness, returning me home to the middle of Trump-supporting Middle America.

Write faster.

CHAPTER TWO

THE EDUCATION OF DONALD TRUMP

"Some men see things as they are and say, why; I dream things that never were and say, why not?"

—*Robert F. Kennedy quoting George Bernard Shaw*

MAY 2014

As I sit across from Donald Trump at his desk in his twenty-sixth-floor Trump Tower office, the question of the day revolves around Thomas Piketty, the French economist in the news because of his book *Capital in the Twenty-First Century*—in which Piketty lauds state intervention in capitalism and the restriction of the accumulation of wealth, which he sees, according to *The Wall Street Journal*, as morally illegitimate. Trump, arguably then the most prominent capitalist in America, if not the world, is appalled. He answers:

> *"Well, you're not going to have very many people working in this world if that were the case. People need the incentive and it's a tremendous incentive. And a thing like that would destroy jobs. It would destroy health, various health plans, various health plans. It would destroy education. It would destroy the world as we know it in free market societies. Which, and many of them are doing extremely well. You need the incentive to create wealth, and that incentive brings about jobs and all of the other things that jobs need. And it's also jobs with substantial income for people and families. It's not just jobs where they can live, it's jobs where they can live really well. Which includes medical, which includes education, which includes so many things that go along with it. So that would be a disaster for people that partook."*

Jobs. They are critical in the Trump worldview. How many had he created over the course of his career? I ask.

> *"Oh, tens of thousands. Even now, I mean, in four weeks I start, I start work on Pennsylvania Avenue in Washington, D.C. right between the Capitol and the White House. Right smack…the best location, the Old Post Office, and we're creating tremendous numbers of jobs. We're, you know, basically rebuilding it as one of the great hotels of the world. And…see, there's a thing you couldn't do without tremendous incentives and all of the other… you know, it's a very expensive project. A lot of people are going to be employed, a lot of jobs created. And as you know, I'm in the process, pretty close to finishing up Trump National Doral, what was Doral and—eight hundred acres right in the middle of Miami, so you know, we have tremendous jobs. We have jobs going up all over the world. No, I love what I'm doing, and I have a lot of fun doing it."*

And he has a prediction for the November elections. Unlike those forty-nine establishment Republicans the left-wing think tank Think Progress had gleefully quoted as predicting disaster for the GOP in 2014 because of the Ted Cruz-led effort to defund Obamacare by shutting down the government in 2013, Trump has an altogether different view of what is coming.

> *"We have a very big election coming up, and the Republicans are going to do very well in this election because of Obamacare and, I think, the lack of respect for the country. The country's in a very much different place than it was previously because of what's happened with respect to Obama, and it's really disastrous what's going on. So I do think the Republicans are going to have a massive victory, much bigger than anyone understands. And a lot of that is also because of the disaster known as Obamacare."*

In fact, when the smoke cleared from the 2014 elections, Republicans gained nine Senate seats, returning them to the majority, and won a net gain of thirteen House seats, giving them their largest majority since 1928—a full eighty-six years earlier.

As it turned out, not for the last time, Trump was right. The "political experts" were wrong. It was a glimpse of Trump's political acumen from outside the Beltway. What about this outsider-versus-insider business? I ask. What does he think of that?

> *"Well there's another thing. I went to New Hampshire recently for David Bossie and the group and you know, the two groups, they were terrific groups. And I made a speech. And I was told by everybody that it was the best speech, it had the biggest applause, by far the biggest applause. By the way, I was the only one on the front page [of* The New Hampshire Union Leader*], and a couple of the articles said, well they were just totally, they said, 'Mr. Trump had a smattering of applause.' And I'm saying to myself, 'What is…?' I had a five-minute standing ovation when I finished. And nobody else got that. Um, you know, again they have to reflect what's going on. And even people up there said, 'Wow. That was amazing!' 'Cause they actually said, 'He had a spattering of applause,' meaning, like, you know, people are applauding and falling asleep. The fact is, you know, I do draw big crowds. I think that…you know it would be very interesting, because if I ran it would be much different than any other candidate, because I'm a businessperson; I've done a great job. I built an incredible company and an exciting company, you know a company with really exciting things, and it would be a very much different campaign than the campaigns of politicians."*

Why? I ask.

> *"These are people that run for office professionally. They run if they lose; if they win, they just keep running. And they make a living running. You know, they take some of the money, they live off that money. With me it would be a very much different campaign; I would have something very strongly in mind. It would be about making this country great again. The word 'again' being a very important word. And it would be 'Make America Great Again,' because we are heading in the wrong direction.*

We are being laughed at throughout the world. We are not being led properly, and our country is in serious trouble."

Later, Trump circles back to the idea of "Make America Great Again," adding:

"One of the things that I feel strongly about is 'Make America Great Again…Make America Rich Again.' You can't be great if you're not rich. And when I see the Republicans wanting to cut Social Security, wanting to cut Medicare, wanting to cut Medicaid—you know, all of it, they want to cut Medicare down to a level, and they want to tinker with Social Security, and they want to do all these things. By the way the Democrats never mention this, they want to do a big number on Medicaid. I feel differently. I feel that I want to make this country—if I were president—I'd want to make this country so rich. We have such potential that you wouldn't have to take away and start cutting people's Social Security and Medicare. Now you want to take all the fraud and abuse out, which is a huge number, by the way. It has to run properly…. What I would do is make the country strong and rich. And once you make the country rich, you don't have to worry so much about cutting people's medical care and cutting Social Security and the kind of things that Paul Ryan and others are talking about. Because I don't think, frankly, that they are doing the right thing. I think that people have worked all their lives, you have many great people in this country, and I don't think they should be talking about cutting their…different elements of life after a certain period of time. So, and that's something you are not hearing from Republicans. And by the way, unless our country is going to be rich again, you're going to have no choice but to cut everything and cut it down to the bone. And I don't want to see that happen."

For anyone paying attention to Donald Trump in 2013 and 2014—and almost the entire Old Order political community that occupied and ran the Swamp was not—his words were an almost uncanny harbinger of events to come, and a reminder of whence he came.

His younger self, he had told me in our first meeting in 2013, had crossed the East River from Queens, disregarding his father's advice that the Trumps were from Queens and he should not go into the glistening, intimidating world of Manhattan real estate. Young Donald ignored his father's advice, followed his dreams, rented an apartment in Manhattan, and printed up business cards that read "The Trump Organization." It was a Manhattan organization that had no one in it but himself. Business card in hand, he recalled, the outsider from Queens set out to make deals in Manhattan, laying a one-man siege to—and eventually conquering—what the presidential chronicler Theodore H. White had once called "the heart of the Eastern Establishment...the Perfumed Stockade." Or, as it were, the crown jewel of the American Old Order.

Trump had succeeded beyond all measure. By October 2013, he was starring at *The American Spectator*'s annual Washington dinner—actually costarring with Texas senator Ted Cruz. I had flown down from New York with him at his request, our departure from Trump Tower momentarily delayed when his mere appearance in the building's tourist-laden lobby produced a mob scene of autograph- and selfie-seekers. I introduced him to the crowd that night at the *Spectator* dinner, the audience standing and applauding as he stepped forward to the tune of "New York, New York." After the usual preliminaries, he moved directly to the events of the moment.

For the past thirteen days, Senator Cruz had been leading a fight that resulted in an effective shutdown of the federal government, because neither funding for fiscal 2014 nor a continuing resolution that would carry the government through the crisis had been approved. The Texan had been under withering attack from Old Order Republicans and others, all of them predicting disaster for the GOP in the 2014 elections as a result of Cruz's actions—which revolved around keeping the GOP's promise to defund Obamacare.

As noted, the far-left blog Think Progress had published a list with the headline "49 Republicans Who Say Shutting Down The Government Over Obamacare Is A Big Mistake."

The list was a who's who of the Old Order GOP establishment that included names like Senator John McCain, Congressman Paul Ryan, governors or former governors Chris Christie, Jeb Bush, Mitt Romney, and more, plus a long list of conservative pundits including ex-Bush "forty-three" staffers Karl Rove, Nicolle Wallace, and David Frum.

Cruz is sitting a few feet in front of Trump this evening, and will follow him on the podium. Among other things, Trump says this, towards the end addressing Cruz directly:

> *"I just want to mention that over the last few weeks, because of what has been going on, a lot of people...I wrote a book called* Art of the Deal, *and people think I know about negotiation, and the press would call me and ask, 'What do you think of what's going on with the Republicans and the Democrats?' I hated to see what was happening, because conservatives and the Republicans were not sticking together. And I said, and I said it very loudly, that had they been together, had they been uni-fied...one of the Senators came out with a very famous quote, 'We can't win.' That was the exact quote. 'We can't win.' Had they stuck together, you would have made one hell of a deal. And you wouldn't be in the position where you're being crit-icized right now. So, Senator, hang in there, Senator...hang in there, Senator. But it wasn't easy for you, I can tell you. They were sniping at your heels, and I'm not talking about the Democrats. Just keep it going."*

He went on to talk about America's "being scoffed at" around the world, and said he thought Obamacare would "die of its own weight." Famously in the day, the new government website for Obamacare had opened as a disaster. He wondered why competent high-tech companies hadn't been hired to set it up—instead of its being a "disaster." It was "one hell of an embarrassment," he said—but the upside, he thought, was that it might aid a Republican victory in 2014. He went on to talk of the problems of illegal immigration.

In other words, both in his talk with me and his speech that night, what was said was the forerunner of what the country would hear from him from the day he announced his candidacy two years later, in 2015. And it was, notably to me, very well received when he said it at the *Spectator* dinner. *Very* well received.

The evening drew to its inevitable close. Surrounded by the crowd, smil-ing and shaking hands, Trump edged his way back to the escalator, out to the waiting SUV, and returned to the airport named for the fortieth president, who had arrived in Washington thirty-two years earlier to wage political war against the capital's ruling class of Old Order insiders—a war known to history as the "Reagan Revolution."

After Trump stepped aboard, the small Citation quickly took off and climbed into the darkness on the short trip to Manhattan, and to the waiting limousine that would return him to Trump Tower and the Old Order Swamp domain that is Manhattan. The town had no idea that its capture by Trump years earlier would provide the base for his forthcoming assault on the Swamp's headquarters—Washington, D.C., the city of presidential monuments and Old Order insiders.

The next day *The Washington Post's* coverage of the man who had been mobbed by tourists in New York and given a standing ovation by conservatives in Washington was exactly nothing.

CHAPTER THREE

WHAT THINK YE OF ME? PANIC: COLLAPSE OF THE OLD ORDER

"On a sudden, the Earth yawns asunder, and amid Tartarean smoke, and glare of fierce brightness, rises Sansculottism, many-headed, fire-breathing, and asks: What think ye of me?"

—*Thomas Carlyle in* The French Revolution

JANUARY 20, 2017

It was just over three years since that October evening when Donald Trump had quietly entered and departed this city of presidential monuments and Old Order insiders, unnoticed by *The Washington Post* and the Swamp's cluster of major media. Now he had returned, this time to be inaugurated as the forty-fifth president of the United States. Overcoming what many saw as impossible if not laughable odds, Trump had pulled off the greatest political upset since 1948's victory by Harry Truman over Thomas E. Dewey. Many thought Trump's triumph in one of the country's most tumultuous campaigns was even greater than 1948's—the hands down upset win in all of American election history. I certainly did.

The Old Order's *New York Times* left no doubt that it understood the importance of Trump's inauguration. The paper correctly if warily noted:

> *Mr. Trump's ascension amounted to a hostile takeover of a capital facing its most significant disruption in generations. While officially a Republican, he has taken on leaders of both parties and, with no prior political career of his own, made clear that he saw himself as the ultimate outsider not beholden to the current system....*
>
> *Mr. Trump said the inauguration was not merely the transfer of power from one president to another. "We are transferring*

power from Washington, D.C., and giving it back to you, the people," he said.

"For too long," he continued, "a small group in our nation's capital has reaped the rewards of government while the people have borne the cost. Washington flourished but the people did not share in the wealth." He added, "That all changes starting right here and right now."

On this inaugural day of the Trump era, jubilant Trump supporters, the "forgotten men and women" of America, as Trump had called them, flooded the streets of Washington, many wearing the trademark red hats bearing the phrase "Make America Great Again."

In France in 1789—the time of the French Revolution—the Old Order was called the *ancien régime.* The British historian Simon Schama would describe it this way:

Virtually as soon as the term was coined, "old regime" was automatically freighted with associations of both traditionalism and senescence. It conjured up a society so encrusted with anachronisms that only a shock of great violence could free the living organism within. Institutionally torpid, economically immobile, culturally atrophied and socially stratified, this "old regime" was incapable of self-modernization.

To say the least, as the 2016 campaign unfolded, it became clear to any woke observer that the Old Order of American elites had come to be viewed by Trump-supporting "new populists" as fitting Schama's description of the French *ancien régime* exactly. The American Old Order is filled with "traditionalism"—and not in a good way. It is senescent—in both its thinking and its reaction to events. It is "encrusted with anachronisms" (as in, "This is the way it has always been done"), "institutionally torpid" (unable or slow to respond to problems) and, most assuredly, "socially stratified." (There is "us," and then there is "them"—another way of describing the phenomenon that so resembles the social stratification of an American junior high school.)

But many in Washington that day were angry—viscerally so—at Trump's day of triumph. The American *ancien régime*—the American Old Order in all its many manifestations across the country—was angry, resentful, and in full panic mode.

"They started throwing bricks at first, then they started throwing the trash bin but that didn't work, then they picked up metal spikes and just started smashing the windows out," he said. "They had all that stuff in their backpacks."

The speaker was fifty-six-year-old Ronald Dye, identified in a story in the U.K.'s *Telegraph* as a customer at a downtown Washington Starbucks on January 20. *The Telegraph* added that Dye "said he hid under tables at Starbucks as 300 to 400 protesters swept past, some stopping to hurl bricks." Over 200 people were arrested.

There was, of course, video, which provided clear images of a briskly marching black-hooded mob racing along a Washington street, smashing the plate-glass windows of the famously liberal Starbucks before moving on to do the same to an adjacent Bank of America in a stark, violent testament to the furies the new president's election had unleashed. As if not satisfied with that, the protestors torched a limousine. Ironically, the limo belonged to one Muhammad Ashraf, a legal American immigrant—who also happens to be a Muslim. Ashraf's company did not have riot insurance for the car, which, he said, would cost $70,000 to replace.

Days before the inauguration, Georgia congressman John Lewis, a decided hero of the civil rights movement of the 1960s, bloodied at Selma, had let loose with a tirade attacking the new president as not a "legitimate president." Lewis was long past his days as a young civil rights hero, morphing into the personification of an Old Order lion, Democratic establishment version. Trump, in the style his rebellious "forgotten man" voters had come to love, hit back instantly, tweeting: "Congressman John Lewis should spend more time on fixing and helping his district, which is in horrible shape and falling apart (not to mention crime infested) rather than falsely complaining about the election results."

Pass the smelling salts. The Old Order stirred.

Nearly seventy members of Congress, reported *The Washington Post*, were now intent on noisily boycotting Trump's inauguration. All of them were Democrats. A number of them cited the president-elect's attack on Lewis as their reason, saying nothing about Lewis's initial, unprovoked attack on Trump. One tweet or press release after another gushed forth from these officials, variously and always piously proclaiming the new president as "a unique threat to the Constitution and to our country" or that his "rhetoric + actions" were "far beyond the pale."

In a classic illustration of Old Order hypocrisy, Democratic members of Congress issued statements attacking the new president. Minnesota's Keith Ellison hit Trump for stirring hate—the self-same Ellison who had been revealed as an ally of the anti-Semitic Louis Farrakhan. Michigan's John Conyers said the president needed to "grow up." By the end of the year, Conyers would be forced to resign as a result of multiple allegations of sexual harassment brought by female staff members, one of whom accused her boss of summoning her into his office while wearing only his underwear.

The day after the inauguration would bring a much more spectacular manifestation of Old Order panic, as hundreds of thousands of angry liberals employed one of their favorite tactics—the massive "march" that in this case was organized as a women's march on Washington. Pop star Madonna said that she was thinking of "blowing up the White House," while actress Ashley Judd read a poem proclaiming herself a "nasty woman!"

As it happened, I had some time off CNN's air and, with a friend, walked along Constitution Avenue to see what was up. In some cases, I was recognized and sharply asked what I was doing there or, more bluntly, angrily told to get out. Other marchers wanted to talk, which I was happy to do (as well as pose for selfies!). I was a child of the '60s, and the whole event had an air of a '60s reunion. Sure, there were young people there. But most assuredly there were men and women who clearly were themselves children of the '60s, and I had the vague feeling they had been doing the march of the moment through the decades, protesting every Republican president from Nixon on through Reagan, both Bushes, and now Trump. The causes had evolved from Vietnam to the nuclear freeze to anti-Iraq War or pro-choice and now anti-Trump marches.

Indeed, pro-life women spoke up to say that they had been quite deliberately excluded from the march, decidedly a nasty bit of non-inclusion. In fact, the marchers were the Old Order personified. And in typical "Tinker to Evers to Chance" style—as in the poem about the early-twentieth-century baseball players for the Chicago Cubs who epitomized relentlessly effective teamwork on the field—organizers organized, the marchers marched, and the Old Order media gave them reams of favorable coverage.

- A *New York Times* headline: "Crowd Scientists Say Women's March in Washington Had 3 Times as Many People as Trump's Inauguration."
- From CNN: "Protesters rally worldwide in solidarity with Washington march."
- From *TheAtlantic*: "The Inauguration, and the Counter-Inauguration."

Similar headlines were everywhere and, of course, marches were held in liberal enclaves across the country. Not noted at the time was that, to borrow from the "divide by race and gender" style of the left, the election stats showed that Trump had carried 52 percent of white women's votes, 25 percent of Hispanic women's, and 4 percent of black women's, and that Hillary Clinton, the first female presidential nominee, had won a paltry 54 percent of the total female vote, hardly a resounding endorsement of voting by gender. There were many reasons why Clinton was not being inaugurated this day, and later she would give as one of those reasons a refinement of her infamous campaign characterization that Trump supporters were a "basket of deplorables." This time, she said, her problem had been with white women who had "tremendous pressure from fathers and husbands and boyfriends and male employers not to vote for 'the girl'" and an "ongoing pressure to vote the way that your husband, your boss, your son, whoever, believes you should." The inherent racism, not to mention sexism, in that remark was as stunning as it was not surprising.

The presence of Old Order music star Madonna, actress Judd, and others in Washington was merely a slice of the Old Order dominion that was the entertainment industry in its refusal to celebrate the new president. Stars like the predictably liberal Alec Baldwin and Mark Ruffalo led a demonstration in front of New York's Trump International Hotel and Tower in New York. *Variety* also reported that "Judd Apatow, Jane Fonda and Joseph Gordon-Levitt are among those planning to participate in a 'Love-a-Thon' on Facebook Live, an event organized by several tech executives and former staffers for Hillary Clinton. The event will raise money for groups such as Planned Parenthood and the American Civil Liberties Union." Note well the last group, which will resurface shortly in our story.

In the world of academia, one college after another had students going out of their way to voice their anger at Trump's swearing-in. At the predictable Swamp that is the left-wing University of California at Berkeley, there was a "campus-wide" class walkout. But there were also anti-Trump demonstrations at Swamps—er, campuses—ranging from Ohio State to Florida State, to the University of Texas, to Philadelphia's Temple University, and more.

In the sports world, while Trump had received the endorsements of some notable sports figures, including Indiana University's famous basketball coach Bobby Knight, as well as Curt Schilling, the legendary Red Sox pitcher, soon enough CNN was reporting that "from Super Bowl winners, basketball MVP's, boxing champions, ballet dancers, Olympic medalists in soccer, figure skating and fencing, and sports legends like Billie Jean King and Kareem Abdul-Jabbar" there had "formed a passionate chorus protesting the state of American politics." Which is to say, the Swamp that is the sports division of the Old Order couldn't abide the new president.

Then there was the Swamp of Old Order American science. The Canadian Broadcasting Company (CBC) offered this headline about the American scientific community: "Scientists protest Trump inauguration with #USofScience on Twitter: Concern over Trump's views on science and policies prompt tweets."

Its story began: "Scientists from across the U.S. are taking to Twitter, concerned about the incoming president's views on science."

Not to be left out were illegal immigrants—their demands being part of the reason Trump's forgotten Americans were so exercised to begin with. In Oregon they held a protest-the-inauguration rally that was set to attract "hundreds of illegal immigrants" living in the state. The rally, a week before the inauguration, was attended by the state's senior U.S. senator, Democrat Ron Wyden.

While the "Resistance," as it was quickly called, garnered much media attention, nothing was said of an increasingly glaring fact.

An era was ending. An era dominated by the American Old Order. Whether it was reacted to with violence, congressional boycotts or marches in Washington and elsewhere, whether it was in the Swamps of the media, academia, science, sports, or Hollywood, the era of America as dominated by these various manifestations of the Old Order was ending—coming apart at the seams, in some cases.

As millions of Trump supporters across the country demonstrated on Election Day, the Old Order was so supremely—arrogantly—overconfident that it had been absolutely blind to what had been coming. But that most assuredly did not mean it wasn't capable of taking on the new president. In fact, while the Old Order, its leaders and rank-and-file soldiers, didn't understand what they were seeing when they were seeing it in real time in 2016, now they were awake—awake, alarmed, and angrily spoiling for a fight.

The central issue of the 2016 campaign that few had foreseen—the war against the American Old Order—had now been rung as a political bell. It was in fact ringing loud and clear this inauguration day—with one Swamp War after another looming, as in Jefferson's words about the coming conflict over slavery, "like a firebell in the night." As Robert Bork noted, this Swamp War was really about an Old Order obsession with dominance of the general American culture—and the battle in the new Trump era was on in earnest.

*　*　*　*　*

Perhaps most ironically, the Old Order came under attack in 2018 from maybe the oldest of Old Orders—the far left and socialists. In June 2018, *The New York Times* ran this headline: "Alexandria Ocasio-Cortez: A 28-Year-Old Democratic Giant Slayer."

Ocasio-Cortez had challenged longtime New York Democratic congressman Joe Crowley for nomination in a primary. And, in an upset, won. The *Times* reported of her victory:

> *She has never held elected office. She is still paying off her student loans. She is 28 years old. "Women like me aren't supposed to run for office," Alexandria Ocasio-Cortez said in a viral campaign video released last month.*
>
> *They certainly weren't supposed to win.*
>
> *But in a stunning upset Tuesday night that ignited the New York and national political worlds, Ms. Ocasio-Cortez, a Bronx-born community organizer and member of the Democratic Socialists of America, defeated Representative Joseph Crowley, a 19-year incumbent and Queens political stalwart who had not faced a primary challenger in 14 years.*
>
> *Mr. Crowley, who is twice Ms. Ocasio-Cortez's age, is the No. 4 Democrat in the House of Representatives and had been favored to ascend to the speaker's lectern if Democrats retook the lower chamber this fall.*

In truth, it is not unusual for twentysomethings to be elected to Congress. The required minimum age to be a member of the House is twenty-five, and Ocasio-Cortez was already three years past that. What made her triumph so startling to some was her defeat of a certified Old Order congressman, Democratic Party establishment version.

Here's where this gets interesting. Ocasio-Cortez is, as the *Times* duly if warily noted, a member of the Democratic Socialists of America. In the wake of her victory, National Public Radio set out to explore the worldview of the DSA. Not surprisingly, here's how one socialist sums up his beliefs in NPR's piece:

> *"I think we just need to realize that the end goal is, ultimately, like social control of the means of production," said Joe Cernelli, a founding member of that West Virginia DSA chapter. "You know we don't just want to improve capitalism, we will ultimately want to get rid of it."*

That's not just his idea; the DSA views capitalism as an oppressive system—"We see it as fundamentally undemocratic," as DSA National Director Maria Svart put it. Here's how she sums up what the group wants:

"When it comes right down to it, we believe people need to be able to live a dignified life. I mean, there are certain things that should not be left up to the market," she said.

Removing some parts of the economy from the forces of the free market, for example. In other words, socialism.

Got it.

Trump was not impressed. As evidenced in that 2014 interview with me, he had long been on record saying that socialism is a failure. In fact, when I had probed about President Obama's role in getting some Americans to think socialism was a good thing, he answered:

> *"The president has absolutely poisoned people's minds. And he's using a very populist approach where, you know, everybody can live very nicely and nobody has to work. This has always been a country based on work. The sad fact is that this is not the first time this has happened to a country, and those countries have all failed eventually. And it's only upon the failure that some-*

thing can come out of it, because it's very hard to beat the rheto-ric of 'Gee whiz, you know, we're gonna give…we're gonna have an income redistribution in this country.' Problem is nobody's going to be working. That's when it gets corrected, historically. And that's something that shouldn't happen to us. Hopefully we don't have to go down that path.

"But when it gets fixed is when it blows up. And it will blow up, if that's going to be the case. But the minds of so many have been poisoned by President Obama that it's really an incredible thing. An incredible thing has taken place."

Trump's answer then would doubtless not change in a discussion of Alexandria Ocasio-Cortez today. In fact, in his 2019 State of the Union address, he made his view emphatically clear, saying, "America will never be a socialist country." Whether in a book by a French socialist in 2014 or in a campaign by a young American socialist in 2018—not to mention the collapse of socialist Venezuela—the principle is the same. And in a very real sense, socialism is the oldest of the Old Orders in America today.

As opposed to Trump's slogan "Make America Great Again," socialism is about, to use a current example of centuries of socialism's failures, making America Venezuela. Or Cuba. Or worse.

One thing can be said with certainty: Donald Trump is no fan of socialism—and he will be ready to do battle with its newly rising advocates on the left in whatever Swamp War they may show up in over the rest of his presidency.

CHAPTER FOUR

BATTLE STATIONS:
THE SWAMP ATTACKS

"A desperate disease requires a dangerous remedy."

—*Guy Fawkes*

leven days after the new president took office, *The Washington Post* ran the headline "Resistance from within: Federal workers push back against Trump."

The story reported:

> *Less than two weeks into Trump's administration, federal work-*
> *ers are in regular consultation with recently departed Obama-*
> *era political appointees about what they can do to push back*
> *against the new president's initiatives. Some federal employees*
> *have set up social media accounts to anonymously leak word of*
> *changes that Trump appointees are trying to make....*
>
> *At a church in Columbia Heights last weekend, dozens of*
> *federal workers attended a support group for civil servants seek-*
> *ing a forum to discuss their opposition to the Trump adminis-*
> *tration. And 180 federal employees have signed up for a work-*
> *shop next weekend, where experts will offer advice on workers'*
> *rights and how they can express civil disobedience.*

That this would happen, shocking as it should seem, is not a surprise. As Jonathan Swan, then of *The Hill,* reported in late October 2016 as the Clinton-Trump campaign neared its tumultuous ending:

> *Federal government employees are opening their wallets to help*
> *Hillary Clinton beat Donald Trump on Nov. 8.*

Of the roughly $2 million that federal workers from 14 agencies spent on presidential politics by the end of September, about $1.9 million, or 95 percent, went to the Democratic nominee's campaign, according to an analysis by The Hill.

This is another way of saying that the bureaucrats who run the so-called permanent government in Washington were and are liberal activists as much as they are government employees. They are Swamp Warriors.

The nation's capital, so goes the legend, was built on a swamp. In fact, Washington historian Don Hawkins disputes the legend, saying that within "the original city's boundaries…only about 2 percent of the total area fits the definition of a swamp." Even so, there is no dispute that the city has long since left behind its once durable reputation as a sleepy, provincial backwater that was, in the words of John F. Kennedy, a city of "Northern charm and Southern efficiency." If Los Angeles was built on the movie industry, Detroit on cars, and Houston and Dallas on oil, Washington's "industry" is government. And government has been booming. If nothing else, Washington, D.C., is not just the nation's capital. It has become the Swamp. The capital of America's Old Order.

But what does the Swamp look like? What makes it the Swamp? A geological swamp is a murky wetland generally fed by a larger water source, and depending on where it is located it can be alive with some combination of alligators, snakes, turtles, frogs, fish, and trees, the latter dead and alive. The Washington version of this—in which the alligators and snakes and the rest come in human form—has a source as well, and it isn't the surrounding Potomac and Anacostia Rivers. It's big government.

The arrival of Franklin D. Roosevelt's big government enthusiasts of the New Deal in 1933 took the occasional expansion of government as practiced in earlier administrations and supercharged it. The formula for Washington's growth rose always from a felt need for government to do *something* to assist this or that group of Americans with whatever problem of the moment seemed overwhelming and demanding of governmental assistance. In 1933 it was the Great Depression, as it became known. And in response, Washington was flooded with big government enthusiasts determined to remake America from the top down.

To pick just one example (there are hundreds) for illustrative purposes of how the Swamp metastasizes, the provision of housing is typical. "I see one-third of a nation ill-housed, ill-clad, ill-nourished," FDR proclaimed in his own second inauguration in January 1937 as he recounted his administration's first term and the promise of his second. He added that the "government of the United States can do the things the times require."

This vision of government's "doing something" about housing expressed itself in congressional passage of the National Housing Act of 1934, which established the goal of making housing and mortgages affordable for Americans. It gave birth to two federal agencies, the Federal Housing Administration and the Federal Savings and Loan Insurance Corporation. Not satisfied with this, the Roosevelt administration persuaded Congress to pass the United States Housing Act of 1937, which put the federal government in the business of subsidizing local public housing.

In 1938, FDR created the Federal National Mortgage Association—aka Fannie Mae, in Swamp bureaucratic language. The idea: putting the U.S. government into the business of providing mortgage money to banks to ease financing costs for consumers.

Thus it was that the federal government began its serious entry into the world of housing, with later presidents slowly expanding what FDR had begun. By 1965, President Lyndon Johnson, an ardent FDR admirer who was first elected to Congress from Texas as a staunch Roosevelt supporter in a 1937 special election, was establishing the United States Department of Housing and Urban Development. HUD, as it became known in the Washington big government vernacular, would soon be housed in a ten-story concrete-and-glass leviathan built in the aptly named Brutalist style of architecture that itself now houses almost 9,000 federal employees in the building and across the country. The department is home to sixteen "offices" and two agencies, and in 2015 had a budget of $48.3 billion. HUD employees are paid an average of $100,123 a year. (And from 1990 until January 20, 1993—the day the Bush forty-one administration gave way to the Clinton era—I worked in the HUD headquarters as a congressional aide to HUD secretary Jack Kemp. It is indeed a very big place.)

In 1970, Congress passed, with the support of Republican president Richard Nixon, the Emergency Home Finance Act of 1970, which in turn created the Federal Home Loan Mortgage Corporation or, in more Swamp bureaucratese, Freddie Mac.

Both Fannie Mae and Freddie Mac would become central bureaucratic players—not to the good—in the Great Recession financial crisis of 2008. It was an all-too-typical tale from the Swamp, and the particulars have been detailed repeatedly, notably in the book *Reckless Endangerment: How Outsized Ambition, Greed, and Corruption Led to Economic Armageddon.* Written by *New York Times* business reporter Gretchen Morgenson and Joshua Rosner, a partner at the independent research firm Graham Fisher & Co., the book is a harrowing tale of the heart of the Swamp that grew from the original government involvement in the housing industry and quickly and inevitably became mired in the typical Swamp culture of Old Order elites in the worlds of Washington lobbying.

What Roosevelt and his successors had set in motion was, among other things, a magnet for lobbyists, as the 2008 financial crisis would so vividly illustrate. Firms registered and counted as housing lobbyists today number over 600, employing numbers small and large, collectively when not individually grossing millions. Thus on two fronts—federal employees and lobbyists—the natural order of things in Washington, D.C., was set. With the addition of fifteen Cabinet departments with their own concrete-and-glass leviathans, thousands of employees, and billions in budgetary allotments and attracting their own army of specialized lobbyists by the end of another big government presidency—Obama's—Washington, D.C., on the day Donald Trump was inaugurated, was indeed a very wide and deep Swamp of Old Order insiders.

The massive infusion of cash, much of it extracted from Americans taxpayers regularly reminded of this fact every April 15 as checks are written to the federal bureaucracy that is the IRS, changed not just the economic profile of the city but its psychology. The District of Columbia website boasts "the Washington, DC metro area is the strongest economy in the United States."

And so it is. The city overflows with first-class restaurants and watering holes that themselves are overflowing with well-to-do customers who earn their money in government, lobbying, the media or related consulting jobs for those seeking to influence government or get elected to it.

Once a cultural wasteland, the city is now a prime entertainment hub with offerings ranging from Broadway plays and film premieres to the National Symphony and the Washington National Opera, with performances at the Kennedy Center or historical settings unique to the nation's capital, from

Ford's Theater to the U.S. Capitol lawn or the grounds of the Washington Monument. The NFL's Washington Redskins and Major League Baseball's Washington Nationals share the sports pages with the NBA's Washington Wizards and the National Hockey League's Washington Capitals.

Not to be left out is the media. Well beyond the influence of the home-town *Washington Post*, as the center of American political power, the town is flooded with national and state media outlets and their much-in-demand personnel. If Manhattan is the center of the financial and media world, Washington is home to thousands of journalists and staff charged with filling the airwaves and cyber and print pages of everything from the four broadcast networks (ABC, CBS, NBC, and PBS) and three cable outlets (CNN, Fox, MSNBC) to the *Post*, *The Washington Times*, the *Washington Examiner*, *The Washington Free Beacon*, and every American and foreign news outlet imaginable. Predominantly liberal, journalists in Washington are like actors in Hollywood—everywhere.

All of this, of course, is reflected in Washington's neighborhoods. Members of Congress live side by side with journalists, bureaucrats, lobbyists, White House aides, and consultants. The force of all this has transformed the town's psychology, however initially inadvertent when the capital was first formed, into a bipartisan sense of "us versus them." "Us" refers to those who live "inside the Beltway." "Outside the Beltway" are "them," meaning those who live, metaphorically and literally, outside the locale—but not the powerful reach—of those inside the Beltway.

Collectively this not only produces a Swamp of a town wholly preoccupied with its own importance—the jobs, political power, and status of its denizens—but has also created a mesmerizing Swamp psychology of the herd, or a Swamp groupthink whose real method of communication is virtue signaling. (It has even impacted romantic life, with various publications running stories that the love lives of young Trump aides frequently crater the instant it is revealed they work in the Trump administration.)

As Donald John Trump took the oath of office on that cold January day, another vision of his that the sophisticated political observers of this town could not see until it was too late was that the Queens outsider who had once conquered the "Perfumed Stockade" that was Old Order Manhattan against all odds was now assuming the ultimate insider job that the Washington Swamp had to offer.

In an openly bipartisan fashion, the infuriated and resentful insiders of the Swamp's Old Order seethed, junior high school style. The cool kids had lost the election, and they didn't like it one bit.

"There are a whole lot of career attorneys who are determined not to let their work get dismantled, by working twice as hard, by just being total pains in the butt if people try to undo their work," said an anonymous "Justice Department official," as *HuffPost* (formerly the *Huffington Post*) described its source. In fact, *HuffPost* unwittingly provided a window into just how contemptuous federal bureaucrats can be of an elected president—not to mention the American people who elected them and, oh yes, pay their salaries.

- From the Department of Veterans Affairs came this: "I cannot, in good conscience, work for either the bozo-elect or whoever he may appoint as the new secretary of the VA. Honestly, I cannot accept the thought of having to look at photos of these clowns when I walk into my office in the morning."

- "Am I going to be an unwitting enabler of war crimes under this administration?" wondered a source from the Pentagon's Defense Intelligence Agency.

- "Yes, we're worried that our president might actually turn out to be a fascist. That's a not-insignificant cause for concern."—a Department of Labor bureaucrat.

- "I would take George W. Bush any day over this. I would take him in a heartbeat. Right now."—an EPA bureaucrat.

- And by 2019? There was this story in anti-Trump *The Daily Beast*. The headline: "Treasury Department Chaos Leads to Exodus of Key Staffers." The story? Staffers complaining the senior Trump-appointees would "overlook their professional assessments on key policy-related topics"—and so they quit.

Behold the Swamp mentality.

So how does it work in practice? This way.

Recall that the Trump administration's secretary of education is Michigan conservative and education activist Betsy DeVos. Which is to say she is at odds with the liberal education agenda that is so dear to the hearts of not just liberal education activists outside the department but also those of the bureaucrats inside the department.

DeVos had barely been confirmed when, a little over two weeks after Trump's inauguration, she scheduled a visit to a school in Washington. On arriving—presto!—protestors! CNN's headline was "Protesters block Betsy DeVos from entering DC public school."

The CNN report said:

> *Protesters briefly blocked Education Secretary Betsy DeVos as she tried to enter a public school in Washington on Friday morning.*
>
> *Demonstrators holding signs greeted DeVos when she arrived at Jefferson Middle School Academy in southwest Washington, not far from the Department of Education building.*
>
> *When she headed toward the school's entrance, the protesters stood in front of her, video from CNN affiliate WJLA showed.*
>
> *DeVos then turned around and walked away, the video showed, with one protester walking beside her shouting, "Go back! Shame, shame" as she got into an SUV and drove off.*

Score a small victory for the Swamp. But there would be, of course, more to come. (And remember—this is only the Department of Education!)

President Trump, as with all presidents, has to produce a budget for the federal government. This is a massive document with the particulars of federal budgeting, which I learned close up as a young congressional staffer for Pennsylvania congressman Bud Shuster, a member of the House Budget Committee. But in the Trump era, the budget was part of a Swamp War all of its own.

Before the document was released, mysteriously *The Washington Post* ran back-to-back stories on two different days in May 2017 detailing proposed budget cuts in the Department of Education. The first headline screamed "Trump's first full education budget: Deep cuts to public school programs in pursuit of school choice."

The story—utterly typical of the breed of Swamp hysteria over threats to the cherished Old Order way of doing things—began this way:

> *Funding for college work-study programs would be cut in half, public-service loan forgiveness would end and hundreds of mil-*

lions of dollars that public schools could use for mental health, advanced coursework and other services would vanish under a Trump administration plan to cut $10.6 billion from federal education initiatives, according to budget documents obtained by The Washington Post.

The administration would channel part of the savings into its top priority: school choice. It seeks to spend about $400 million to expand charter schools and vouchers for private and religious schools, and another $1 billion to push public schools to adopt choice-friendly policies.

President Trump and Education Secretary Betsy DeVos have repeatedly said they want to shrink the federal role in education and give parents more opportunity to choose their children's schools.

The next day the *Post* picked up from where it had left off the day before, with the headline "Here are K-12 education programs Trump wants to eliminate in 2018 budget."

This jewel of Swamp warfare begins:

Mental health services. Civics and arts programs. International education and language studies. Anti-bullying activities. Gifted and talented initiatives. Full-service community schools.

These are some of the K-12 education programs that President Trump is proposing be eliminated in his first full budget, as explained in a story published on The Washington Post's website, here.

Now here's where the story gets interesting. What is on display here is exactly—again—the "Tinker to Evers to Chance"-style teamwork that is reflexive Swamp warfare. In this case the ball was first picked up by organizers (Tinker), who arrange for a protest to harass and embarrass the secretary in front of television cameras. Eventually the ball—the early details of the education budget—gets thrown to an anonymous insider bureaucrat—Evers. And in turn, the insider bureaucrat, a crafty Swamp warrior, throws to Chance in the form of a leak to *The Washington Post*. And presto! The *Post* runs stories depicting DeVos as Cruella de Vil, the seriously wicked villain from the novel-based Disney cartoon classic *101 Dalmatians* who wants to kidnap puppies to make coats out of their fur. Cruella de Vil's name, of course, is taken from the words "cruel" and "devil," and she is the epitome of sheer meanness. Note well, again, how that second *Post* story about DeVos's wanting to eliminate various federal education programs began: "Mental health services. Civics and arts programs. International education and language studies. Anti-bullying activities. Gifted and talented initiatives. Full-service community schools."

Got that? The Swamp's message to all Swamp Warriors is crystal clear. Betsy DeVos is soooooo cruel and devil-like, so mean, mean, mean, that she wants to kill mental health services for needy children, not to mention take away their "civics and arts programs" and "international education and language studies." As if that isn't cruel and mean enough, on top of that she wants to leave the children of America at the mercy of school bullies by—*gasp!*—scrapping "anti-bullying activities"!

The script at this point calls for DeVos—humiliated, scorned, and mocked—to retreat. Maybe to resign and go home to Michigan in shame. But this Trump appointee, very much in the spirit of Trump himself, decides to—*gasp!*—punch back.

The *Post*, aghast, ran this headline—which was, but of course, based on a leak from inside the Education Department's bureaucracy: "Education Secretary Betsy DeVos asked whether leakers could be prosecuted, internal report shows."

That's right. DeVos had the audacity to want to know if whoever was leaking internal Education Department documents could be prosecuted—which sent the Swamp Warriors crazy. The answer from the department's assistant inspector general for investigations appeared to be that, well, there was no policy in place to provide for this. But he recommended policies to do just that.

Score this one small Swamp War as a victory for Betsy DeVos. But it would be a mistake to think her victories will stop her tangles with the Swamp Warriors of the Education Department. They will go on, for sure, for her entire tenure as secretary.

And it would be a mistake to see this Old Order attitude as simply belonging to liberals in the Swamp bureaucracy.

* * * * *

Welcome to the world of Never Trumpers.

It started out innocently enough, and it has occasionally happened before in the history of presidential politics. A candidate emerges from a series of hard-fought primaries to lead the delegate count for a presidential nomination. The losers grumble. There is a last-ditch effort to have the candidate's intra-party opponents defeat him. It fails. Then the losers rally to the winner.

In 1960, the Democratic Party's old guard was less than thrilled at the emerging young Massachusetts senator John F. Kennedy. Not only was Kennedy a mere stripling as a forty-three-year-old, but he was also Catholic. There had never been a Catholic president—but there had been Al Smith, the 1928 Democratic nominee who was both Catholic and clobbered by the GOP's Herbert Hoover. Too many party oldsters remembered the Smith disaster and saw Kennedy as repeating it. Former president Harry S. Truman denounced him, going as far as to resign his Missouri delegate seat to the party convention when it became obvious that Kennedy might capture the nomination at the convention—in fact, Truman charged that the nomination had been "rigged" for JFK. In spite of triumphs in the key primary states of Wisconsin and West Virginia, Kennedy was challenged all the way through a floor fight at the Democratic Convention, not winning until the roll call got to "W" on the ballot—with Wyoming finally putting him over the top. Significantly, the different factions got together, with the old guard's Texas senator Lyndon Johnson, the Senate majority leader, put on the ticket as JFK's running mate. The ticket won in the fall.

In 1976 some in the Democratic Party establishment, aghast at the idea that ex-Georgia governor Jimmy Carter, a party outsider, was on the verge of winning the party's nomination, formed the ABC coalition—Anybody But Carter. It failed. The establishment's Minnesota senator Walter Mondale, like LBJ, went on the ticket as the vice presidential nominee to soothe the old guard. The party insiders finally rallied to their nominee, and Carter went on to win the presidency.

There are exceptions, of course. In 1964 one establishment Republican after another refused to support Senator Barry Goldwater after the conservative Arizonan won the GOP nomination to take on President Lyndon Johnson. While it is doubtful Goldwater would have won an election that took place not quite a year after President Kennedy was assassinated—few Americans had an appetite for a third president in four years—still it was notable that so many prominent Republicans went out of their way to so ostentatiously withhold support from their party's nominee. Goldwater lost in a landslide.

So there was nothing particularly unusual about grumbling from Republican Party insiders when Donald Trump, against all odds, won the GOP nomination. As with Kennedy and Carter, Trump selected a popular party favorite—the conservative Indiana governor Mike Pence—as his running mate. And right about there, the similarities between past presidential nominees and the winning Trump stop.

It was a remarkable sight in the beginning. Letters or statements began popping up in primary season opposing Trump. *National Review* published statements from various prominent conservatives opposing Trump in January 2016 under the headline "Conservatives Against Trump." Yet a number of those people—although not all—had a change of heart later and boarded the Trump train.

More ominous was the report in March 2016 that ninety-five former national security officials from several Republican administrations had signed a letter saying they would never vote for Trump. By August there was yet another letter, after Trump and Pence had been nominated, which said, among other things:

> *The undersigned individuals have all served in senior national security and/or foreign policy positions in Republican Administrations, from Richard Nixon to George W. Bush. We have worked directly on national security issues with these Republican Presidents and/or their principal advisers during wartime and other periods of crisis, through successes and failures. We know the personal qualities required of a President of the United States.*
>
> *None of us will vote for Donald Trump.*

As Trump gained steam, members of the GOP's Never Trump cabal went out of their way to attack him.

"He is an authoritarian blending nationalist and tribalist impulses, which historically has never worked out well for the nation that goes in that direction or the people in that nation," said Erick Erickson, the founder of the conservative site *Red State*.

Said William Kristol over at the conservative *Weekly Standard*:

> *I've made my "never Trump" argument to other Republicans. The strongest counter-argument is, oh, you're electing Hillary. I don't think it's correct. I think the nomination of Donald Trump is what is most likely going to elect Hillary. And I think having a strong, alternative conservative would actually help Republicans down-ballot, and actually maybe in the presidential election, as well.*

Kristol would spend his time in 2016 trying to induce a conservative somebody—a conservative anybody—to join the race as a spoiler. Had his efforts been successful, Hillary Clinton would have been elected. And sadly—I had contributed to the *Weekly Standard* in 2002 and certainly liked and respected Bill Kristol and his crew—the Never Trump brand the magazine adopted proved in late 2018 to be fatal. Unable to sustain itself or find backers, it went out of business.

Famously, longtime conservative columnist George Will not only denounced Trump but, once it became clear that Trump would be the Republican nominee, made a point of announcing he was leaving the Republican Party. "After Trump went after the 'Mexican' judge from northern Indiana then [House Speaker] Paul Ryan endorsed him, I decided that in fact this was not my party anymore."

After Will made his announcement, former Bush forty-three White House speechwriter David Frum took to the pages of the left-leaning *Atlantic* to vent, saying in part: "The Republican Party is ill, and it has been ill for a long time. But quitting won't help: An American political party can only be reformed from within."

One of the more vocal Never Trumpers was a Republican consultant named Rick Wilson. Writing in the *New York Daily News* in August 2016, Wilson made it plain that he knew with certainty that Trump was going to lose. What Wilson took to the pages of one of the most vocal anti-Trump papers in the country (a serious contest) was a demand that Trump get absolutely clobbered so that he and his supporters could never rise again. His headline: "Beat him like a drum: Donald Trump must not just lose in November; to correct the institutions he's broken, he must suffer a humiliating defeat."

Calling Trump "the single worst major party nominee in modern history," Wilson went on to say in this jewel of a *Daily News* Op-Ed, this:

> *And so, now, here we are: As revealed by poll after poll, Americans feel worn down by the dirty, ugly character of the dirty, ugly candidate at the top of the GOP ticket.*
>
> *It's not just that, in the wake of the Democratic Convention, Hillary Clinton has surged ahead in national polls by seven, nine, 15 points.*
>
> *She is far ahead in every state poll that matters. A Friday poll put her up slightly in Georgia, which has been reliable Republican territory in the last five elections....*
>
> *Those of us who believe, who know, that Trump is dangerous can't just settle for him being beaten in November. We need to ensure that he is on the business end of a decisive, humiliating defeat—so that the terribly divisive forces he has unleashed are delivered a death blow.*

In concluding, Wilson insisted that Trump supporters had "dragged one of America's great political parties from the back of a truck."

Not to put too fine a point on it, but Rick Wilson could not have been more wrong than if he believed babies come from storks. Wilson is typical of the elitists of the Republican Party who had managed to drive the party into not just a ditch but a political hole the size of the Grand Canyon. And there is nothing new about this either.

All the way back in 1948, Republican elites of the day were not just opposed to Democratic president Harry Truman—they were *offended* by Truman and his style. They saw him as a joke, mocking him with lines like "To err is Truman" and "I'm just mild about Harry." He was seen as "common" and crude, a crass, ugly, bullying little man whose very presence in the Oval Office was soiling the White House.

The Rick Wilsons of the day were advising New York governor Thomas E. Dewey, the GOP nominee, to be the opposite—and Dewey needed no persuading. Told that party workers wanted him to conduct a blistering, hard-edged campaign against the blunt-spoken president who was earning the nickname "Give 'em hell Harry" for his scorched-earth tactics, Dewey replied: "That's not what we are going to do…. I will not get down into the gutter with that fellow." Famously, Truman won in the upset of the century.

In 2018, Wilson wrote a book titled *Everything Trump Touches Dies*. Having been proved 1,000 percent wrong with his Trump predictions in 2016, he was now lashing out at those who were 1,000 percent right. At the top of his list was Sean Hannity. For six pages Wilson rages on, saying that Hannity is (among other things) "a shallow, dangerously stupid man" and "a disaster in every way but the ratings" who has "enlisted a clown college of Fox contributors like Newt Gingrich and Geraldo Rivera." Recall, this ranting by Wilson is directed towards the commentator (Hannity) who saw what Wilson missed by a country mile. He also aims at the ex–speaker of the House (Gingrich) who led a successful political revolution to take back the House from Democrats for the first time in forty years, something establishment Republicans and their consultants of the day could not and did not do.

Notably, in the style of a Dewey advisor, Wilson has reserved a section of his book to rant about Trump's lack of dignity. The message: the GOP is all about style, and Trump doesn't have it. As always, lots of these Republican Old Order consultants advise presidential candidates to play by the Marquess of Queensberry Rules—and are always shocked when they lose. Then they go out and do the same things in the next election—with the same results.

As the criticism of Trump gained steam in 2015, I made a point of taking a look back in GOP history. Where had I heard these predictions of disaster by establishment Republicans before? In July 2015, with Trump's campaign barely a month old, I wrote about them in a *Spectator* column titled "Yes, Trump Can Win."

- **Former Republican president Gerald Ford** in 1980: "I hear more and more often that we don't want, can't afford to have a replay of 1964." If the Republican Party nominates Ronald Reagan, "it would be an impossible situation" because Reagan "is perceived as a most conservative Republican. A very conservative Republican can't win in a national election." Asked if that meant Ford thought Reagan couldn't win, Ford replied to *The New York Times*: "That's right." The *Times* story went on to observe that Ford thought "Mr. Reagan would be a sure-loser in November" and that Reagan held "extreme and too-simple views."

- **Illinois Republican senator Charles Percy** said Reagan's candidacy was "foolhardy" and would lead to a "crushing defeat" for the Republican Party. "It could signal the beginning of the end of our party as an effective force in American political life," he said.
- **Republican vice president Nelson Rockefeller** dismissed Reagan as "a minority of a minority" who "has been taking some extreme positions."
- **New York Republican senator Jacob Javits:** He said Reagan's positions are "so extreme that they would alter our country's very economic and social structure and our place in the world to such a degree as to make our country's place at home and abroad, as we know it, a thing of the past."
- **The liberal Republican Ripon Society:** "The nomination of Ronald Reagan would McGovernize the Republican Party."

These predictions of doom for the GOP by the party's Old Order grandees of the day were echoed, but of course, across the Old Order media spectrum anytime Reagan was discussed as a potential GOP nominee. As here:

- *The New York Times:* Reagan's candidacy is "patently ridiculous."
- *The New York Times:* "The astonishing thing is that this amusing but frivolous Reagan fantasy is taken so seriously by the news media and particularly by the President (Gerald Ford). It makes a lot of news, but it makes no sense."
- *The New Republic:* "Ronald Reagan to me is still the posturing, essentially mindless and totally unconvincing candy man that he's been in my opinion ever since I watched his first try for the Republican nomination evaporate in Miami in 1968."
- *The New Republic:* "Reagan is Goldwater revisited.... He is a divisive factor in the party."
- *Harper's Magazine:* "That he should be regarded as a serious candidate for President is a shame and an embarrassment for the country at large to swallow."
- *Chicago Daily News:* "The trouble with Reagan, of course, is that his positions on the major issues are cunningly phrased nonsense—irrationality conceived and hair-raising in their potential mischief...."

Here comes Barry Goldwater again, only more so, and at this stage another such debacle could sink the GOP so deep it might never recover."

- *Time:* "Republicans now must decide whether he represents a conservative wave of the future or is just another Barry Goldwater calling on the party to mount a hopeless crusade against the twentieth century."

- *Newsweek:* Ronald Reagan is "a man whose mind and nerve and mediagenic style have never been tested in Presidential politics and may not be adequate to the trial."

- *National Review* (**a conservative magazine**): "Reagan's image remains inchoate.... At the outset of his campaign, his image is largely that of the role-playing actor—pleasant on stage, but ill-equipped for the real world beyond the footlights. Reagan does not yet project the presidential image. He is not seen as a serious man." An *NR* columnist dismissed Reagan by saying simply: "He's not a serious man."

- *Manchester Union Leader* (**a conservative New Hampshire paper**): Reagan "lacks the charisma and conviction needed to win."

- *Pravda,* **the official newspaper of the Soviet Union:** Reagan is a "dinosaur from the 'cold war'.... It is strange that there are still fish in the sea that are tempted by this putrid bait."

What is crystal clear for any conservative who is awake is that the battle between conservatives and GOP establishment types has been raging for decades. Way back there in the mists, in 1950, Tom Dewey, the leader of the GOP's Eastern establishment, which had managed to lose the presidency twice with Dewey as the nominee, insisted that if the party went down the conservative path, "the Republicans would lose every election and the Democrats would win every election." As seen with those predictions of doom for the GOP in Reagan's days, nothing has changed today in terms of the "wisdom" of GOP establishment types.

Rick Wilson, for sure, was not the only one who predicted disaster for Trump. Political experts and journalists foresaw disaster. From the Bush wing of the party came this from Karl Rove, writing in *The Wall Street Journal*:

> *The response of GOP candidates to Mr. Trump should be guided*
> *by the June 23 Fox News Poll showing that 64% of Republicans,*

69% of conservatives and 55% of tea party members consider his candidacy a sideshow. An analyst at the FiveThirtyEight website pointed out that Mr. Trump has the worst favorable/unfavorable ratings of 106 presidential candidates since 1980, worse than even Al Sharpton and Jesse Jackson. Mr. Trump is disliked by 57% of his own party....

Mr. Trump could become the 2016 version of Missouri Rep. Todd Akin, who tarnished the GOP brand in 2012 with an offensive statement about rape. Republican leaders from Mitt Romney on down immediately condemned his words, but swing voters were persuaded that every Republican believed what Mr. Akin said.

Over at NBC, Perry Bacon wrote:

Donald Trump is almost certainly not going to be the Republican presidential nominee, and his candidacy puts the Republican Party in a quandary over its rules for which candidates to include in debates.

Trump has obvious disadvantages. He has never run for another office or held another government post, as nearly all modern presidents have. The Republican Party has at least a dozen candidates with stronger credentials than Trump.... He is unlikely to win a single primary.

Then there was this from *The Washington Post*'s Chris Cillizza—who is now a political analyst for CNN:

There's a tendency when someone like Donald Trump announces that he is running for president to view—and analyze—him through the same lens that we do for the other men and women actively seeking the presidency. What's his policy vision? Who's in his political inner circle? What would a Trump presidency look like?

Asking any of these questions gives Trump a benefit of the doubt that he simply doesn't deserve: That a path exists for him to be president.

It doesn't. Not even close.

Mitt Romney, the party's 2012 nominee—who had gone out of his way to seek Trump's endorsement that year—took to the University of Utah's Hinckley Institute to launch a scathing attack on the man he had so badly wanted to endorse him four years earlier. Among other things, Romney said:

- "First on the economy. If Donald Trump's plans were ever implemented, the country would sink into prolonged recession."
- "Here's what I know. Donald Trump is a phony, a fraud. His promises are as worthless as a degree from Trump University."
- "Now let me turn to national security and the safety of our homes and loved ones. Mr. Trump's bombast is already alarming the allies and fueling the enmity of our enemies. Insulting all Muslims will keep many of them from fully engaging with us in the urgent fight against ISIS, and for what purpose?"
- "Think of Donald Trump's personal qualities. The bullying, the greed, the showing off, the misogyny, the absurd third grade theatrics. You know, we have long referred to him as "The Donald." He's the only person in the entire country to whom we have added an article before his name, and it was not because he had attributes we admired."
- "Now, Mr. Trump relishes any poll that reflects what he thinks of himself. But polls are also saying that he will lose to Hillary Clinton."
- "And let me put it very plainly. If we Republicans choose Donald Trump as our nominee, the prospects for a safe and prosperous future are greatly diminished."
- "Of course, a Trump nomination enables her victory. And the audio and video of the infamous Tapper-Trump exchange on the Ku Klux Klan will play 100,000 times on cable and who knows how many million times on social media."

As events played out, Romney's predictions of what would happen if Trump were the nominee, not to mention what would result from his policies if elected president, turned out to be an exercise in spectacular political misjudgment. And as to the Frum charge that the Republican Party was ill? It seems to me that the Republican Party is ill from departing from Reagan's conservatism and replacing it with Old Order preservation politics that GOPers of the Frum type have long advocated.

On—and on and on—went this surge of what became known as the politics of "Never Trump." In September 2016, with the Trump-Clinton battle now in full swing, the left-leaning *HuffPost*, which earlier had started keeping a list of the "group of Republican officials, operatives, and conservative intellectuals" who were flatly refusing to endorse the Trump-Pence ticket updated the list to just shy of fifty. The list included former presidents Bush forty-one and forty-three, former Florida governor Jeb Bush, 2012 GOP nominee Romney, and an assortment of moderate Republican governors, senators, and members of Congress.

The lack of support from the Bushes reminded me of an observation made by former Reagan White House political director Ed Rollins, who signed on to co-chair the pro-Trump Great America political action committee in 2016. In his memoir *Bare Knuckles and Back Rooms: My Life in American Politics*, Rollins wrote the following of Reagan's selection for vice president, the moderate and establishment Republican George H. W. Bush, whom Reagan had just defeated for the 1980 GOP presidential nomination. After describing the Reagan-Bush ticket as a "shotgun marriage" of the conservative and establishment wings of the GOP, Rollins says he thought of Bush as a "Trojan Horse. The enemy (the establishment) was in our (conservative) camp." He adds: "In the end, Ronald Reagan had won the battle and handed his sword to the losers…. At the very outset of the revolution, the seeds had been sown for its undoing."

Indeed, Reagan biographer Steven F. Hayward would note this of the Reagan-Bush differences after the 1988 election, as the transition began from the Reagan presidency to that of Bush: "But the first order of business for the Bush transition was turning out all of the Reaganites as quickly as possible…. Newt Gingrich cautioned, 'We are not Bush's movement.'"

In late November 2018, former president George H. W. Bush, ninety-four, passed away. Without question, he was a man of great and high character and most certainly a genuine American hero. As president he safely guided the Cold War to its conclusion and memorably assembled a first-class coalition of thirty nations to drive Iraq's Saddam Hussein out of Kuwait. The stumbling block that helped defeat the Bush re-election in 1992 was breaking his famous campaign pledge "Read my lips: no new taxes." In truth, Bush forty-one's breaking of that pledge is typical of moderate Republicans in domestic American politics—there is, as Tom Dewey, John McCain, Mitt Romney, and others have repeatedly demonstrated over the decades, an instinct to be like Democrats, just a little less so. Time after time this urge proves fatal for the GOP.

The Reagan Revolution, among other things, remade both the Republican Party and the government along Reagan's conservative ideological lines—and the Bush Republicans, who had previously been Ford Republicans or Nixon Republicans or Eisenhower and Dewey Republicans—were determined to bring the party back into what they saw as the moderate mold.

Nowhere was the GOP branch of the Old Order better exemplified than in a story from *Politico* in early 2015, as former Florida governor Jeb Bush began his campaign. The headline:

> "Bush courts D.C. lobbyists: His allies are being asked to raise $50,000 each for the likely 2016 hopeful."

The story began:

> *Jeb Bush's wooing of Washington has officially begun.*
>
> *The former Florida governor held two meetings with association executives and lobbyists Tuesday at the National Association of Wholesaler-Distributors headquarters, outlining his thinking about running for president and taking questions from veteran GOP operatives.*
>
> *Bush is expected to hold a similar meeting Wednesday with another group of Republican allies. He is slated to return to Washington in February as part of 60 fundraisers across the country his team has planned.*

The Bush campaign did indeed raise lots of money from Old Order establishment insiders—over $100 million. And it utterly flamed out. Voters wanted—were demanding—someone who would shatter the Washington Old Order status quo and clean out the Swamp. This was something neither Jeb Bush nor any other establishment type had the slightest intention of doing. The Never Trumpers not only never got this, but they made a point of signing on to oppose Trump's decidedly Reagan-style conservative agenda.

Now the Trump Revolution was at hand. Donald Trump was not Ronald Reagan. As I would say often enough on CNN, there are no duplicates of anyone; all human beings are unique. But Trump's pledges to appoint conservatives to the Supreme Court, cut taxes, and conduct a foreign policy of Reaganesque "peace through strength" were all decidedly conservative—and most assuredly would not be acted on in a Hillary Clinton administration. Yet it made no difference to various Bushies or to Romney and others. While there were indeed some serious Reaganites on various lists—including, on the *National Review* list, perhaps the most loyal of them all, former Reagan attorney general Edwin Meese, a truly honorable soul—it was the more establishment GOP names that seemed to stand out.

There was something glaringly obvious about all of this, even if the media was unable or unwilling to pick up on it. When one added all these lists of non-endorsers and signers of indignant Never Trump letters together, what did they collectively represent? Not all of them, but overall—particularly that list of ninety-five national security "experts" who actually boasted about their records with the Bushes and Nixon?

Yes indeed, a number of these people had morphed, perhaps inevitably given their establishment credentials, into classic Swamp Warriors. They themselves had become the high priests of the Old Order, and their virulent Never Trump letters—the letter from the ninety-five national security types in particular—were virtual symbols of their Old Order status. And they found an eager audience on cable networks like MSNBC and CNN. MSNBC loved to spotlight former McCain senior advisor Steve Schmidt. Having failed to elect McCain president, Schmidt now spends his time telling the world that Trump—who won his presidential election—is incompetent. Ya can't make this stuff up.

Former self-described "conservative" turned Never Trumper Max Boot put his Never Trumpism in book form, like Wilson and others. Reading it is an exercise in understanding just how various Republicans over the decades have revealed that when push came to shove, they were not only not Republicans, but they were most assuredly not conservatives. The late British prime minister Margaret Thatcher used to focus on this same problem with British Conservatives. In her memoirs, Thatcher says of some of her fellow Tories (after stating the obvious about the British Labor Party—that it is devoted to socialism):

> *The Tory Party was more ambivalent. At the level of principle,*
> *rhetorically and in Opposition, it opposed these (socialist) doctrines*

and preached the gospel of free enterprise with very little qualifica-
tion. Almost every post-war Tory victory had been won on slogans
such as 'Britain Strong and Free' or 'Set the People Free.' But in the
fine print of policy, and especially in government, the Tory Party
merely pitched camp in the long march to the left. It never tried
seriously to reverse it. Privatization? The Carlisle State Pubs were
sold off. Taxation? Regulation? Subsidies? If these were cut down at
the start of a Tory government, they gradually crept up again as its
life ebbed away. The welfare state? We boasted of spending more
money than Labour, not of restoring people to independence and
self-reliance. The result of this style of accommodationist politics,
as my colleague Keith Joseph complained, was that post-war pol-
itics became a 'socialist ratchet'—Labour moved Britain towards
more statism; the Tories stood pat; and the next Labour government
moved the country a little further left. The Tories loosened the corset
of socialism; they never removed it.

This is a thumbnail description of Old Order establishment Republicans
in America. Heaven forbid if one actually tried to "remove the corset" of big
government socialism from the Swamp.

Some Never Trumpers have even bought into the Old Order's insistence
on identity politics, or as I call it, the grandson of slavery and the son of
segregation. In Max Boot's book *The Corrosion of Conservatism: Why I Left
the Right*, Boot illustrates the problem exactly. He accuses Trump of racism
and cites as an example "when Trump launched a crusade against African-
American NFL players who kneeled during the national anthem to protest
police brutality." Boot points to this Trump statement made at a September
2017 rally: "Wouldn't you love to see one of our NFL owners when someone
disrespects our flag to say, 'Get that son of a bitch off the field right now...
he's fired!'"

This criticism of Trump—and Boot was far from alone in making it, as
the left was enraged as well—is a classic of the Old Order's systemic racism.
Trump never said one word about race. It is Boot and the other Trump critics
who have looked at these players—all of them multimillionaire professional
athletes, a category that has no color—and reduced them to their skin color.

In 2018, following the Trump summit in Helsinki with Russia's Vladimir
Putin—which was blasted by many Old Order national security and foreign

policy "experts"—Fox's Tucker Carlson delivered a withering analysis. He said, in part:

> *"With remarkable speed and intensity, the media, the foreign policy establishment, both political parties have come together as one to attack the president for his meeting yesterday with the Russian president Vladimir Putin. Anderson Cooper, John McCain, Mitt Romney—they all described the President's remarks about Russia as disgraceful. Former CIA Director John Brennan called those remarks 'treasonous' and grounds for impeachment. Nancy Pelosi and Chuck Schumer announced that Trump was being blackmailed by a foreign power. Others accused him of being a sleeper agent, a spy. One member of Congress from Tennessee called for a military coup against the presidency."*

Tucker went on to note Trump's correction remarks the next day as doing the necessary "genuflecting before US intelligence agencies whose judgment must never be questioned." What made the president buckle:

> *"...is amazing...and ominous. The people who are yelling the loudest about the Russians being our greatest enemy and Trump is their puppet happen to be the very same people who have been mismanaging our foreign policy for the past two decades. The people who invaded Iraq and wouldn't admit it was a mistake. The people who killed Muammar Gaddafi for no obvious reason and prolonged the horrible Syrian Civil War and then threw open the borders of Europe. The ones still defending the pointless Afghan conflict and even now planning new disasters around the world in Lebanon, Iran, and yes in Russia. These are the people who have made America weaker and poorer and sadder. The group whose failures got Trump elected in the first place. You would think by this late date they would be discredited completely and unemployable, wearing uniforms and picking up trash by the side of a turnpike somewhere. But no, they're not. They're hosting cable news shows, they're holding high positions of influence at the State Department. They run virtually*

every nonprofit public policy institution in Washington. They are still in some sense in charge of our national conversation. And naturally they hate the idea of rethinking or correcting any of the countless blunders they have made over the years. And that's one of the main reasons they hate Trump, because he calls them on those blunders...[and] on the big questions Trump is indisputably right. The Cold War is over. The world has changed. It is time to rethink America's alliances and to act in our own interest for once."

He closed by adding what many Trump supporters had begun to conclude:

"This is about democracy, whether or not voters rule their country. It turns out the very people telling you they are saving our democracy are working overtime to destroy it—and scolding you as they do."

Carlson went on to mention one of the uncomfortable facts of the Swamp. Why the focus on Russia and not, say, Saudi Arabia or China? He pointed out that many in Washington are getting rich from the Chinese and the Saudis. Latin Americans clean their homes and watch their kids. No one is getting rich from Russians, unless one counts the Clintons. Only with the murder of Jamal Khashoggi, a Saudi journalist who had written for *The Washington Post* and was brutally killed when visiting the Saudi embassy in Turkey, did this attitude begin to change.

Rush Limbaugh, as well, understood what was really going on with the cascade of Swamp media resentment washing over Trump after Helsinki. In answering a caller who was admiring Trump's blunt-speaking ways versus the usual ambiguity of other politicians, Limbaugh said:

"Well, I think you're partially right. You're on the right track. I think in this particular area where basically they don't like the way Trump talks, is what you're saying, and the reason is because he's too direct, that's certainly true, but I think it goes farther than that. I think we're dealing with class arrogance. I think the media considers themselves part of the political class in Washington.

"And they are an equal part. They're on the same elite level as the politicians and the bureaucrats that they cover.

"In fact, in many of the media's minds they may be on a higher level, given they may have more power because they, in their minds, can destroy whoever they want to destroy. Whereas a bureaucrat has to go undermine people and backstab and this kind of thing. The media can do that right out in the open.

"As part of this arrogance of class, there is a proper way of speaking and there's a proper way of behaving. And there's also, if you're Republican, there's a proper way to acknowledge that you know that you're second-tier establishment, that you're not in the elite. And Trump blows all that up. And he makes no effort to ingratiate himself in their world. Instead, he walks in and is in the process of blowing up their world.

"He's blowing up their very restrictive class distinctions. He's blowing up the way they talk about things inside the Beltway. He's blowing up diplomacy. He's blowing up foreign relations. And it's being done in a way these people can't figure out. For the life of them, they can't understand straight talk. To them, straight talk is thuggery, it's insulting, and it's mysterious. And so Trump is like an invader, an alien, and he's gotta go."

Right there is a superb description of what the unspoken core complaint about Trump by Republican Establishment Never Trumpers really is all about. The plain-spoken Trump is guilty of many things, in their eyes. But first and foremost, Trump offends their sense of style and class. He had every opportunity with personal wealth and an Ivy League education—the University of Pennsylvania's Wharton School of Finance—to be one of them. He refused. Not unlike, over a half century earlier, the plain-spoken Harry S. Truman offended Thomas E. Dewey and the establishment Republicans of that day. Trump is not one of them—but he could have been—and in fact he couldn't care less. Which, naturally, angers Never Trumpers even more. It is yet again the junior high school-clique mentality hard at work.

Rick Wilson rants about the virtue of the Never Trumpers. In fact, the comparisons he makes of Trump supporters to all sorts of historical bad guys is in fact the way I certainly see the Never Trumpers. They—the Jeff Flakes, and the consultant/commentator types like Rick Wilson, Steve Schmidt, Max

Boot, and others in the GOP (if they, like Schmidt and Boot, haven't departed the party) are the Neville Chamberlains of American politics. They are all too willing to appease the Old Order leftists and their liberal state and their quest for cultural authoritarianism. Longtime conservative David Horowitz puts it well in an article over at the conservative Center for American Greatness:

> The posture of these NeverTrumpers is transparently self-serving. It preserves their intellectual credentials as "conservatives," and simultaneously takes them out of the line of fire from an increasingly vicious Left whose goal is to destroy Trump and his presidency, and—incidentally—conservative America. Sitting on the fence affords them new career opportunities—appearances on CNN and MSNBC and columns in the New York Times. All that's required is that they avoid taking sides in the political war that is engulfing the country. All this reminds me of a memorable Trotsky sneer about liberals, whom he accused of being reluctant to step into the stream of political conflict because they were afraid to get their moral principles wet.

Yet in fact it is precisely Trump's not being one of the Old Order priests—although he easily could have been one— that was a good part of his attraction to voters. On occasion at his rallies both before and after his election, Trump would mock the way the Old Order expected its presidents to behave, slowing his speech and sounding like a solemn phony who means not a single thing he is solemnly saying. Trump is different—he relishes going after phonies, just as he told me directly, and he meant every word of what he was saying. And his supporters, on a gut level, knew it.

The ultimate irony of the Never Trump movement is that in fact its very resistance created its opposite—what might be called the Always Trump movement. Come hell or high water, whether it was a leaked *Access Hollywood* tape in the campaign or a presidential press conference with Vladimir Putin, the Always Trumpers were sticking by their man. They had had enough of Old Order rule and Swamp War politics. And they had, by God, done something about it.

"A desperate disease requires a dangerous remedy," said the infamous British anarchist Guy Fawkes. Fawkes, a Catholic, had indeed plotted dangerous remedies for British politics. One was to assassinate King James, a

Protestant who was accused of persecuting Catholics, and replace the king with his daughter Princess Elizabeth, who, Fawkes and others hoped, would be less repressive to Catholics. Fawkes was also involved in the "Gunpowder Plot," a plot to blow up the British Parliament building during the opening of Parliament.

In the world of the Swamp, Old Order bureaucrats—such as those plotting against Education Secretary DeVos—and those Old Order Never Trumper Republicans like Wilson, Frum, Schmidt, Boot, and others all view Trump's very being, not to mention his presidency, as some sort of "desperate disease." There isn't a day when they aren't plotting politically dangerous remedies to halt or oust their target from the presidency completely. These would include everything from impeachment to a "Special Counsel" (Robert Mueller) to unproved, wildly vivid allegations of Trump's secretly plotting with Vladimir Putin to steal the 2016 election.

Yet thus far in this particular Swamp War with bureaucrats and Never Trumpers, chalk one up for Trump and his new populists. Which is why, if you listen, you can hear the sound of gnashing teeth all over Washington.

CHAPTER FIVE

SIX WAYS FROM SUNDAY:
THE DEEP STATE WEAPONIZES

"Let me tell you: You take on the intelligence community—they have six ways from Sunday at getting back at you."

—*Senate Minority Leader Charles Schumer*

"That bastard."

—*John F. Kennedy, on
FBI director J. Edgar Hoover*

"**F**—Trump."
"He's not ever going to become president, right? Right?!"
"No. No he won't. We'll stop it."

So went the back-and-forth texts between the deputy assistant director of the Counterintelligence Division of the Federal Bureau of Investigation—Peter Strzok—and the legal counsel to the deputy director of the FBI, Lisa Page. The texts happened in an FBI workplace run by FBI director James Comey.

Oh yes. Did I mention Strzok and Page were having an affair? Or that Strzok also texted Page that "God, Hillary should win 100 million to 0"? Did I mention that Strzok was, at the same time he was texting these anti-Trump, pro-Hillary Clinton sentiments, the very same official inside the FBI who was charged with investigating Clinton? In December 2017, *The Hill* reported:

> *The former FBI official, who was recently fired from special counsel Robert Mueller's Russia team over messages critical of President Trump, reportedly edited a key phrase that removed possible legal implications in former FBI Director James*

Comey's statement about his decision on the Hillary Clinton email investigation.

Peter Strzok, who served as a counterintelligence expert at the bureau, changed the description of Clinton's actions in Comey's statement, CNN reported Monday, citing U.S. officials familiar with the matter.

One source told the news outlet that electronic records reveal that Strzok changed the language from "grossly negligent" to "extremely careless," scrubbing a key word that could have had legal ramifications for Clinton. An individual who mishandled classified material could be prosecuted under federal law for "gross negligence."

On top of that, eventually Americans learned that a "dossier" on Trump—compiled by British spy Christopher Steele, the onetime head of the Russia desk for British intelligence (MI6), and paid for by the Clinton campaign and the Democratic National Committee—was used to obtain a warrant to investigate the Trump campaign under the Foreign Intelligence Surveillance Act (FISA). The FISA judge who issued the warrant was not told of the dossier's blatantly political source. The dossier, filled with unsubstantiated gossip, alleged that the Trump campaign had colluded with Russia to win the 2016 election. None of it was true. It was a blatant attempt by Obama administration officials to influence the 2016 election—and when that failed, to overturn the results.

Not since the reign of J. Edgar Hoover has the FBI seen such a brazen misuse of federal law enforcement power, not to mention such a vivid display of the Old Order's reach. In fact, the Hoover legend is instructive in considering just how widespread were both the desire and the drive of Old Order bureaucrats in the FBI to "f—Trump" in this particular Swamp War.

One small but illustrative tale of how Hoover the wily bureaucrat played the game is discussed at length in Pulitzer Prize-winning author Tim Weiner's book *Enemies: A History of the FBI*. It made *The New York Times* of the day. The story?

During the Kennedy administration, the attorney general was the president's brother Bobby. Bobby and Hoover were legendarily like oil and water. As Kennedy biographer and friend Arthur Schlesinger noted in his biography of RFK: "The center of institutional resistance" to Kennedy's authority as attorney general was the Federal Bureau of Investigation.

The State Department notified the Attorney General that there seemed to be a leak at State that was a constant problem, resulting in the continual questioning of the choice of personnel at State by the hostile senator who chaired the Senate Internal Security Subcommittee. An investigation launched by Kennedy found the leaker, "a high ranking official in the Security Office and a holdover from the McCarthy period"—a reference to the Communists-in-government investigations of the 1950s by Wisconsin senator Joseph McCarthy. The man's name was Otto Otepka, and he was in fact the deputy director of the State Department's Office of Security. It turned out that Otepka was giving classified documents to the counsel for the Senate subcommittee. And as Weiner points out, Hoover and the senator "had an informal and highly secret agreement to share intelligence with each other."

Here's where the tale sounds eerily similar to that of today's ex-FBI director James Comey and the texts of the Trump-hating Peter Strzok and Lisa Page. When confronted, Otepka acknowledged that, in fact, yes, he had been giving the documents to the senator, who in turn shared his information with J. Edgar Hoover. The senator and FBI director were determined to root out suspected Communists in government, and a need was felt to know about just whom the Kennedy administration was hiring. Otepka's admission got him fired by Secretary of State Dean Rusk. Rusk, according to an admiring biography of Otepka by former UPI correspondent William J. Gill titled *The Ordeal of Otto Otepka*, said that his subordinate "was out of bounds." Otepka faced formal charges of dismissal from the State Department, the charges saying, among other things: "You have conducted yourself in a manner unbecoming an officer of the Department of State."

Said Otepka in defiance: "To me, loyalty to…my country is paramount." He added: "I feel it is my higher duty to my country to reveal the security risks that this new Administration is bringing into government. I am willing to break the law and sacrifice my career to bring this practice to a halt."

Did you catch that phrase? This one: "I feel it is my higher duty to my country…"

And where exactly have Americans heard a version of that recently? That's right: the memoir of fired FBI director James Comey, titled *A Higher Loyalty*. Comey's version of a higher duty, a higher loyalty, is exactly the same as Otepka's—an allegiance to "lasting values, most important the truth." Otepka didn't see those values in the Kennedy-era State Department—a highly subjective, not to say partisan, point of view—so he used his official position to deliberately, not to mention subversively, oppose his own bosses and, ultimately, President Kennedy himself. The latter, of course, was the duly elected president of the United States.

The central difference between Otepka and Comey and Comey's anti-Trump allies in the FBI and Justice Department is that Otepka was a conservative anti-Communist, while Comey's Old Order ire was directed at Donald Trump from the left. But make no mistake, their common insistence that they had a "higher duty" (Otepka) or "higher loyalty" (Comey) to save the country from a perceived danger in the White House is identical. It says everything about the mindset of government officials and high-ranking bureaucrats who decide to take the law into their own hands from a duly elected president out of a sense of elitist entitlement.

In 1962, political journalists Fletcher Knebel and Charles W. Bailey II, both longtime members of the Washington press corps for the Washington bureau of Cowles, wrote a bestselling political novel, *Seven Days in May*. The book was such a hit, it was made into a 1964 movie featuring the hot stars of the period: Burt Lancaster, Kirk Douglas, Ava Gardner, and Fredric March. The plot: the chairman of the Joint Chiefs of Staff, Air Force general James Mattoon Scott, played by Lancaster, is so opposed to the incumbent president of the United States, Jordan Lyman (Fredric March), and to Lyman's signing of a nuclear disarmament treaty with the Soviet Union, that Scott and several of his fellow military chiefs plan a coup d'état that would replace the elected president Lyman with...General Scott. General Scott's aide, Marine colonel Martin "Jiggs" Casey (Douglas), stumbles on the plot through a series of odd happenings and goes directly to the president to inform him about Scott and the secret cabal behind the plan.

Eerily the book and film presage the thinking that has now become vividly evident in real life with the collusion among the FBI, CIA, and Department of Justice senior officials plotting to stop Trump. Here are lines from the movie, a conversation between Jiggs Casey and his friend Colonel "Mutt" Henderson, Henderson the executive officer—the deputy commander—in charge of the secret military division that is key to the planned coup. Henderson is not in on the plot—only his immediate superior, a Fascist-minded colonel, is in on the conspiracy. Henderson believes he is genuinely helping to command a long-approved-through-channels unit called ECOMCON—military shorthand for Emergency Communications Control. But he is puzzled about what he is being asked to do.

Henderson: You know, it's funny.

Casey: What?

Henderson: We seem to spend more time training for seizure than for prevention.

Like the Commies already had the stuff and we had to get it back.

What Casey eventually realizes is that his friend's unit was never approved by the president, and in fact "seizing" is exactly the role the ECOMCON unit is supposed to play. Specifically, its purpose is the seizing of the emergency communications of private American television and telephone companies— to "take back" communications lines for the new military junta on the seventh day of May when it runs its coup that will seize the presidency itself from its lawful occupant. In the end, their plot discovered, the fictional President Lyman fires General Scott, and his coconspirators, the military chiefs of staff, resign in disgrace.

Substitute the names of the characters in the book and film with the now uncovered anti-Trump plotters in the FBI, CIA, and Justice Department, and it becomes instantly clear just how serious the plot to do in Trump is— first when he was a candidate and now that he's the president. In real life it isn't right-wing military leaders leading this cabal, characters with the real-life titles of chairman of the Joint Chiefs of Staff, chief of staff of the Army, chief of staff of the Air Force, and commandant of the Marines. (In *Seven Days in May*, the Navy declines to join the plotters.)

In the real-life drama revolving around Trump, the main characters are Old Order civilian bureaucrats with titles like director of the FBI (Comey), deputy director of the FBI (Andrew McCabe), deputy assistant director of the Counterintelligence Division of the FBI (Peter Strzok), director of the CIA (John Brennan), deputy attorney general (Sally Yates), and associate attorney general (Bruce Ohr). They were aided in their task by the British ex-spy, MI6 officer Christopher Steele. Individually and collectively they were about "seizing" the presidency to "get it back" from Trump and his new populist legions who had quite legitimately won the election.

And as in *Seven Days in May*, there has been a string of prominent firings, resignations, and demotions, in this case more than two dozen in the FBI and the Department of Justice alone.

The question here is not, "Did this happen?" "This" being the Old Order's attempted sabotage of the Trump campaign and the Trump presidency. The evidence is overwhelming that it did. The real question is why. Why did this happen?

The answer can be found in a look back at that previously cited quote from the theologian Reinhold Niebuhr, written at the time of the Great Depression: "There is nothing in history to support the thesis that a dominant class ever yields its position or privileges in society because its rule has been convicted of ineptness or injustices."

Niebuhr's point applies with particular pointedness to the *why* of today's Old Order and its raison d'être for acting as it did and does in relation to Donald Trump. As is indicated by the title of Comey's book, the warriors of the Old Order in the FBI, the Justice Department, and the CIA had a "higher loyalty" than their oath of office and the Constitution. Their higher loyalty was and is to the Old Order, to the Swamp—and to the power and privileges it bestows.

Comey himself, illustrating exactly Niebuhr's point of why he did what he did, has acknowledged his motives. As reported by *The Hill*:

> *Former FBI Director James Comey acknowledged on Tuesday that he did not confront President Trump on false statements during meetings with him.*
>
> *Comey said he did so because he wanted to remain in his role as the nation's top cop.*

Well of course. That is the *why* of all of this mess. It was and is all about keeping the power and privilege of an Old Order high priest. And the participants, with increasing desperation, went to increasingly extreme ways of doing this.

Yet another case in point: former Obama director of the CIA John Brennan.

In August 2016, Bloomberg reported that if "Hillary Clinton wins the U.S. presidential election in November, John Brennan would like to continue his post as director of the Central Intelligence Agency." Exactly. So how to go about winning the presumed next president's confidence?

Gregg Jarrett, the legal and political analyst for Fox News, in a detailed analysis of Brennan in Jarrett's bestselling book *The Russia Hoax: The Illicit Scheme to Clear Hillary Clinton and Frame Donald Trump*, says this after noting the difficulty in uncovering duplicity in an agency "cloaked in stealth and secrecy." The subject: then director Brennan's role in spreading the phony "dossier" on Donald Trump. Writes Jarrett, quoting a senior aide to the House Intelligence Committee: "'John Brennan did more than anyone to promulgate the dirty dossier. He politicized and effectively weaponized what was false intelligence against Trump.'"

"What exactly did Brennan do?" Jarrett asks. The aide quickly details exactly the game the ex-CIA director played.

- Brennan was one of the first to "have access" to the phony dossier.
- He "alerted the FBI" so that it would open a Trump-Russia investigation.
- He told "top members of Congress" that Russia was trying to elect Trump.

Jarrett goes on to quote Stephen Cohen, professor emeritus of Russian Studies at New York University and Princeton. Cohen wrote of Brennan in the left-wing magazine *The Nation*:

> Brennan played a central role in promoting the Russiagate narrative, briefing members of Congress privately and giving President Obama himself a top-secret envelope in early August 2016 that almost certainly contained [British ex-spy Christopher] Steele's dossier.
>
> In short, if these reports and Brennan's own testimony are to be believed, he, not the FBI, was the instigator and godfather of Russiagate. Certainly, his subsequent frequent and vociferous public retelling of the Russiagate allegations against Trump suggest that he played a (and probably the) instigating role. And, it seems, a role in the Steele dossier as well.

Jarrett also correctly identifies Comey as the "man who, more than any-one else, is responsible for the most notorious hoax in modern American history." The hoax was designed to block the Trump campaign from winning, and when that failed, to use the investigative powers of the FBI and the Justice Department to overthrow the duly elected president.

Along the way, Brennan (the ex-CIA director) and Comey (the fired FBI director) have said things like this:

Brennan tweeted:

> *Donald Trump's press conference performance in Helsinki rises to & exceeds the threshold of "high crimes & misdemeanors"... It was nothing short of treasonous. Not only were Trump's comments imbecilic, he is wholly in the pocket of Putin. Republican Patriots: Where are you???....*

He added this to MSNBC host Rachel Maddow:

> *"Are the Republicans on the Hill...going to wait for a disaster to happen before they actually find their backbones and spines, to speak up against somebody who clearly, clearly is not carrying out his responsibilities with any sense of purpose and common sense...I think right now, this country is in a crisis in terms of what Mr. Trump has done and is liable to do."*

Comey, speaking with ABC's George Stephanopoulos:

> *Comey: I think he's morally unfit to be president.*
>
> *Stephanopoulos: You can't say for certain that the president of the United States is not compromised by the Russians?*
>
> *Comey: It is stunning and I wish I wasn't saying it, but it's just—it's the truth. I cannot say that. It always struck me and still strikes me as unlikely, and I woulda been able to say with high confidence about any other president I dealt with, but I can't. It's possible.*

Who does this sound like? The fictional General James Mattoon Scott from *Seven Days in May.*

General Scott: This country's in trouble...deep trouble. Now, there are two ways we can handle this. We can sit here on our duffs and...ask for divine guidance and hope for it. Or we can...or we can what?

The "or what" for General Scott and his fellow plotters is a military coup overthrowing the elected president of the United States. They are openly contemptuous of the elected civilian authority—the president—chosen freely by the American people. Indeed, the FBI's Peter Strzok was openly contemptuous of the American people themselves, as revealed when he texted his FBI paramour that he could "smell" Trump supporters while in a Virginia Walmart.

So too, as is clearly on the record, are Brennan, Comey, and their fellow plotters and schemers openly contemptuous of Donald Trump—to the point that, like General Scott, they spent considerable time using their various high offices to first stop the election of a candidate they did not like and, when that failed, doing what they could to overturn the results and drive the new president from office.

To say the least, Brennan's conduct alone is a sharp departure from that of his predecessors, who conducted their CIA and post-CIA careers by the nonpolitical book. President Trump, aware that Brennan still possessed top security clearance despite being well out of government, revoked his security clearance. The result?

In a classic illustration of Niebuhr's point that "there is nothing in history to support the thesis that a dominant class ever yields its position or privileges in society," the "dominant class" of Old Order warriors raced to defend Brennan's—and their own—"position or privileges in society." In this case, the privilege at hand was a security clearance.

In a typical "Tinker to Evers to Chance" combination, Brennan made his charge, Old Order buddies stepped forward, and *The Washington Post* gave them the forum to attack the president. In a style that eerily and uncomfortably echoes the *Seven Days in May* theme of military leaders threatening the duly elected commander-in-chief, retired rear admiral William McRaven— who was in charge of the Navy Seal mission that killed Osama bin Laden— sent in an op-ed to the Old Order *Post*, which obligingly ran it with the headline "Revoke my security clearance, too, Mr. President."

In a classic demonstration of Old Order Swampiness, the letter says in part:

Dear Mr. President:

Former CIA director John Brennan, whose security clearance you revoked on Wednesday, is one of the finest public servants I have ever known. Few Americans have done more to protect this country than John. He is a man of unparalleled integrity, whose honesty and character have never been in question, except by those who don't know him.

Therefore, I would consider it an honor if you would revoke my security clearance as well, so I can add my name to the list of men and women who have spoken up against your presidency.

After taking a condescending swipe at the outsider president, McRaven goes on to lecture:

A good leader tries to embody the best qualities of his or her organization. A good leader sets the example for others to follow. A good leader always puts the welfare of others before himself or herself.

Did you catch that part that says a "good leader sets the example for others to follow"? Did McRaven really think that Brennan's hyper-political game-playing with the dirty dossier was an example of being a "good leader" in the United States government? Really?

After another swipe at Trump's leadership, the retired admiral closes by saying:

If you think for a moment that your McCarthy-era tactics will suppress the voices of criticism, you are sadly mistaken. The criticism will continue until you become the leader we prayed you would be.

One doesn't know whether to laugh or cry at this. The blunt message here to the president of the United States is that the Old Order elites have privilege—in this case security classifications after they leave government. And if the president messes with their privileges, they will scream bloody murder and stamp their feet until they are returned. Worse still, they tried to claim that the president was out to "suppress the voices of criticism," a laughable untruth. Everyone has the right to free speech; no one has the right to a security clearance. Brennan faced zero restrictions on his speech. Not one.

More amusingly, in a telling recognition of Trump's smarts, Bloomberg's Eli Lake took note that far from silencing Brennan, Trump would laser in on Brennan's words and actions to create what television loves best: a hero and a villain, with Trump using Brennan as a foil. The showdown, I would add, vividly illustrated Trump's politically popular war against the Old Order and the Swamp—not to mention specific Swamp creatures like Brennan.

To show the Old Order's hand in even more detail in this Swamp War, a letter was signed and issued by sixty former CIA officials that said in part:

> *All of us believe it is critical to protect classified information from unauthorized disclosure. But we believe equally strongly that former government officials have the right to express their unclassified views on what they see as critical national security issues without fear of being punished for doing so.…*
>
> *Our signatures below do not necessarily mean that we concur with the opinions expressed by former Director Brennan or the way in which he expressed them. What they do represent, however, is our firm belief that the country will be weakened if there is a political litmus test applied before seasoned experts are allowed to share their views.*

Not to be outdone, incredibly, CBS soon ran the headline "Top former intelligence bosses sign letter supporting John Brennan."

The story said:

> *Thirteen former senior intelligence officials, including 12 former CIA directors and deputy directors and one former director of national intelligence, have signed a letter of support for former CIA director John Brennan, calling the signal sent by the White House's decision to strip him of his security clearance "inappropriate" and "deeply regrettable."*

Incredibly, the letter said:

> *[W]e all agree that the president's action has nothing to do with who should and should not hold security clearances – and everything to do with an attempt to stifle free speech.*

You don't have to agree with what John Brennan says (and…not all of us do) to agree with his right to say it, subject to his obligation to protect classified information.

Let's be crystal clear here. At no time—ever—did the president restrict John Brennan's right to free speech. He was and is at this moment free to say whatever he wants. But neither John Brennan nor any of his predecessors nor any of those sixty CIA analysts have a God-given Constitutional right to classified information when they leave government. In fact, the idea that they all consider this privilege some sort of "right" is extraordinarily dangerous to the country. Effectively they are demanding that America become an aristocracy with themselves as an Americanized version of a hereditary nobility.

Rest assured, this Old Order attitude of privilege is thoroughly bipartisan. Here's another excerpt from that CBS report on Brennan:

Former homeland security and counterterrorism adviser to President George W. Bush Fran Townsend, who is also a CBS News senior national security analyst, said clearances did not generally merit revocation for political reasons. "The notion that you're going to pull somebody's clearance because you don't like what they did in government service or you don't like what they say is deeply disturbing and very offensive, frankly," she said.

Not to pick on Townsend, but quite clearly it never seems to cross her mind that government officials' insisting they are entitled to keep their government privileges after departing government is "deeply disturbing and very offensive, frankly." It is the very height of Old Order elitism.

* * * * *

In September 2018, North Carolina congressman Mark Meadows released a letter he had written to Deputy Attorney General Rod Rosenstein. There had been, after much back-and-forth, a release of documents that included internal texts between the FBI's Peter Strzok and Lisa Page. Meadows's astonishing letter reads:

Dear Mr. Rosenstein:

As you may know, we recently received a new production of documents from the Department providing greater insight into FBI and DOJ activity in the 2016 election and the early stages of the Trump presidency. Our review of these new documents raises grave concerns regarding an apparent systemic culture of media leaking by high-ranking officials at the FBI and DOJ related to ongoing investigations.

Review of these new documents suggests a coordinated effort on the part of the FBI and DOJ to release information in the public domain potentially harmful to President Donald Trump's administration. For example, the following text exchange should lead a reasonable person to question whether there was a sincere desire to investigate wrongdoing or to place derogatory information in the media to justify a continued probe.

April 10, 2017: Peter Strzok contacts Lisa Page to discuss a "media leak strategy."

Specifically the text says: "I had literally just gone to find this phone to tell you about media leak strategy before you go."

April 12, 2017: Peter Strzok congratulates Lisa Page on a job well done while referring to two derogatory articles about Carter Page. In the text, Strzok warns Page two articles are coming out, one which is "worse" than the other about Lisa's "namesake." Strzok added: "Well done, Page."

The Meadows letter goes on to specifically cite articles that have appeared in *The Washington Post* in the same April 2017 time frame that set off a "flurry" of articles "suggesting connections between President Trump and Russia."

Notably, Meadows discovered that newly unearthed documents from the Justice Department "indicate DOJ officials, specifically Andrew Weissmann, participated in unauthorized conversations with the media in the same time period. Evidence suggests senior officials at the FBI and DOJ communicated with other news outlets beyond the *Washington Post*, as well."

In short, here is the "Tinker to Evers to Chance" Old Order teamwork on display in this Swamp War. From Lisa Page to Peter Strzok to the appropriate media outlet and—presto!—a false story that attempted to discredit the president of the United States was on the move in the "mainstream" media.

Leaks to the media were in fact how the Old Order played their game of targeting the president for removal. In a May 2018 column of my own at *The American Spectator* on the subject titled "Deep Stategate: The Sweetheart Leaks" I noted that investigative reporter and Fox contributor Sara Carter had reported this:

> *Over the past week, a mountain of leaks regarding classified information regarding the FBI's operation into the Trump campaign have been shared with The Washington Post and The New York Times. Many lawmakers and sources closely connected to the FBI and DOJ this reporter has spoken with believe the leaks came from the DOJ and Bureau in an effort to stay ahead of the story and frame the narrative.*

By September 12, 2018, Lee Smith at RealClearInvestigations (RCI) had a lengthy detective-style piece posted that followed the trail of leaks from the "anti-Trump leakers." Smith begins his investigative report by saying:

> *A trail of evidence appearing in major news outlets suggests a campaign to undermine President Trump from within the government through illegal leaks of classified information, and then to thwart congressional investigators probing the disclosures....*
>
> *Past and present U.S. officials say the template for the leak campaign can be traced back to the Obama administration's efforts to sell the 2015 Iran nuclear deal, which made the press reliant on background conversations and favorable leaks from government officials. Obama adviser Ben Rhodes told The New York Times in 2016 that "we created an echo chamber" that "helped retail the administration's narrative."*

"That same configuration," said Michael Doran, a senior official in the George W. Bush White House, "the press, political operatives, newly minted experts, social media validators—was repurposed to target Trump, his campaign, transition team, then presidency." The echo chamber's primary instrument in attacking the current White House, said Doran, "is the Russia collusion narrative."

The RCI investigation revealed that the leak strategy came in two stages. First "was an offensive operation aimed at disrupting Trump's agenda, especially through leaks alleging connections between his campaign and the Russians." The second phase "has been more defensive, pushing back against congressional oversight committees that had uncovered irregularities in the FBI's investigation of Trump." And notably there was this: "This second phase has also included articles and opinion pieces – some written by journalists who have published classified information – dismissing suspicions of an orchestrated campaign against Trump as, to use the phrase invoked in a recent *New Yorker* article, a 'conspiracy theory.'"

Note well the phrase "conspiracy theory."

By mid-September 2018, more texts between the FBI's Strzok and Page surfaced, plainly illustrating the extensive leaks that were coming from Old Order government bureaucrats in a decided *Seven Days in May*-style conspiracy campaign to run a silent coup against the elected president of the United States. Samples from a Fox News exclusive:

> *Page: Oh, remind me to tell you tomorrow about the times doing a story about the rnc hacks. ["RNC" is a reference to the Republican National Committee.]*

> *Strzok: And more than they already did? I told you Quinn told me they (sic) pulling out all the stops on some story. [Quinn was described by Fox this way: "A source told Fox News 'Quinn' could be referring to Richard Quinn, who served as the chief of the Media and Investigative Publicity Section in the Office of Public Affairs. Quinn could not be reached for comment."]*

> *Strzok: Think our sisters have begun leaking like mad. Scorned and worried, and political, they're kicking into overdrive.*

Fox reported this of the "sisters" reference:

> *Retired FBI special agent and former FBI national spokesman John Iannarelli told Fox News it could be a reference to another government agency.*

"Sisters is an odd phrase to use," Iannarelli told Fox News Wednesday. *"It could be any intelligence agency or any other federal law enforcement agency. The FBI works with all of them because, post 9/11, it's all about cooperation and sharing."*

Again, why do all of this? There is only one answer—and it is the very same answer that is at the core of all of the Old Order's "Resistance" efforts. Donald Trump and all those millions of Americans who voted for him were and are seen as a mortal threat to the privileges of position and power that Old Order Swamp Warriors have seen as uniquely and deservedly belonging to them as Old Order elites. And they would use every ounce of their power and privilege in a major Swamp War to destroy that threat.

* * * * *

Nowhere is there a bolder example of just how the Old Order works than in the case of CNN pro-Trump commentator Paris Dennard.

In August 2018, the issue of security clearances for former government officials came front and center as the president quite publicly cut off the clearance for ex-Obama CIA director John Brennan. On CNN, on Anderson Cooper's show with Jim Sciutto subbing, my former colleagues ex-CIA analyst Phil Mudd and Dennard went at it on the issue.

Dennard made the utterly obvious factual point that those with security clearances can monetize them after leaving government. The clearances bring value to private-sector consulting gigs, as Fox News accurately reported during the controversy, saying that "security clearances can also provide a financial bump for some in the private sector." Mudd went ballistic, taking it personally.

In the aftermath, President Trump saw this exchange and tweeted about it, saying he had "just watched former Intelligence Official Phillip [sic] Mudd become totally unglued and weird while debating wonderful" Paris Dennard, who "destroyed him." The president wondered if "Mudd is in no mental condition to have such a Clearance. Should be REVOKED?"

What was very curious about the Mudd-Dennard exchange on CNN—and is very telling about how the Old Order operates—was what followed. Their heated discussion, along with the president's response, went, as they say, viral. The media reported on it everywhere. This happens in the media world, no big deal. Except…

Recall this from New York senator Charles Schumer, the Senate's Democratic minority leader: "Let me tell you: You take on the intelligence community—they have six ways from Sunday at getting back at you."

Hmmm.

Within days of this exchange between Paris Dennard and Phil Mudd, in which Dennard was being praised by the conservative media, with the president himself taking note, suddenly—out of the blue in *The Washington Post*, in the style of "Tinker to Evers to Chance"—appears a story with this headline: "Trump called this White House defender 'wonderful.' He was fired from his previous job for alleged sexual harassment."

This jewel of an Old Order hit piece began:

> *A conservative commentator who was lauded by President Trump this week as "wonderful" and who has argued that past sexual indiscretions should have no bearing on Trump's presidency was fired from Arizona State University four years ago for making sexually explicit comments and gestures toward women, according to documents and a university official.*

So it went from Tinker—Arizona State University—to Evers—*The Washington Post*—and then the put-away was delivered by Chance—CNN. *The Hollywood Reporter*'s headline: "CNN Suspends Contributor Paris Dennard Following Sexual Misconduct Report."

And…poof! There goes another CNN Trump supporter (in addition to myself and later Ed Martin and Jason Miller) who dared to make a challenge to the Old Order way.

The fact that Dennard is black recalls, as Candace Owens of Turning Point USA, a conservative activist group, pointed out, the famous Clarence Thomas statement when Thomas was faced with the similar double standard in his confirmation hearing. Which, again, was this (emphasis added):

> "And from my standpoint as a black American, *as far as I'm concerned, it is a high-tech lynching for uppity blacks who in any way deign to think for themselves, to do for themselves, to have different ideas, and* it is a message that unless you kowtow to an old order, this is what will happen to you. You will be lynched, destroyed, caricatured by a committee of the U.S. Senate, rather than hung from a tree."

Paris Dennard would not "kowtow to an old order" in the style of those in that Grisham novel/film version who kowtowed to the Mafia law firm Bendini, Lambert and Locke, for fear of being killed. There right on the set of CNN was Paris Dennard, an ex-Bush forty-three White House aide with all kinds of Old Order opportunities spread out before him, choosing to leave "The Firm" of the Old Order—which in Dennard's case meant defending President Trump on CNN in a discussion about revoking security clearances. And within days—*boom.*

The Old Order—from Arizona State to *The Washington Post* to CNN—made him pay the price. It was a price paid for directly challenging on CNN the practice of Old Order intelligence officials' keeping their privileges—security clearances—after leaving government.

An illustration of the way the Old Order plays the game doesn't get any more graphic than that.

* * * * *

The Washington Post editorial of August 11, 2018, had this headline: "Don't fall for Trump's latest whataboutism."

"Whataboutism"—which is answering a charge by saying "what about X?"—is liberalspeak for "double standard." In this instance, the subject was the charge—by now the very old and decidedly unproven charge—that the Trump campaign had colluded with Russia to steal the 2016 election. The editorial began:

> PRESIDENT TRUMP *tweets it repeatedly: Yes, there was collusion with Russia—except the real colluders were Hillary Clinton and the Democratic Party. The president was back at it again Thursday, quoting a conservative cable host's asser-tion that "Hillary Clinton & the Democrats colluded with the Russians to fix the 2016 election." This inflammatory argument may play well with the president's supporters and others inclined to believe the worst about Ms. Clinton. But the claim that Ms. Clinton's 2016 opposition- research activities were on the same moral or legal plane with the Trump team's direct interac-tions with Russians represents a preposterous effort to confuse and distract.*

As an exercise in Old Order media gaslighting and fake news, the *Post*'s editorial was utterly typical. It went on in this vein at length and included this line: "When the information he was gathering on Mr. Trump seemed alarming, Mr. Steele informed the Federal Bureau of Investigation about his concerns." And the FBI used these "concerns"—the phony dossier, which the *Post* at least admits was "opposition research"—to obtain a FISA warrant that in turn was used to spy on the Trump campaign. And the latter was done without informing the FISA judge that this was nothing more than campaign "oppo research."

What's missing? What's missing is the proverbial elephant in the room.

The purpose of this book is to explore the *how* and *why* behind Old Order Swamp Wars against President Trump and the American people who elected him. It's not the purpose here to break news on the anti-Trump cabal in the FBI, the CIA, and the Department of Justice. Serious journalists like investigative reporter and Fox News contributor Sara Carter, Fox legal and political analyst Gregg Jarrett, and *The Hill*'s John Solomon, all of whom have been relentless in their digging, all of which in turn has been showcased on Sean Hannity's radio and TV shows, have long since debunked exactly the fake news with which the *Post* was trying to gaslight its readers. So too has *The Wall Street Journal*'s Kimberley Strassel.

But here's one excerpt from Jarrett's seriously detailed book on the subject, *The Russia Hoax*, that helps illustrate the problem facing Americans. Jarrett says (emphasis added):

> *As director of the Federal Bureau of Investigation, Comey launched a dilating investigation into Donald J. Trump in the summer of 2016. There was not a whiff of credible evidence to legally justify the probe. So, in a deception worthy of a solid street hustle, Comey labeled it a "counterintelligence matter." The clever feint allowed for a covert criminal investigation in search of a crime, reversing and bastardizing the legal process. This is what abuse of power looks like.*

Bingo. And Gregg Jarrett is not alone in revealing that there was in fact collusion between the Clinton campaign and the Russians. California congressman Devin Nunes, the chair of the House Intelligence Committee, has been leading the House committee's investigation into the charge and has said quite plainly: "The truth is that they [Democrats] are covering up that Hillary Clinton colluded with the Russians to get dirt on Trump to feed it to the FBI to open up an investigation into the other campaign."

So again, the question here is not, "Did this happen?" In spite of the gaslighting by *The Washington Post*'s editorial board and so many other Old Order media allies, yes, in fact, the real Russia collusion was done not just by the Clinton campaign, but by senior-level Old Order bureaucrats whose goal was to prevent the election of Donald Trump. When that failed, the goal became stealing his presidency by forcing him out of office in the fashion of a silent coup d'état.

But in their maniacally driven Old Order desire to get Trump, the coup planners in this Swamp War wound up hitting a different target altogether—themselves.

The question here is not, "*Did* these Old Order bureaucrats do what they did?" The question is, "*Why* did they do it?" Why in the world would senior American bureaucrats ever, ever embark on such a seriously disturbing mission as substituting their own political desires for those of a freely voting American people?

The answer is as simple as it is obvious. All of this was done in the service of the elites of the self-selected American Old Order. As with the Grisham novel's Mafia-run law firm of Bendini, Lambert and Locke, the object was to protect and preserve the power and privileges of an Old Order that will do anything—say anything—to protect that power and those privileges. They saw this power and these privileges—security clearances are but one form— as being directly threatened by candidate—not to mention president— Donald Trump.

And in the style of the "Tinker to Evers to Chance" baseball players, teamwork in this defense was on full display.

In *The American Spectator* in August 2018, the day after the FBI finally fired Strzok, contributing editor George Neumayr wrote about the coup-minded Old Order members. At the time, former associate deputy attorney general Bruce Ohr had not yet testified to Congress on his role (and that of wife Nellie!) in all of this. He has now done so, opening yet another can of worms about this bureaucratic attempt at a silent coup. Neumayr wrote (emphasis added):

> *Bruce Ohr, on the other hand, still hasn't testified before Congress. Apparently, he will appear before it later this month. So he is still picking up a DOJ check. Ohr was the number four man in Obama's Justice Department. His boss was the anti-Trump saboteur Sally Yates. During the 2016 campaign, Ohr and Yates, among many others, had turned the DOJ into a branch office of Hillary's headquarters. Ohr's wife, Nelly [sic], worked for Hillary's opposition research firm, Fusion GPS. The media has reported that Bruce Ohr, starting in January 2016, served month in and month out as a conduit for Hillary's chief opposition researcher, the former British spy Christopher Steele. Steele might as well have had an office next to Ohr's at DOJ.*
>
> *The DOJ corruption on display here is staggering, and were the roles reversed, were it a Republican Justice Department spying on a Democratic presidential campaign (with, say, Lee Atwater calling Ed Meese's deputy every month to check in on the spying), the Ohrs and Strzoks would be run out of DC on a rail. As it is, they can count on at least a few years of well-paid punditry at CNN and MSNBC.* The ethos of official Washington supports all things dastardly toward Trump. Spy on him, tape him, raid his lawyer's office, harass his family, fabricate stories about him—anything goes. He is to be treated, according to official Washington, like, or perhaps even worse than, a foreign occupier.
>
> *If James Comey deserves the gold medal for sanctimonious phoniness, Sally Yates surely deserves a silver. What a low, nasty partisan, who dressed up her vicious hack work for Hillary at Trump's expense in the pompous garb of the "independence of the Justice Department."* Yates was engaged in nothing less than a three-stage coup against Trump: first, she joined Peter Strzok, Christopher Steele, and John Brennan in trying to "stop" Trump from winning; then, once he won, she allowed Ohr to continue collecting dirt from Steele in the hopes of preventing Trump's inauguration (not to mention her entrap-

ment of Michael Flynn, based on her Eddie Haskell-like concern about "Logan Act violations"); finally, once Trump did enter office, she used her Justice Department perch to defy his Travel ban, a ban that the Supreme Court has thoroughly vindicated. How are Yates and her pitiful subordinate Bruce Ohr any different from crooked officials in some Latin American banana republic?

Answer: They are not different.

Disturbingly, there was a vivid illustration of the banana republic mind set at work in the Mueller investigation. Former Trump ally Roger Stone, a longtime Republican political consultant, was indicted on charges that had nothing to do with the investigation's original purpose - uncovering supposed Trump-Russia collusion in the 2016 campaign. Of a sudden, early one morning, gun toting FBI agents descended en masse on Stone's house as if they were there to arrest a violent drug lord. As Fox News legal analyst Judge Andrew Napolitano correctly noted:

"They're looking to squeeze Roger Stone, that's the reason for the Gestapo-like tactics last Friday morning at his house where they sent twice the number of people to arrest him as the Department of Defense sent to kill Osama bin Laden. It just isn't supposed to happen in America unless the government has some ulterior motive for using brute force. In this case, they want to try and terrify Stone into cooperating with them."

All of this scene was conveniently covered by on-the-scene cameras from CNN. Gestapo tactics is precisely the correct term for this kind of stunt.

But as occasionally happens in banana republics, a coup attempt can backfire, with lethal consequences for the coup plotters.

As noted, at the end of *Seven Days in May*, the president, now understanding the details of the coup that was planned to remove him from office, demands and gets the resignations of all those involved, and General Scott is fired.

As of this writing, FBI director James Comey has been fired. (In December 2018 he testified to the House Judiciary Committee—and stunningly said, "I don't recall," "I don't remember," or "I don't know" a full 245 times.) So too has Comey's deputy, Andrew McCabe, been fired. McCabe, as I write this, is under investigation by a grand jury. Comey's chief of staff, James Rybicki, has quit the Bureau. FBI chief legal counsel James Baker was initially reassigned and finally resigned. Eventually Deputy Assistant Director for Counterintelligence Peter Strzok was fired. His lover and fellow anti-Trumper, FBI lawyer Lisa Page, has resigned. Sally Yates is gone from the Justice Department, with Bruce Ohr hanging on by a thread. Rabidly partisan CIA director John Brennan is reduced to hurling tweeted barbs at Trump from the safety net of the Old Order media outlet that is MSNBC.

On September 5, 2018, *The New York Times* published an anonymous op-ed that echoed the plotters in *Seven Days in May*. The headline:

"I Am Part of the Resistance Inside the Trump Administration: I work for the president but like-minded colleagues and I have vowed to thwart parts of his agenda and his worst inclinations."

The article begins:

> *President Trump is facing a test to his presidency unlike any faced by a modern American leader.*
>
> *It's not just that the special counsel looms large. Or that the country is bitterly divided over Mr. Trump's leadership. Or even that his party might well lose the House to an opposition hellbent on his downfall.*
>
> *The dilemma—which he does not fully grasp—is that many of the senior officials in his own administration are working diligently from within to frustrate parts of his agenda and his worst inclinations.*
>
> *I am one of them.*

What comes to mind here in answer to that op-ed, and as the stunning revelations of anti-Trump plotting by the heads of the CIA and FBI and others in government are uncovered, is this rebuke by the fictional president Jordan Lyman in *Seven Days in May*. In a final Oval Office confrontation with the treacherous General James Scott, President Lyman listens to an arrogant Scott justify his intended coup by speaking of the "voice" of the American people. The president responds in the film as follows:

> *"Where the hell have you heard that voice? In freight elevators? In dark alleys? In secret places in the dead of night? How did that voice seep into a locked room full of conspirators? That's not where you hear the voice of the people. Not in this republic.*

"You want to defend the United States of America? Then defend it with the tools it supplies you with, its Constitution. You ask for a mandate, General, from a ballot box. You don't steal it after midnight when the country has its back turned."

In real life, that "voice" spoke to Old Order bureaucrats-turned-conspirators in the shadowy texts sent from the dimly lit recesses of the FBI building, the hushed whispers of conspirators at the Department of Justice and in CIA headquarters. Hearing voices of a "higher loyalty" and desperate to keep their Old Order power and privilege, when America had its back turned, trusted government officials tried to steal a mandate given by the American people at the ballot box.

In the style of the Old Order, these Swamp Warriors launched the ultimate Swamp War. It was a Swamp War designed, like the plot of *Seven Days in May,* to overturn a presidential election with a silent coup that overthrows an elected president. In the words of former Bush forty-one deputy undersecretary of defense Jed Babbin, writing in *The American Spectator,* the things that were done were "abuses of power and crimes." Babbin noted that they were crimes "against our system of law and government. They were perpetrated by employees of the government, under color of law, with the intention of affecting the outcome of an election."

In this Swamp War—a scandal far worse than Watergate that is still unfolding as the battle over consequences rages—President Trump and the millions of Americans who support him are in the fight of modern America's political life. It's one of the most serious fights in America's history since the Civil War.

CHAPTER SIX

FAKE NEWS:
THE GASLIGHTING OF AMERICA

Gregory: You see how it is, Elizabeth.
Elizabeth: I see just *how it is, sir.*

—from the film Gaslight

2014

Donald Trump was disgusted. The subject? The dishonesty of the American media. As we sat in his Trump Tower office on the skyscraper's twenty-sixth floor, a grand view of Central Park was stretched out behind and below him. Interviewing him for *The American Spectator*, I noted that Republicans had complained frequently that their presidential nominees didn't fight back when the liberal media went after them. If he ran for president in 2016, how would Trump deal with a media that would be out to defeat him? In short, how would he deal with a press that has been relentlessly hostile to Republican nominees—and presidents—for decades?

Without missing a beat, the future candidate focused on his own recent comments about Donald Sterling, the owner of basketball's Los Angeles Clippers. Sterling was in the news because a girlfriend had released a private tape of Sterling making racist comments. Trump replied to me:

> *"Well, I see firsthand the dishonesty of the press, because proba-*
> *bly nobody gets more press than I do. As an example, last week*
> *I was on a Fox program, a Fox show, and I very much lam-*
> *basted Donald Sterling. And then at the very end I said: 'On*
> *top of which, he has the girlfriend from hell.' And the haters and*
> *the very dishonest reporters who have their own agenda, they*
> *didn't cover what I said about Donald Sterling. They only took*
> *'the girlfriend from hell' and they said, 'Oh he's not blaming*

Donald Sterling. He's defending Donald Sterling. He's blaming the girlfriend.'

"The press is extremely dishonest. Much of it. Some of it I have great respect for, and they're great people and honorable people. But there's a large segment of the press that's more dishonest than anybody I've seen in business or anywhere else. They are extremely dishonest and very dishonorable people. And the one thing you have to do is you have to inform the public of that. The public has to know about the dishonesty of the press, because these are really bad people and they don't tell the truth and they have no intention of telling the truth. And I know who they are and I would expose them 100 percent. And I will be doing that. I mean, as I go down the line, I enjoy exposing people for being frauds and, you know, I would be definitely doing that. I think it's important to know. Because a lot of the public, they think, oh, they read it in the newspaper, and therefore it must be true. Well much of the things you read in the newspaper are absolutely false and really disgustingly false.

"HuffPost, which is a total fraud, had a headline: 'Donald Trump Defends Donald Sterling.' Oh it's disgusting. It's all over the place. Fifty percent of the press had me defending the guy when actually I said he should be thrown out of [the NBA] and stuff like that. They actually pretended like I didn't speak the first...you know, 95 percent of what I said didn't exist. Really dishonest reporting. But that's just a case of what's going on with the press. They're very, very dishonest. Much of it. And I can't say all of it. Some of it's great. But, you know, right or wrong, Jeff, I don't mind being criticized if they're right. But when they make up, when they fabricate things, and they fabricate something—and the only good thing about this one was it was fresh, it was current, and people actually went back because they were looking to do a number on me, but they got the transcript and said, "Wow! This is really a stretch. This is a tough one." And we made a lot of people look bad. You gotta fight 'em. You gotta fight 'em. I wish the libel laws were stronger. I really do. Because you could have so much fun with it. No, you could have so much fun with it. They're so dishonest."

Four years later almost to the day, now in the White House, President Trump tweets this:

> *The Fake Mainstream Media has, from the time I announced I was running for President, run the most highly sophisticated & dishonest Disinformation Campaign in the history of politics. No matter how well WE do, they find fault. But the forgotten men & women WON, I'm President!*

Later, in an August 2018 interview with Fox's Ainsley Earhardt, the president had this exchange:

> *Earhardt: Is the press the enemy of the people?*
>
> *Trump: No, not at all, but the fake news is, and the fake news is comprised of—it's a lot. It's a big chunk. Somebody said, "What's the chunk?" I said, "80 percent?" It's a lot. It's a lot. If I do something well, it's not reported, other than in the 20 percent.*

He also said, "I mean, *The New York Times* cannot write a good story about me. They're crazed. They're like lunatics."

Long before Trump targeted "fake news," it was clear that he had given serious thought to how he would deal with the media if he ran for president. Not to mention if he became president. As well he should have. In fact, when then private citizen Trump said to me in 2014 that "many of the things you read in the newspaper are absolutely false and really disgustingly false," he was more correct historically than perhaps even he knew.

What Trump was describing in 2014 was a tactic called gaslighting, and the term would be commonly used by the time he became president. The term derives from the common title to two films, 1940's and 1944's *Gaslight*. The plot centers around a husband who so manipulates his wife into believing things that are not true that she comes to doubt her own sanity. It is a term that fits exactly what Trump accuses today's media of doing: pushing "fake news"—news that is completely untrue yet is presented to Americans to make them believe it is fact.

* * * * *

It was July 1964, and the Republican Party was gathering in San Francisco to nominate Arizona senator Barry Goldwater as its presidential candidate. Goldwater, a conservative, had emerged as the nominee after a tumultuous primary face-off against the liberal Eastern Republican establishment of the day, defeating, first, New York governor Nelson Rockefeller and, when "Rocky" withdrew, Pennsylvania governor William Scranton.

As Goldwater prepared to give his acceptance speech that week, the GOP convention, as Goldwater would later recount in his memoirs, "opened in an uproar." Why?

CBS News correspondent Daniel Schorr, reporting from Munich, Germany, had taken to the CBS TV airwaves to report that Goldwater had "accepted an invitation to visit, immediately after the convention... Berchtesgaden, Hitler's onetime stamping ground." Schorr added that Goldwater was set to speak to a German group he identified as being aligned with the German "right wing." He reported on a Goldwater interview in the German press:

> It is now clear that Senator Goldwater's interview with Der Spiegel, with its hard line appealing to right-wing elements in Germany, was only the start of a move to link up with his opposite numbers in Germany.... Thus there are signs that American and German right wings are joining up, and the election campaign is taking on a new dimension.

Which is to say—and no one in the day missed it—CBS through Schorr was gaslighting Americans to make them believe that Barry Goldwater, a sitting United States senator, the new Republican nominee for president of the United States, who had served as a pilot in the Army Air Force during World War Two and was at that moment a Major General in the United States Air Force Reserve—not only was some kind of Nazi, but that he was headed to Germany after the convention to speak to a group that CBS suggested was, as Goldwater said in his memoirs, "a breeding ground of neo-Naziism." In fact, Goldwater wasn't even leaving the country after his nomination, much less headed to Germany to hang out at "Hitler's onetime stamping ground" and give a speech to a supposed group of latter-day would-be Nazis. Decades later, still furious at the blatant CBS lie, Goldwater would write in his memoirs: "The CBS broadcast was false, and Schorr's was the most irresponsible reporting I've witnessed in my life. *The New York Times* followed with an untrue account of its own."

In the day, Goldwater was even blunter. You might even say he sounded Trumpian. On July 17, 1964, *The New York Times* described Goldwater's view of the press—and the *Times* itself—as follows:

Senator Charges Lies to the Press; Accuses Some News Media of 'Utter Dishonesty'

SAN FRANCISCO, July 17 (UPI)—The Republican Presidential nominee, Senator Barry Goldwater, has charged in an interview that some of the news media have resorted to "utter dishonesty" and "out-and-out lies" in reporting his campaign activities.

"Newspapers like The New York Times have to stoop to utter dishonesty in reflecting my views. Some of the newspapers here in San Francisco like The Chronicle—that are nothing but out-and-out lies. Now if they disagree with me, fine, that's their right."

He was also critical of the Columbia Broadcasting System [CBS], claiming the network had "pulled three sneakers on me that I'll never forgive them for."…

He said the network, in one example, had reported he was going to Germany after the convention to "return to the site of the Führer's point of starting and start my campaign there, that I had an invitation to speak in Germany to a rightwing group, [and] that my effort would be to cement the relations between the extremist groups in America and Germany."

"This is nothing but—and I won't swear but you know what I'm thinking—a dad-burned dirty lie," he said.

What Goldwater was fuming about was…fake news. CBS and the *Times* were gaslighting Americans about Goldwater, trying to make them believe something that was completely not reality. Yes, Barry Goldwater was in fact a World War Two hero, a major general in the Air Force Reserve, a senator, presidential nominee, good dad and good husband, and all the rest. But "forget all that" was the real message from CBS and the *Times*. The move was on to gaslight Americans into the not-so-subtle belief that Barry Goldwater was in fact some sort of secret Nazi or some such other horrific thing, a crazy bigot who would plunge the nation and the world into war through alliances with "the German right wing." One can only wonder what Goldwater would think when a future senator from Arizona, Jeff Flake, would take to the Senate floor to denounce President Trump for, among other things, accusing the press of exactly what Goldwater did in 1964: lying. Lying deliberately and willfully. Apparently for Flake it was okay to ignore Goldwater's saying the same thing as Trump on this subject—the difference is that in his lengthy Senate speech, Flake never attacked Arizona icon Goldwater for saying the same thing as Trump. Imagine that.

In 1964, Donald Trump was eighteen years old. The terms "fake news" and "gaslighting" were decades away from modern use. But in fact that is exactly what Goldwater had to deal with—fake news and gaslighting. Trump was also not the first and certainly not the last GOP nominee who would have to deal with what Goldwater was already calling a year earlier—in 1963!—the media's "liberal bias."

Four years before the Goldwater convention, then vice president Richard Nixon had been the Republican nominee, facing off against the Democrats' nominee, Massachusetts senator John F. Kennedy. Famously, Kennedy won in a squeaker—with questions raised about an election stolen in Chicago and Texas. But there was a telling aspect of the Kennedy-Nixon campaign when it came to the media of the day, and it was captured this way by the late Theodore H. White in his Pulitzer Prize-winning account of the campaign, *The Making of the President 1960*. Wrote White of the traveling press corps that was covering JFK:

> *By the last weeks of the campaign, those forty or fifty national correspondents who had followed Kennedy since the beginning of his electoral exertions into the November days had become more than a press corps—they had become his friends and, some of them, his most devoted admirers. When the bus or the plane rolled or flew through the night, they sang songs of their own composition about Mr. Nixon and the Republicans in chorus with the Kennedy staff and they felt that they, too, were marching like soldiers of the Lord to the New Frontier.*

The 1960 campaign was a full fifty-six years before Donald Trump would be the successful Republican nominee in 2016. Yet without doubt the pattern of the modern media's dealings with any Republican nominee—let alone Donald Trump—was already plainly evident. And whether he knew the specifics of the 1960 press corps' behavior as they accompanied JFK—"marching like soldiers of the Lord to the New Frontier"—or whether he knew then that CBS and *The New York Times* had falsely portrayed Barry Goldwater as a would-be Nazi to gaslight Americans, he was more than aware of just how the two most recent Republican nominees had fared in the media.

By the time of our conversation in 2014, Republicans had watched the candidacies of two moderate, press-friendly Republicans crash and burn. John McCain, as the Republican Party's 2008 presidential nominee, in particular was a media favorite in his self-assigned role as the "maverick" senator from Arizona. Yet once nominated, McCain was buried in a sea of gaslighting "news" stories.

A *Politico* headline: "John Lewis, Invoking George Wallace, says McCain and Palin 'playing with fire.'"

McCain, insisted Lewis, was "sowing the seeds of hatred and division, and there is no need for this hostility in our political discourse." Which is to say, Lewis implied that Senator John McCain was a racist.

Then there was this one from *The New York Times*: "For McCain, Self-Confidence on Ethics Poses Its Own Risk."

In that article, the candidate who joked that his political base was the media suddenly stood accused of having an affair with a female lobbyist, Vicki Iseman. This, in turn, set off the inevitable avalanche of stories with gaslighting headlines like these:

- ABC News: "McCain Denies Report Claiming Lobbyist Link"
- *The New York Times:* "McCain refutes article detailing close ties with woman lobbyist"
- *US News & World Report:* "McCain Denies Allegations of a Relationship with Iseman"
- *The Guardian:* "The Real McCain: Paul Harris uncovers the dark side of John McCain"

Iseman, to her immense credit, was so incensed about the untruth of the stories that she sued the *Times*. Eventually a settlement was reached—after the campaign was long over, of course—and the *Times* printed this statement: "The article did not state, and *The Times* did not intend to conclude, that Ms. Iseman had engaged in a romantic affair with Senator McCain or an unethical relationship on behalf of her clients in breach of the public trust." It was good for Iseman—she deserved the retraction—but way too late for McCain.

Four years later, the upright, straight-as-an-arrow GOP moderate and Mormon Mitt Romney got nominated, and in a blink the gaslighting of yet another GOP nominee began. The gaslighting headlines included these:

- *The Washington Post*: "Mitt Romney's prep school classmates recall pranks, but also troubling incidents"
- *Time:* "Romney's Cruel Canine Vacation"
- ABC News: "Dog on Roof? What Was It Like for Romney's Pooch?"
- Mediaite: "Brutal New Ad Blames Mitt Romney For Death Of Steelworker's Wife"

In other words, once the media's favorite Republican candidates (against other, more conservative Republicans) were nominated and seen as a potential threat to a Democratic nominee—first Senator Barack Obama in 2008 (McCain) and then President Obama in 2012 (Romney)—the media that heretofore had written favorably of moderates McCain and Romney turned on a dime to savage them. McCain the Vietnam War hero was gaslighted to become McCain the racist, the womanizer, the pal of greedy lobbyists who also had a "dark side." Romney, the handsome moderate Republican governor whose dad had stood with Martin Luther King while himself a moderate governor, was gaslighted into being Romney the racist, the bullying teen who beat up a gay classmate, the coldhearted SOB who cruelly put his dog on a car roof in a cage, and, in an Obama ad replayed endlessly in the media, the man who coldly cut off health insurance for the dying wife of a steelworker after Romney's Bain Capital took over the plant.

Oh yes. When Senator McCain died in August 2018, the media overflowed with tributes—as if their gaslighting depictions in 2008 of McCain as some sort of racist monster who was conducting an affair with a lobbyist and was one greedy guy had never happened. The same happened upon the death of ex-president George H. W. Bush. Hailed as a role model in death, he had been slammed as being a racist, sexist, and more as a very much alive candidate and president. By then the media had President Trump in their sights, and celebrating the deceased McCain and Bush was a useful way to bash Trump.

In both cases McCain and Romney and their campaigns—not unlike Goldwater in 1964—were left to wander befuddled, reduced to playing defense—spluttering some version of "but…but…that's not true" (or in the case of Romney's dog, trying vainly to suggest that the dog's airborne adventure wasn't as bad as it had been made to sound).

Elected Republican presidents from Eisenhower to Bush forty-three had all faced some version of this liberal media blizzard of untruths. One of the standard media attacks on Republican presidents is that they are "dumb." Eisenhower—who planned the D-Day invasion—was routinely portrayed as a man with charm, a big smile…and little if any intelligence. Ford, a star athlete at the University of Michigan, had the misfortune to trip coming down the steps of Air Force One. Instantly he was routinely portrayed as a stumbling, bumbling idiot. *Saturday Night Live*'s Chevy Chase made a career out of depicting Ford as a dimwitted simpleton. Reagan was regularly dismissed as stupid, with liberal writer Gore Vidal sniping that "the Reagan Library burned down and 'both books were lost'—including the one Reagan had not finished coloring." Both Bushes, particularly George W. Bush, were routinely dismissed as dumb. Only Nixon escaped—but instead of portraying him as dumb, the press went with some version of evil.

Democratic presidents are, curiously, routinely judged to be somewhere north of brilliant. JFK, dismissed by some of his senatorial peers as a lightweight playboy, became a seriously brilliant intellectual in the press the moment he was nominated. LBJ was the vastly experienced and crafty legislative genius. Jimmy Carter was the brilliant Naval Academy graduate who knew all there was to know about engineering and things nuclear. The hosannas for the smarts of Bill Clinton and Barack Obama are still gushing.

Suffice it to say, Trump on that pleasant day in May 2014 was well aware of how this game was played in the press, and was well aware of what had happened to both McCain and Romney. He was surely unaware that decades before, GOP nominee Goldwater had bluntly accused some in the media of "utter dishonesty." The terms "fake news" and "gaslighting" were still in the future. But he made plain that he would fight back if these types of moments arrived if he ever ran for president, much less if he got to be president. And he was quite sure they would arrive.

Of the many things that made Donald Trump a unique candidate for president—and a unique president—was the geographic accident of his birth. He was a New Yorker through and through, and his opponents, both in the Republican Party and later in the Clinton campaign, did not grasp that Trump had the best of both worlds when it came to preparing for a presidential race.

The first of Trump's advantages was the fact that he had grown up in Queens with a father in the real estate and construction business, which gave him considerable exposure to blue-collar, everyday working Americans. Second was his time in Manhattan—arguably the center of the global media universe. Over the decades, Trump had dealt with journalists of all stripes, from the serious-minded *New York Times* and *Wall Street Journal* to tabloids like the *New York Post* and the *New York Daily News*. Add in those who worked for magazines both local and national, not to mention television, again both the local and, this being Manhattan, the national networks—and it would be hard, if not impossible, to find a more completely media-savvy candidate. All of that happened well before he was given the opportunity to be a television star himself as host of NBC's *The Apprentice*. There was virtually no aspect of the media—good, bad, or indifferent—that he had not experienced up close and personally.

Time after time after time in his pre-political career, Donald Trump had received media coverage that ran the gamut from good to colorful to miserable. He paid attention. This, in short, was a man who had a serious understanding of the media in all its many facets. He may not have been aware of the Teddy White story about JFK's traveling press corps' seeing themselves as Kennedy's "soldiers of the Lord" marching with JFK to the glories of the "New Frontier." He may well have had no idea that CBS and *The New York Times* had tried to paint Barry Goldwater as some sort of Nazi with stories that might collectively be called the granddaddy of today's "fake news." But he most assuredly was vividly aware that the press was hostile in general to any Republican nominee and any Republican president. He knew without doubt that the press herd with its culture of liberal groupthink would be coming for him. Unlike his Republican predecessors, he was more than willing to dish right back at what was effectively the Leftist State Media.

Suffice it to say, the media didn't like it. Shocking, I know. But also at play in this media-versus- conservative dynamic over the decades since the Nixon campaign of 1960 and the Goldwater campaign of 1964 was a veritable revolution in the media itself.

First, the technology evolved. The reason the CBS "Goldwater is allied with Nazis" gaslighting story was so potent is that CBS was one of only three broadcast television networks, and in the day, it was the dominant one. The liberal media controlled the national memory. Over time, cable news appeared, and in 1996, Rupert Murdoch and Roger Ailes created Fox News—a decided, unabashed, unashamed conservative alternative to the groupthink that runs mainstream media outlets. Eight years before the creation of Fox, Rush Limbaugh led the way into conservative talk radio, with talk radio quickly becoming a staple of American life. Not long after that, the internet appeared, with conservative sites blossoming. Collectively, all of this destroyed the liberal media's monopoly—once and for all.

What it did not destroy was the culture—the liberal mindset—of the "mainstream" media. In fact, with the liberal media's monopoly gone, the liberal mindset in the media became more pronounced, and pretensions of objectivity vanished. Whether the media was covering the Kennedy traveling press corps in 1960 or the Hillary Clinton press corps in 2016, the one fact that never changed over the decades was the herd mentality of the Leftist State Media. By 2016 it was so pronounced that it produced repeated headlines like these:

- *The New York Times:* "Hillary Clinton has an 85% chance to win"
- *The Washington Post:* "No, Donald Trump, beating Hillary Clinton will not be easy for you"
- CNN: "Clinton predicted to beat Trump…due to economics"
- NBC: "Clinton Holds 11-Point National Lead Over Trump: NBC/ WSJ Poll"

On and on and on this went. Sitting on CNN sets night after night— but living in the middle of Pennsylvania—I could clearly see the disconnect. Pennsylvania was awash in Trump signs.

The weekend before Halloween 2016, I had no CNN obligations. So I put my then-ninety-seven-year-old mom in the car for a drive into the nearby countryside to get a pumpkin at a favorite farm stand. As we drove, I noticed something: Trump signs. They were everywhere—in front yards, on street corners, and even hand-painted on barns. I began counting. Hillary signs: one. Trump signs: hundreds. By Monday night, I was in New York to be on CNN with my pals on Anderson Cooper's show. Yet when I mentioned what I thought was a telling political forecast of what was happening in Pennsylvania—a state that had not voted for a Republican in over a quarter of a century—my liberal colleagues dismissed this as anecdotal. I was looking at actual, physical evidence of serious Trump support; they were busy looking at polling data—the latter of which, not to put too fine a point on it, was wildly wrong.

The night before the election, I sat on Anderson's show with colleagues as CNN paused our discussion to show Hillary Clinton's last rally. It took place in front of Independence Hall in Philadelphia, featuring rock stars Bruce Springsteen and Jon Bon Jovi as opening acts for Bill and Chelsea Clinton, Michelle Obama, President Obama, and finally Hillary Clinton herself. Predictably, there were thousands there. And why not? Springsteen and Bon Jovi paired? Of course there would be a crowd! If I had been in the area, I might have gone! My liberal colleagues gushed afterwards at the glorious moment in which the first black president was about to be succeeded by America's first woman president. I noted something else.

In the history of Pennsylvania, Philadelphia—its largest city—has always been politically unpopular in large parts of the rest of the state. It is seen as something of a politically bullying sibling, its sheer size always demanding recognition for its needs before suburbs, rural areas, and Western Pennsylvania. I thought the rally a serious last-minute major political mistake. Whether it was the presence of literal rock stars Springsteen and Bon Jovi or the political rock stars the Clintons and the Obamas, it seemed clear to me that there would be a lot of Pennsylvanians who would roll their eyes at the elitism of the whole event—political and Hollywood/rock-and-roll elites scratching each other's backs. And as all those Trump signs blanketing the state indicated, this rally would spur Trump-supporting Pennsylvanians to show up the next day en masse to elect Trump.

But it wasn't just a lot of my fellow CNNers who were convinced that Hillary Clinton was going to carry the state as part of what came to be called the "blue wall"—Northeastern and Midwestern industrial states that were presumed to be in the Democratic (Clinton) corner. One mainstream media outlet after another—television networks and print publications, not to mention online sources—were certain she was going to be the next president. Blinded by their own political bias, the media across the board got the biggest story of the year—the entire election—completely wrong.

Yet when the election was over, it also became crystal clear that the Old Order media—not just furious and shocked about getting the results wrong but decidedly angry at Trump's being elected—was settling in to do its part in the Swamp Wars. Far from learning from their mistake and resolving to cover the new president fairly, the media would instead ratchet up their defense of the Old Order. They did this for a very obvious reason: the liberal "mainstream" media ("mainstream" today being highly misleading, as the media has long since ceased to be mainstream) had in fact over the decades become the media division of the Old Order itself, or as I call it, it had become the Leftist State Media.. What was "new" about their bias for JFK in 1960 had long since calcified into an instinctive defense of the Old Order's rights, privileges, and long-established ways of doing things. As the Trump era dawned, the Old Order's Leftist State Media would see to it that anyone who was out there attacking the Trump presidency or Trump supporters was going to be made into a hero. Conversely, anyone who defended Trump—whether it was the president himself; a family, Cabinet, or staff member; or anyone else across the spectrum of American life and culture—would become an Old Order media target. I soon learned this, as they say, in an up-close and personal way.

* * * * *

Fox media critic Howard Kurtz, in his recent book on the campaign—*Media Madness: Donald Trump, the Press, and the War Over the Truth*—shares a telltale anecdote about the liberal media's mindset. There are doubtless an infinite number of similar stories, but this one will suffice as an illustration of the kind of press that President Trump was facing from the moment he was sworn in.

The Kurtz story takes place during the campaign, when a Republican National Committee staffer called *New York Times* reporter Jonathan Martin about a particular—and unfavorable—Martin story about Trump. Writes Kurtz: "The reporter shot back, 'You're a racist and a fascist; Donald Trump is a racist and a fascist, we all know it, and you are complicit. By supporting him you're all culpable.'"

Kurtz goes on to write that later in the campaign, in another conversation between the same staffer and Martin, the *Times* reporter "accused the staffer—and everyone working on Trump's behalf—of supporting a racist campaign and a racist candidate."

Alrighty, then! So much for the "objective" Old Order media. And curiously, or maybe not so curiously, in August 2018 it was discovered that newly hired *New York Times* editorial board member Sarah Jeong, whom the paper identified in left-wing segregationist style—er, make that identity politics style—as "a young Asian woman," had posted one tweet after another that were clearly racist. Among them:

- "oh man it's kind of sick how much joy I get out of being cruel to old white men"
- "Dumbass fucking white people marking up the internet with their opinions like dogs pissing on fire hydrants"
- "Are white people genetically predisposed to burn faster in the sun, thus logically only fit to live underground like groveling goblins"

She also called white people "dogs."

I can find no peep that Jonathan Martin angrily resigned from *The New York Times* because the paper had hired a "racist and a fascist." Zip.

Then again, the *Times* issued this statement that said:

> *Her journalism and the fact that she is a young Asian woman have made her a subject of frequent online harassment. For a period of time she responded to that harassment by imitating the rhetoric of her harassers. She sees now that this approach only served to feed the vitriol that we too often see on social media.*
>
> *She understands that this type of rhetoric is not acceptable at* The Times, *and we are confident that she will be an important voice for the editorial board moving forward.*

Hmmm. Unlike CNN, which fired me for mocking Media Matters for its anti-Semitism and racial bigotry, something that had been flagged several times by others, the *Times* quickly defended its new hire on the grounds that, well, she wasn't racist, she was just "imitating the rhetoric of her harassers."

Huh.

While what follows is but one anecdote, it serves well to illustrate the problems President Trump is facing when dealing with Old Order media institutions. This perfect example of how they play the game surfaced almost a year after I left CNN.

Kim Kardashian West of Hollywood fame, the wife of the Trump-supporting rapper and record producer Kanye West, but not a Trump fan herself, came to the White House to discuss prison reform. Trump senior advisor and son-in-law Jared Kushner, whose father, Charles Kushner, has served time in federal prison for tax evasion and witness tampering, as well as making illegal campaign contributions, had taken a serious interest in the issue and reached out to a slew of Trump opponents who shared the goal of prison reform.

Kardashian arrived at the White House, had her time with the president, and met with Kushner and others to discuss the issue. The *Times* dutifully reported that "the reason for Ms. Kardashian West's interest [in prison reform] is the case of Alice Johnson, a 63-year-old Tennessee woman who, according to the nonprofit project Can-Do, was sentenced in 1996 to life in prison on charges related to cocaine possession and money laundering." An Oval Office photo was taken of Kardashian and the president—it was inevitable.

And like clockwork, before the day was out, CNN's Jim Acosta took to the CNN airwaves to denounce the meeting and Kardashian's very presence to discuss the issue. Acosta, one of my former CNN colleagues, chastised Kardashian, saying that her presence to discuss prison reform was not "normal": "She shouldn't be here, talking about prison reform. It's very nice that she is here, but that's not a serious thing to have happened here at the White House."

It took a nanosecond for the ever-observant Joseph Wulfsohn, then of Mediaite and now of Fox News, to find a clip of Acosta personally interviewing another A-list celebrity—musician and actor John Legend—in 2015. The subject: the politically liberal Legend bringing up the issue of prison reform with President Obama during a visit to the Obama White House. Strangely,

Acosta had a completely different reaction then. The CNN banner that was displayed as Acosta spoke to Legend read approvingly: "Musician on a mission." And sure enough, there on the clip was Jim Acosta praising an A-List celebrity—not so coincidentally an Obama friend and supporter—for taking up the serious issue of prison reform with President Obama.

I met Acosta several times during the campaign and afterwards, sharing the inevitable panel duty. He's a smart guy and a nice guy—but the comparison of these two Acosta moments serves to illustrate in snapshot form just how Old Order journalists will quite openly defend Old Order institutions by displaying their reflexive contempt for President Trump. A defense of the Old Order can either be overtly hostile, as was Jonathan Martin of *The New York Times* on those campaign phone calls with the RNC staffer, or it can be deceptive through omission, as was CNN's Acosta in presenting one view of Kim Kardashian West while omitting that he said exactly the opposite about John Legend—when both Kardashian and Legend were lobbying for the same issue and from the same side of that issue, but with two very different presidents.

Both Martin and Acosta are the journalistic descendants of those reporters "marching like soldiers of the Lord to the New Frontier" with John F. Kennedy in 1960. Indeed, *Times* reporter Martin's angry depiction of Trump as "a racist and a fascist"—not to mention his paper's description of Trump as a racist—was the 2016 version of CBS's Daniel Schorr's gaslighting portrayal of Barry Goldwater as a Nazi in 1964.

In neither case was Martin or Acosta's coverage about journalism—a "just the facts" presentation of the news. Acosta didn't simply report Kardashian's presence at the White House to push for prison reform and a pardon for Alice Johnson. Instead, Acosta played liberal pundit, telling the CNN audience, "She shouldn't be here, talking about prison reform. It's very nice that she is here, but that's not a serious thing to have happened here at the White House." That isn't news—that's opinion. Acosta's opinion. It is a small but telling example of how "fake news" works, with Acosta gaslighting Americans into believing there was something very different and very inappropriate about the Kardashian visit—when in fact he himself had praised a liberal celebrity for doing the very same thing with a liberal president.

Martin and Acosta are Old Order activists—Swamp Warriors. They—and their journalistic homes, *The New York Times* and CNN—are about the Old Order and its preservation. Most assuredly they are not alone.

Others make assumptions—as did Martin—that are political. Liberal. They say, as Martin did, "We all know," and they are right. Those of the Old Order media "all know" and believe some version of the same liberal agenda. The Merriam-Webster dictionary defines a cult as "a system of religious beliefs and ritual"—which in many ways describes not just the Old Order but the underlying theology of the Old Order media's secular religion—cult—of liberalism as well.

To challenge that theology is to be attacked as a racist, homophobe, xenophobe, or whatever suits the momentary need of the liberal agenda and the required Old Order defense of the liberal faith. It is the ultimate political example of what Sigmund Freud defined as "projection"—the primitive defense of oneself by projecting one's own impulses onto others.

* * * * *

Examples upon examples of "fake news" and "gaslighting" by the media are out there. For example:

In the summer of 2018, Trump called Don Lemon "the dumbest man on television" after an extensive Lemon interview with NBA star LeBron James, who trashed Trump on Lemon's Friday-night CNN show. Almost instantly—by Sunday morning—there were NBC's *Sunday Today* host Willie Geist and NBC's *Meet the Press* moderator Chuck Todd going straight to the gaslighting routine. As recorded by the Media Research Center's Nicholas Fondacaro on *NewsBusters* (disclosure: I write a weekly media column for the site), the back-and-forth between the two liberal hosts went this way:

> *"Let's talk about that tweet Friday night insulting the intelligence of both LeBron James and Don Lemon at CNN, an African-American television host," Geist prefaced. "Was this more than an attack on somebody he saw insulting him on television? And why does he keep going back to the insult on intelligence when it comes to African-American leaders in this country?"*
>
> *[Chuck] Todd admitted that LeBron did attack the President by saying he never wanted to meet with him, but insisted "there is a troubling pattern here." "Every time he disparages an African-*

American political opponent of some sort, whether they're an athlete or an actual elected official, he always goes to intelligence. Always," he declared.

"It's hard not to notice that pattern and it's hard not to look at it and wonder if there is nefarious motives behind it and some sort of long-term belief system in him or maybe he's just trying to send some sort of dog whistle to his supporters," Todd continued, shifting his smears to Trump voters. He suggested that it really was "just a whistle" for them as opposed to the mystical "dog whistle" only they could understand.

Not long after this, ex-Trump White House aide Omarosa Manigault Newman, a onetime star of Trump's *Apprentice* reality show, was fired by presidential chief of staff General John Kelly. Newman came out with a revenge book that attacked the president and Kelly, among others. She released tapes she had secretly made while in the White House. Trump, in response, called her a "dog," prompting this headline in *The New York Times* that went down the same race-card-playing path as Geist and Todd had gone down: "Trump's 'That Dog' Attack on Omarosa Manigault Newman Is Latest Insult Aimed at Black People."

Really? Unmentioned by Geist and Todd, and by *The New York Times*, was a July 10, 2018, story with the headline "The 487 People, Places and Things Donald Trump Has Insulted on Twitter: A Complete List."

It was published in…yes…*The New York Times*. Among those the *Times* listed as having been Trump targets for their alleged lack of smarts or other faults were these:

1. CNN's Jim Acosta: "Crazy."
2. Supreme Court Justice Ruth Bader Ginsburg: Makes "very dumb political statements about me."
3. Conservative talk-show host Glenn Beck: "Dumb as a rock."
4. CNN commentator and ex-Clinton White House aide Paul Begala: "Dopey."
5. Former vice president Joe Biden: "Crazy Joe."
6. *New York Times* columnist David Brooks: "A dummy" and "one of the dumbest of all pundits," who "is closing in on being the dumbest of them all."

7. *New York Times* columnist Frank Bruni: "Dope."
8. Mika Brzezinski, cohost of MSNBC's *Morning Joe*: "Dumb as a rock," "crazy and very dumb," and "not very bright."
9. Former president Bill Clinton: "Doesn't know much."
10. Hillary Clinton: "Very dumb" and her "brainpower is highly overrated."
11. Ex-FBI director James Comey: "Very dumb" and "he is not smart."
12. Dallas Mavericks owner Mark Cuban: "Not smart enough to run for president" and "dopey."
13. CNN host and columnist S. E. Cupp: "One of the dumber pundits on TV."
14. Actor Robert De Niro: "A very low IQ individual."
15. *New York Times* columnist Maureen Dowd: "A neurotic dope."
16. Former CIA director Robert Gates: "Dopey."
17. New York senator Kirsten Gillibrand: "Lightweight."
18. South Carolina senator Lindsey Graham: "Dumb mouthpiece."
19. *HuffPost* founder Arianna Huffington: "Dummy."
20. Fox analyst Brit Hume: "A dope."
21. GOP consultant Cheri Jacobus: "Really dumb."
22. Ohio governor John Kasich: "Dummy."
23. Former Fox News anchor Megyn Kelly: "Lightweight."
24. *Weekly Standard* editor Bill Kristol: "Dummy," "dopey," and "even dumber."
25. GOP consultant Rick Wilson: "Dumb as a rock."
26. Wisconsin GOP governor Scott Walker: "Not smart."
27. *Washington Post* columnist Jennifer Rubin: "One of the dumber bloggers."
28. NBC's *Meet the Press* host Chuck Todd: "Knows so little about politics."
29. GOP political consultant Stuart Stevens: "A dumb guy who fails @ virtually everything he touches."

I could keep going—and the *Times* did.

But let's stop with this list of thirty Trump targets and revisit what Willie Geist and Chuck Todd said about the Trump attack on Don Lemon.

Geist: Let's talk about that tweet Friday night insulting the intelligence of both LeBron James and Don Lemon at CNN, an African-American television host.... Was this more than an attack on somebody he saw insulting him on television? And why does he keep going back to the insult on intelligence when it comes to African-American leaders in this country?

Todd:...[T]here is a troubling pattern here. Every time he disparages an African-American political opponent of some sort, whether they're an athlete or an actual elected official, he always goes to intelligence. Always. It's hard not to notice that pattern and it's hard not to look at it and wonder if there is nefarious motives behind it and some sort of long-term belief system in him or maybe he's just trying to send some sort of dog whistle to his supporters.

And let's recall that headline for the *New York Times* story about Trump's attack on Omarosa Manigault Newman as a "dog": "Trump's 'That Dog' Attack on Omarosa Manigault Newman Is Latest Insult Aimed at Black People."

What did both Geist and Todd leave out? What did the *Times* article on Newman leave out?

What do all of these Trump targets mentioned here on this list of thirty, a partial list that I took from the larger *Times* list of 487 Trump Twitter targets, have in common? This list of thirty that includes the names of journalists, senators, governors, a Supreme Court justice, an actor, an ex-FBI director, an ex-CIA director, a conservative talk-radio host, Republican consultants, a former president, and a presidential nominee, the last of whom served as a senator and secretary of state? All of them have been attacked by Trump for their intelligence.

And every last one of them is white.

As for calling Newman a "dog," Laura Ingraham took the time to do the serious research the *Times* would not do and came up with a list of names of those who had been called a "dog" by Trump. The list included Mitt Romney, Glenn Beck, George Will, Steve Bannon, Bill Maher, David Axelrod, and Arianna Huffington. As with the list of those whose intelligence Trump has questioned, every last one of them is white.

Which is to say, Geist and Todd and the *Times* are typical of the breed of deliverers of fake news, gaslighting the NBC and *Times* audiences to make them believe that something Trump has done—in these cases, Trump's attack on the smarts of LeBron James and Don Lemon and his calling Newman a dog—he has done exclusively to blacks. When in fact each case was wildly and quite provably untrue.

These stories were, starkly and unvarnished, fake news. Gaslighting. And, irony of ironies, *The New York Times* itself had demonstrated so in chapter and verse with its long list of Trump's tweets attacking various people or institutions who had attacked him.

But why? Why would a couple of responsible journalists and *The New York Times* leave out easily obtainable facts in a news story? And in the *Times* case, they were facts that the very same paper had gone to great length to detail only weeks earlier. Why? The answer is as simple as it is obvious. This is a Swamp War. The Old Order media, of which Geist and Todd and the *Times* are members in good standing, has, as it always has had, an agenda—a political agenda that leans left. Like the long-ago episode in which Daniel Schorr, CBS, and *The New York Times* were gaslighting Americans of the day to believe that Barry Goldwater was a Nazi sympathizer or worse, these journalists were selectively reporting "news" that was deliberately altered to fit their personal political agenda. In this case, their agenda is to paint both Donald Trump and his supporters as racists—something that has been done to literally every Republican president, presidential nominee, and their supporters for decades. What these Old Order journalists—past and present—were and are delivering to America is not "news" but "fake news"—gaslighting, presenting their considerably liberal political opinion in the guise of "news."

This is, sadly, standard operating procedure for the "mainstream" media today. It is why Fox News dominates its left-wing cable rivals and why talk-show host Sean Hannity—who, not coincidentally, has the number-one show on cable news—says that "journalism is dead" in America. In saying this it is important to note that Martin, Acosta, Geist, Todd, and the *Times* are far, far from alone in the gaslighting of America. Examples litter the media landscape.

Over at *The Federalist,* the headline for a Daniel Payne story was "16 Fake News Stories Reporters Have Run Since Trump Won." The titles of the stories run the gamut from (a supposed) "Spike in Transgender Suicide Rates" (there was zero confirmation of what turned out to be an unsubstantiated rumor) to "The Tri-State Election Hacking Conspiracy Theory" to "The 27-Cent Foreclosure." That last one was a false story in *Politico* by Lorraine Woellert, claiming that Trump secretary of the treasury Steven Mnuchin had, while a banker in the private sector, foreclosed on a ninety-year-old woman's home because she was twenty-seven cents off in her payment. In fact, as Payne notes: "The problem? The central scandalous claims of Woellert's article were simply untrue. As the Competitive Enterprise Institute's Ted Frank pointed out, the woman in question was never foreclosed on, and never lost her home. Moreover, 'It wasn't Mnuchin's bank that brought the suit.'" Payne went on to note: "*Politico* eventually corrected these serious and glaring errors. But the damage was done: the story had been repeated by numerous media outlets including *Huffington Post* (shared 25,000 times on Facebook), the *New York Post*, *Vanity Fair*, and many others."

The supposed election hacking story also proved to be bogus. Payne cited *New York* magazine's Gabriel Sherman breathlessly reporting that "'a group of prominent computer scientists and election lawyers' were demanding a recount in three separate states because of 'persuasive evidence that [the election] results in Wisconsin, Michigan, and Pennsylvania may have been manipulated or hacked.' The evidence? Apparently, 'in Wisconsin, Clinton received 7 percent fewer votes in counties that relied on electronic-voting machines compared with counties that used optical scanners and paper ballots.'" After this story ran, *FiveThirtyEight*, Nate Silver's statistical analysis site, had Silver explaining that it was "demographics, not hacking" that explained the curious voting numbers. "Anyone making allegations of a possible massive electoral hack should provide proof, and we can't find any," he wrote. As Payne noted in his *Federalist* piece: "Additionally, Silver pointed out that the *New York Magazine* article had misrepresented the argument of one of the computer scientists in question."

But it would be a mistake to think that these fake news stories are limited to tales about Trump.

As with Goldwater, simply being a conservative will make you a target of gaslighting and fake news.

In the immediate aftermath of the 2012 Aurora, Colorado, movie theater shooting that killed twelve and wounded another seventy—four years before Trump's election—ABC's Brian Ross went on the air to say that the name of the shooter—James Holmes—matched the name of a "Jim Holmes" who was listed on a website as being a member of the Colorado Tea Party in Aurora. In fact, the report was false—the Jim Holmes in the Tea Party was someone completely different. The shooter was age twenty-four; the Tea Party member fifty-two. It was fake news—for which ABC and Ross later apologized. But make no mistake, the idea driving the story was gaslighting the ABC audience into believing that the conservative Tea Party is somehow prone to violence, so therefore it would be logical that a shooter came out of the Tea Party.

Examples like these of Old Order media figures aggressively and repeatedly trying to gaslight their respective audiences abound.

Another example with NBC's Chuck Todd involved me. When the "news" emerged in a court appearance of ex-Trump lawyer Michael Cohen that Cohen was friends with Fox's Sean Hannity, the "mainstream" media, Todd included, whipped themselves into a self-righteous frenzy. First of all, for anybody who has listened to Hannity over the years, as I have, this was not news. Hannity had spoken of Cohen from time to time, identifying him on-air as a friend. The media tried to paint this—erroneously—as a situation in which Cohen was Hannity's lawyer. This was flatly untrue. That did not stop Todd from saying, as reported by NPR's David Folkenflik per *Mediaite*:

> *I am stunned that Fox had no punitive response. Not a "Sean Hannity must disclose every night," not a "he can't cover this story," not a "he's been suspended for a week," nothing! Not a single thing. They are saying this is okay for anybody that works at Fox News.*

Noting this, I wrote a column on Hannity's website (yes, disclosure: I write columns there) citing a *Politico* story from 2014 that said:

> *NBC Meet the Press host Chuck Todd has a wife who's active in Democratic Party strategic communications, and sometimes donates to Democrats. In 2012, Kristian Denny Todd contributed $2,500 to Sen. Tim Kaine. Todd never felt any need to disclose this during his three recent Kaine interviews on NBC (August 7, September 18, and October 23).*

I also cited a *NewsBusters* story on Todd that said:

> *But Maverick Mail & Strategies, the firm Mrs. Todd founded in 2007 with fellow James Webb aides Steve Jarding and Jessica Vanden Berg, did heavy lifting for openly socialist Bernie Sanders for President this year. Open Secrets shows a bill for $1.992 million made in ten payments to Maverick from January to April. Todd has never disclosed this business relationship in 11 Sanders interviews this year. (If the work began in 2015 before the payments, Todd failed to disclose any tie in six Sanders interviews in the second half of 2015). We didn't even count any Todd interviews with Sanders on MSNBC.*

In other words, there was Chuck Todd criticizing Fox News for not punishing Hannity for supposedly not disclosing his relationship with Cohen—which in fact Hannity had done. Meanwhile Todd himself had clients of his wife's firm on his own show without disclosing that relationship. I watched a tape of *Meet the Press* with both Bernie Sanders and James Webb on the show, and there was not a solitary mention of their ties to Chuck Todd's wife. So I wrote it up.

Chuck Todd was livid with me, taking to *The Bernie and Sid Show* on New York's 77 WABC radio to denounce me as a "lackey," fuming: "What I take offense to on that is that's my wife, that's not me. I think it's a ridiculous place that we're in in society that it's guilt by association."

Of course, creating "guilt by association" is what Chuck Todd had just tried to do with Hannity and Cohen—as it were, making sauce for the Fox and Hannity gander, but not for the NBC and Todd goose.

With this in mind, it was amusing to read many months later that Chuck Todd had taken to the pages of *The Atlantic* to go after Fox News. The headline:

"It's Time for the Press to Stop Complaining—And to Start Fighting Back: A nearly 50-year campaign of vilification, inspired by Fox News's Roger Ailes, has left many Americans distrustful of media outlets. Now, journalists need to speak up for their work."

Furious with President Trump's repeated attacks on the "dishonest" media, Todd actually zeroed in on the late Fox founder Roger Ailes, blaming the media's low standing with the public on Ailes, whose political career had begun with advising then-candidate Richard Nixon on the use of television in the 1968 campaign.

Todd begins by doing exactly what he did with the fake news of Trump's having "a troubling pattern" of disparaging African Americans by attacking their intelligence: he plays the race card, writing, "Figures such as Rush Limbaugh, Matt Drudge, and the trio of Sean Hannity, Tucker Carlson, and Laura Ingraham have attained wealth and power by exploiting the fears of older white people." As with lots of liberals, Todd is obsessed with judging people by skin color.

With race thus injected into this and with Todd completely omitting that his own media gig at NBC, one suspects, pays very well (and why should anyone care about the race of his—or anyone's—audience?), Todd moves on to start the gaslighting (emphasis mine), saying, "Much of the current hand-wringing about this rise in press bashing and delegitimization has been *focused on the president, who—as every reporter in America sadly knows—has declared the press the 'enemy of the people.'*"

Hello? Recall the interview cited above with President Trump and Fox's Ainsley Earhardt, in which this was said (emphasis mine):

> *Earhardt:* Is the press the enemy of the people?
>
> *Trump:* No, not at all, but the fake news is*, and the fake news is comprised of—it's a lot. It's a big chunk. Somebody said, "What's the chunk?" I said, "80 percent?" It's a lot. It's a lot. If I do something well, it's not reported, other than in the 20 percent.*

The boldness of this kind of thing is what always astonishes me. There is a "mainstream" journalist writing an article saying that Trump "*has declared the press the 'enemy of the people,'*" when the president is out there—on videotape no less—saying that the press is *not* the enemy of the people "*but the fake news is.*"

Amazingly, in pointing the finger at Fox for bias, Todd ignores a rather large elephant in the room: his own network, MSNBC. No less than Bill O'Reilly picked up on this, writing in a column:

> *What is also striking about Chuck Todd's media analysis is that he, himself, works on the most biased news operation in*

American history: MSNBC. Yet, Todd ignores that fact entirely while lambasting Fox News for commentary he considers inflammatory. Maybe Chuck Todd might want to dial in his own operation from time to time.

To be clear, Chuck Todd is far from alone in the world of liberal media bias. He is merely a symbol of it. And to be perfectly clear, I don't think he is a bad guy. But he is most assuredly an Old Order liberal guy who pretends to be objective when he decidedly is not objective. That moment reporting on a false "troubling pattern" that depicts Trump as a racist who "disparages an African-American political opponent of some sort" because "he always goes to intelligence" illustrates the point of his liberal bias and addiction to fake news exactly.

This is the problem with the "mainstream" media writ large. No one cares that they are on the left. What has so alienated Americans about the Old Order media—President Trump foremost among them—is the insistence on presenting Old Order liberal far-left journalism as somehow "just the facts" neutral and objective when it is anything but. Well beyond Chuck Todd or any one individual liberal in the media, Old Order gaslighting with fake news is in fact a serious problem in modern-day America. It is an equally serious mistake to believe that this will cease the moment Donald Trump is no longer president.

* * * * *

If you can't gaslight 'em, get 'em off the air!

That, effectively, is the unspoken motto of the Old Order when it comes to dealing with conservatives or Trump supporters who have any kind of an audience on television, radio, or social media.

From Media Matters to Apple, YouTube, Twitter, Google and Facebook, the move is on to stop free speech simply because the liberals who run the censoring operation in question don't like what they hear. The attitude was expressed succinctly by New York mayor Bill de Blasio when he told the U.K. *Guardian*:

"If you could remove News Corp from the last 25 years of American history, we would be in an entirely different place."

In his view, without the malign influence of Murdoch's media empire and its conservative Trump-supporting Fox News "we would be a more unified country. We would not be suffering a lot of the negativity and divisiveness we're going through right now. I can't ignore that."

In other words, if the once ironclad liberal monopoly on news had not been broken by Fox, all would be right with the world. NBC's Chuck Todd with his article expressing outrage at Fox is professing exactly the same sentiment as the leftist Mayor de Blasio: if only they could get rid of Fox News, all would be right with the media world.

The unhappy fact that Americans—conservatives and Trump supporters in particular—have to face is the viscerally authoritarian nature of the Old Order in and out of the media. Media Matters for America all by itself has conducted campaigns to take one prominent conservative after another off of television or radio. Over time the group has targeted Rush Limbaugh, Bill O'Reilly, Sean Hannity, Laura Ingraham, Tucker Carlson, Don Imus, Glenn Beck, and Lou Dobbs for removal from their respective shows. It has succeeded with O'Reilly, Imus, Beck, and Dobbs, when the latter was at CNN. (And oh yes, it came for me as well at CNN.) Recently, the authoritarian-minded left-wing, anti-free press group Sleeping Giants has joined the jihad against the First Amendment and a free press.

As Tucker Carlson and Vince Coglianese reported in *The Daily Caller*:

High profile though these victories against conservatives were, Media Matters has perhaps achieved more influence simply by putting its talking points into the willing hands of liberal journalists. "In '08 it became pretty apparent MSNBC was going left," says one source. "They were using our research to write their stories. They were eager to use our stuff." Media Matters staff had the direct line of MSNBC president Phil Griffin, and used it. Griffin took their calls.

Stories about Fox News were especially well received by MSNBC anchors and executives: "If we published something about Fox in the morning, they'd have it on the air that night verbatim."

But MSNBC executives weren't the only ones talking regularly to Media Matters.

"The entire progressive blogosphere picked up our stuff," says a Media Matters source, *"from Daily Kos to Salon. Greg Sargent [of* The Washington Post*] will write anything you give him. He was the go-to guy to leak stuff."*

"If you can't get it anywhere else, Greg Sargent's always game," agreed another source with firsthand knowledge.

Reached by phone, Sargent declined to comment.

"The HuffPo guys were good, Sam Stein and Nico [Pitney]," remembered one former staffer. *"The people at Huffington Post were always eager to cooperate, which is no surprise given David's long history with Arianna [Huffington]."*

"Jim Rainey at the LA Times took a lot of our stuff," the staffer continued. *"So did Joe Garofoli at the San Francisco Chronicle. We've pushed stories to Eugene Robinson and E.J. Dionne [at* The Washington Post*]. Brian Stelter at the New York Times was helpful."*

"Ben Smith [formerly of Politico, *now at BuzzFeed] will take stories and write what you want him to write,"* explained the former employee, whose account was confirmed by other sources. Staffers at Media Matters *"knew they could dump stuff to Ben Smith, they knew they could dump it at Plum Line [Greg Sargent's* Washington Post *blog], so that's where they sent it."* Smith, who refused to comment on the substance of these claims, later took to Twitter to say that he has been critical of Media Matters.

In other words, a number of these organizations—some of them not blogs but serious journalism outlets—were participating and allying themselves with an authoritarian minded organization. An authoritarian organization—tainted with charges of anti-Semitism—whose objective is to shut down a free press.

Now this anti-free-press cancer has metastasized to social media.

A case at hand as I write this centers on the conspiracy-minded Alex Jones of *Infowars*, who was removed from Twitter in September 2018. He has been banned from other social media platforms as well. I don't agree with Jones, but it clearly isn't just nutty conspiracies that have made him a target for the authoritarian-minded. It's his support of Trump. Writing of the similarities between Jones and the infamous Trump-hating FBI official Peter Strzok, *The Wall Street Journal's* Daniel Henninger observed:

> *After Apple removed his podcasts, similar bannings came from Facebook, Alphabet's YouTube, Microsoft Corp.'s LinkedIn, Spotify and Pinterest. When Mr. Jones tried to escape to Vimeo, it also took down his videos....*
>
> *The* Infowars *banishers said Alex Jones had violated their rules. Rules about what? Hate speech. Not the psychopathologies littering the web. Not its epidemic of illogic. Not its rampant political paranoia. They monitor just one thing: hate speech.*
>
> *There is a problem here, and like nearly all problems today, it's political.*
>
> *Hate speech, contrary to media convention, is not a settled concept. It is difficult to define in ways that are clear or legally precise. Identifying hate speech, especially for the purpose of banning it, is often a judgment call. And at its increasingly familiar worst, a rush to judgment.*
>
> *If there were more balance or good faith in the arguments over the content of speech, one might credit the left's concerns about injury and harm. Instead, what is happening on campuses reveals the reality.*
>
> *On speech issues, academics have developed Stockholm syndrome. When liberal and progressive professors come under assault from student mobs for "hurtful" speech, their colleagues fall silent, shun them, or sell them out. Why should the rest of us regard hate-speech rules as anything but a political weapon?*

"Speech issues" are in fact now full-fledged Old Order Swamp Wars. All over the country, the battles to shut down Trump supporters and conservatives are raging. From Facebook's telling the Trump-supporting video bloggers Diamond and Silk that their content was deemed "unsafe" to the "shadow banning" of prominent conservatives, the authoritarian nature of the left has manifested itself repeatedly.

In September 2018, Breitbart scored a scoop by obtaining an in-house video of Google executives taken in the aftermath of the 2016 election. The story reported, in part:

> *Co-founder Sergey Brin can be heard comparing Trump supporters to fascists and extremists. Brin argues that like other extremists, Trump voters were motivated by "boredom," which he says in the past led to fascism and communism.*
>
> *The Google co-founder then asks his company to consider what it can do to ensure a "better quality of governance and decision-making."*
>
> *VP for Global Affairs Kent Walker argues that supporters of populist causes like the Trump campaign are motivated by "fear, xenophobia, hatred, and a desire for answers that may or may not be there."*
>
> *Later, Walker says that Google should fight to ensure the populist movement – not just in the U.S. but around the world – is merely a "blip" and a "hiccup" in a historical arc that "bends toward progress."*
>
> *CEO Sundar Pichai states that the company will develop machine learning and A.I. to combat what an employee described as "misinformation" shared by "low-information voters."*

This revelation came on the heels of news, in an exclusive of Tucker Carlson's, that Google had deliberately and silently tried to influence the election by getting out the supposedly pro-Hillary Latino vote. *Breitbart* would also later get that story, with reporter Matt Boyle noting:

> *An email chain among senior Google executives from the day after the 2016 presidential election reveals the company tried to influence the 2016 United States presidential election on behalf of one candidate, Democrat Hillary Rodham Clinton.*
>
> *In the emails, a Google executive describes efforts to pay for free rides for a certain sect of the population to the polls—a get-out-the-vote for Hispanic voters operation—and how these efforts were because she thought it would help Hillary Clinton win the general election in 2016. She also used the term "silent*

donation" to describe Google's contribution to the effort to elect Clinton president.

The executive, Eliana Murillo, Google's multicultural marketing department head, was stunned after the election to discover that in the Google push to get Latinos to the polls, the company had miscalculated the amount of support in the Latino community *for* Trump—which turned out to be a quite healthy 29 percent of the Latino vote. As Tucker Carlson accurately notes:

> *This wasn't a get-out-the-vote effort or whatever they say. It wasn't aimed at all potential voters. It wasn't even aimed at a balanced cross-section of subgroups. Google didn't try to get out the vote among say Christian Arabs in Michigan or say Persian Jews in Los Angeles—they sometimes vote Republican. It was aimed only at one group, a group that Google cynically assumed would vote exclusively for the Democratic Party. Furthermore, this mobilization effort targeted not only the entire country but swing states vital to the Hillary campaign. This was not an exercise in civics, this was political consulting. It was in effect an in-kind contribution to the Hillary Clinton campaign.*

This is a startling example of the Old Order's reach in the drive to silently gaslight Americans into believing that Google is simply a nonpartisan social media search engine, when in fact it is clearly culturally and politically obsessed with its own Old Order politics. The failed Google attempt to make a "silent donation" to the Clinton campaign—a donation based on the Old Order's most basic of racial obsessions—is impossible to ignore.

But it wasn't just "silent donations" from the world of high-tech at work in gaslighting Americans. Incredibly, violence was in the mix—and the accompanying reluctance of the Old Order media to report the threatened and actual violence against Trump supporters.

Over at *Breitbart*, John Nolte began keeping a list of physical attacks on Trump supporters. By July 2018, he had found over 500. Here are but ten of them:

- A Trump supporter's car has all four tires slashed in Philadelphia.
- Members of the left-wing terrorist group Antifa follow and harass commentator and activist Candace Owens.

- A Trump supporter is punched in Hollywood.
- Anti-Trump protesters in California target a legal immigrant's cafe over Trump support and hurl feces.
- A seventy-six-year-old man is assaulted by anti-Trump thugs in San Diego.
- A brick is thrown through the front door of the Wheeling, Illinois, township Republican headquarters.
- A Florida man is attacked over a Trump flag in his yard.
- The co-chair of Women for Trump receives death threats after a CNN appearance.
- A burned animal carcass is left on a Trump staffer's porch.
- A woman is brutally attacked in a restaurant over support for Trump.

In Chicago, Suzanne Monk and her husband, Alexander Duvel, owners of Worlds of Music Chicago, were compelled to close their store because they came out in support of Trump. Writing in a letter to *Crain's*, a business paper in Chicago, Monk said:

> *For 24 years, I have loved living in Chicago with my husband, a native Chicagoan. I have loved doing business in Chicago. The food, the sports, the culture and the arts, and the diversity of people have been a fertile ground for our life, and I have been proud to call myself a Chicagoan anywhere I went in the world.*
>
> *But for the last year I have not loved living in Chicago. I am ashamed of you, Chicago, and the intolerance you now accept in the name of politics.*
>
> *You see, I am a Trump supporter. My husband is a Trump supporter, too. And because we support Trump, we no longer feel proud, or safe, being in this city.*
>
> *Chicago, you have always been a Democrat-run town, but this year you have become a one-party city terrorizing anyone not in your party for their beliefs. From the constant protests blocking roads and businesses, to the attacks on Trump supporters, to the verbal and online bullying going on every day across this city, Chicago, you have made it quite clear that Trump supporters are not welcome. When my fellow Chicagoans praised the riot at UIC*

that shut down the Chicago Trump rally I attended, I was angry and ashamed.

You have made it quite clear, there are two choices for Trump supporters in Chicago: Be silent about your politics or be bullied for them.

In September 2018, California Republican congressional candidate Rudy Peters was campaigning at a booth at the Castro Valley Fall Festival, just outside of Oakland. All of a sudden, a hostile man, later revealed as thirty-five-year-old Farzad Fazeli, charged Peters, hurled a cup of coffee at him, threatened to kill him, and pulled a switchblade—which fortunately did not open. The man finally ran when Peters physically defended himself with a campaign sign. He was caught and charged.

The gaslighting moment quickly arrived, as reported here by Nicholas Fondacaro at *NewsBusters*:

> *Republican Congressional candidate Rudy Peters, who's running against Democratic incumbent Eric Swalwell in California, was attacked by an assailant wielding a "switchblade" while campaigning at the Castro Valley Falls Festival on Sunday. The news of the attack reached national attention Tuesday afternoon yet none of the major network broadcasters (ABC, CBS, and NBC) thought it was worth mentioning.*

Laura Ingraham, who has no time for Old Order media gaslighting, immediately devoted an entire show—a full hour—to the topic of the left and its use of violence. She went out of her way to pair Peters and Louisiana Republican and House Majority Whip Steve Scalise—the latter almost shot to death by a man who was an avid follower of MSNBC. (Disclosure: I participated later on the show.) It is notable what Scalise said about the Peters attack and the mainstream media:

> *"If this was going on on the right, you know what would happen, Laura. Every mainstream media outlet would be reporting this, calling on each one of us [to comment]. They'd have microphones in our faces: 'Will you denounce it?' And you know what? I would denounce it. I'd denounce anything that happens on either side.*

"But you don't see that enough from the left, and it needs to happen more and they need to be challenged. Where are these liberal talk-show hosts that yell and scream and rave if their incitement is actually leading somebody to go and commit violence and resort to violence? That's not what this country's about."

What all of this so vividly illustrates is just how far the Old Order will go to preserve itself. Whether in the Old Order social media companies at the top of the elite scale or the most obscure of Old Order street thugs, the authoritarian mentality inherent in these Swamp Wars is running rampant.

Notably, Connecticut Democratic senator Chris Murphy tweeted this after the Alex Jones censorship was announced:

Infowars is the tip of a giant iceberg of hate and lies that uses sites like Facebook and YouTube to tear our nation apart. These companies must do more than take down one website. The survival of our democracy depends on it.

In other words, as Sean Davis, an editor at the conservative *Federalist* has observed, Murphy's thuggish message to Silicon Valley was really, "You'd better ban these websites, or else."

Perhaps the most perceptive suggestion for dealing with social media bans came from *National Review*'s David French. French is no Trump supporter; indeed, he was pushed by some Never Trumpers as a last-minute candidate to stop a successful Trump candidacy. But in an op-ed in, of all places, *The New York Times*, French suggests that the best way for social media companies to deal with the Alex Joneses of the world is through new standards that look to American legal guidelines for libel and slander. He points to the obvious: "'Hate speech' is extraordinarily vague and subjective. Libel and slander are not."

Therein lies the central point. "Hate speech" is being used as a club with which to beat conservatives and Trump supporters into oblivion.

In August 2018, *The Boston Globe* ran a call for papers around the country to run editorials on the same day denouncing Trump for calling out the media as "fake news" and "the enemy of the people." (Actually, again, Trump's point is that fake news is the enemy of the people, but hey.) Proclaimed the *Globe*:

A central pillar of President Trump's politics is a sustained assault on the free press.

The greatness of America is dependent on the role of a free press to speak the truth to the powerful. To label the press "the enemy of the people" is as un-American as it is dangerous to the civic compact we have shared for more than two centuries.

Well, no. As the president expressly made clear to me in 2014, what he goes after is dishonesty in the press. That dishonesty was freshly illustrated in 2018 with the NBC story that tried to gaslight Americans into believing Trump attacks the intelligence of blacks—and therefore is a racist—when in fact he has routinely said the same things about one white person after another. The "civic compact" that the *Globe* cites depends on getting facts. The reason the media has lost the public's trust is because it is intent on making up "facts" and trying to gaslight Americans into believing that fake news is true.

The good news? Conservatives know this. Trump supporters know this. But most important, Donald Trump himself knows this—and long before he ran for president, he was on record as saying so to me. And as the campaign by various social media companies picked up speed, President Trump called them out in a tweet:

Social Media Giants are silencing millions of people. Can't do this even if it means we must continue to hear Fake News like CNN, whose ratings have suffered gravely. People have to figure out what is real, and what is not, without censorship!

Which is to say, the president was speaking up for a free press. And who objected? Why, someone from CNN! Oliver Darcy took to CNN's money section to say:

With his tweet, and others before it, Trump has signaled that he and his Republican allies would continue to paint tech giants like Facebook and Twitter as villains in a longstanding culture war used to excite the conservative base....

The narrative is unlikely to go away anytime soon. The politicians and media outlets on the right that push it do not seem moved by the facts. Instead, they seem more interested in a narrative that resonates with and whips up the conservative base, which is comprised by a swath of the country that feels they are under attack in the great American culture war.

Social media is nothing more than technology—and fairly new technology at that. But Darcy seems clueless that, as demonstrated by the case of CBS's and *The New York Times'* gaslighting Americans in 1964, claiming that Barry Goldwater was playing footsie with would-be Nazis in Germany, the attitude of liberals running big media operations has been around for decades. And it isn't just the media executives, either. As Teddy White noted of members of the press who were covering JFK in the 1960s, they who "felt that they, too, were marching like soldiers of the Lord to the New Frontier," liberal bias from reporters is hardly new.

So we end here where we began, repeating this quote from the future president himself (emphasis mine):

> "The press is extremely dishonest. *Much of it. Some of it I have great respect for, and they're great people and honorable people.* But there's a large segment of the press that's more dishonest than anybody I've seen in business or anywhere else. And the one thing you have to do is you have to inform the public. The public has to know about the dishonesty of the press, because these are really bad people and they don't tell the truth and have no intention of telling the truth. And I know who they are and I would expose them 100 percent. And I will be doing that. *I mean, as I go down the line, I enjoy exposing people for being frauds and, you know, I would be definitely doing that. I think it's important to know. Because a lot of the public, they think, oh, they read it in the newspaper, and therefore it must be true. Well many of the things you read in the newspaper are absolutely false and really disgustingly false."*

In this Swamp War, in which fake news and gaslighting (not to mention ignoring the violence of the left, as in the lack of coverage of the assault on Rudy Peters) are the primary weapons of the media, Donald Trump at a minimum has fought and made it a draw. In fact, it is not unreasonable to suggest that he is winning outright.

CHAPTER SEVEN

TACKLING THE NFL

"We're proud of our country. We respect our flag."

—President Trump, responding to
NFL players who knelt during the
playing of the national anthem

AUGUST 30, 1865

A new White House tradition was stirring as President Andrew Johnson hosted the Brooklyn Atlantics and the Washington Nationals, two of America's premier amateur baseball clubs, at the White House. Four years later, President Ulysses S. Grant invited the professional baseball team the Cincinnati Red Stockings to be his White House guests. In 1910, President William Howard Taft became the first president to throw out the first pitch at a Major League game, this one at Washington's National Stadium. "Baseball is our national game," proclaimed President Calvin Coolidge, who promptly hosted the Washington Senators at the White House. So ingrained in American culture had baseball become that after the attack on Pearl Harbor and the American entrance into World War Two, when baseball's commissioner, Judge Kenesaw Mountain Landis, inquired of President Roosevelt whether the game should be suspended for the duration of the war, FDR replied: "I honestly feel that it would be best for the country to keep baseball going." It did.

Which is to say, the tradition of presidents celebrating professional sports is an old one—a very old one. John F. Kennedy of Boston became the first president to host an NBA champion. Doubtless not coincidentally, the champs that year were the Boston Celtics. On and on went this quite bipartisan tradition of inviting famous athletic champions to celebrate at the White House with the president of the moment. It gathered even more steam in 1980 when President Jimmy Carter became the first president to host a winning Super Bowl team—the Pittsburgh Steelers—and a winning World Series team, the Pittsburgh Pirates.

But as ESPN notes, the Super Bowl tradition really took off in the years of the Reagan presidency.

> *It was Ronald Reagan, however, who made the practice of honoring championship teams at the White House a regular occurrence. Reagan had a cooler full of popcorn dumped on him by New York Giants linebacker Harry Carson, evoking the team's famous Gatorade celebration, in February 1987. The following year, Reagan threw a pass to Washington wide receiver Ricky Sanders.*

As a young White House aide, I was in attendance for those Reagan celebrations of the New York Giants and the Washington Redskins. To this day I have no idea what the political opinions were of the players of those two teams. Conservative? Liberal? Reagan fans? Not Reagan fans? No one knew—and if they did, no one cared. In fact, the Giants' visit to the Reagan White House in 1987 came as the president was smack in the middle of the hotly controversial Iran-Contra scandal. But all of that was put aside for the Giants' ceremony. The moment was about celebrating excellence in sports. It was not about politics.

These events were by then the latest manifestation of an old presidential tradition, combined with the celebration of sport and sportsmanship. Fast-forward to President Trump's inviting a National Football League Super Bowl winner to the White House. This was a president who had almost purchased the Buffalo Bills and in fact, for a while, owned the New Jersey Generals in the nascent United States Football League years earlier. He loved football. What could possibly go wrong in the Trump presidency with this very old tradition?

Enter yet another Old Order Swamp War, this one played out in the Swamp otherwise known as the world of professional sports.

* * * * *

The 2016 election was over by one day.

On November 9, Detroit Pistons coach Stan Van Gundy, in Phoenix to lead his team against the Phoenix Suns, gave an interview to the hometown *Detroit Free Press*. In it, he threw caution to the wind and went on a remarkably hostile rant about something that had nothing whatsoever to do with sports, with basketball, or with his team's prospects that night against the Suns. His topic: president-elect Donald Trump. The headline: "Detroit Pistons' Stan Van Gundy Goes off on Trump: 'Brazenly Racist.'"

From the story:

> *"I don't think anybody can deny this guy is openly and bra-zenly racist and misogynistic," Van Gundy said. "We have just thrown a good part of our population under the bus, and I have problems with thinking this is where we are as a country."*

The coach didn't stop there, plowing on with his own brand of racial supremacy.

> *"I understand problems with the economy. I understand all the problems with Hillary Clinton, I do. But certain things in our country should disqualify you. And the fact that millions and millions of Americans don't think that racism and sexism dis-qualifies you to be our leader, in our country... We presume to tell other countries about human-rights abuses and everything else. We better never do that again, when our leaders talk to China or anybody else about human-rights abuses.*
>
> *We just elected an openly, brazen misogynist leader and we should keep our mouths shut and realize that we need to be learning maybe from the rest of the world, because we don't got anything to teach anybody.*
>
> *It's embarrassing. I have been ashamed of a lot of things that have happened in this country, but I can't say I've ever been ashamed of our country until today. Until today. We all have to find our way to move forward, but that was- and I'm not even trying to make a political statement. To me, that's beyond politics.*
>
> *You don't get to come out and talk about people like that, and then lead our country and have millions of Americans embrace you. I'm having a hard time being with people. I'm going to walk into this arena tonight and realize that-especially*

in this state-most of these people voted for this guy. Like, (exple-
tive), I don't have any respect for that. I don't.
    ... We should be ashamed for what we stand for as the
United States today. That's it for me. I don't have anything to
say about the game tonight."

In a handful of minutes, the Pistons coach had denounced, slandered, and insulted not only the new president-elect, but any and all Americans who had voted for him, beginning with Trump's Arizona supporters who would gather that night to watch the Pistons play the Suns. Notably, Van Gundy did not condemn the basketball fans of another Trump-supporting state—the Detroit Pistons' home state of Michigan. He did, however, note that he lived in a Michigan county that supported Clinton.

The Van Gundy episode was far from being the only sports-related one. As the election receded and the actual Trump presidency dawned, one coach or professional athlete after another leapt at the chance to go public with their open hostility for the new president, his supporters, or both. As Trump supporters include millions of fans of various teams, effectively the coaches and athletes were going out of their way to assail their own fans as racists, bigots, and more. It is a classic, if startling, illustration of just how deeply the mind-set of the elitist Old Order has penetrated wide-ranging American society. A Swamp War had broken out in professional sports—and the self-anointed Swamp Warriors didn't give a damn who knew or who cared. Even more to the point, in the style of John Grisham's book *The Firm*, one had the sense that for the athletes to get along with their peers or teammates, there was an unsubtle pressure on them to rant against Trump—or there would be social, if not contractual, problems.

Being coaches or stars of America's favorite sports, their views won them headlines—as they clearly knew would happen. The headlines and quotes included these, as reported respectively by Bob Kravitz, a sports columnist for NBC's Indianapolis affiliate WTHR, and the web site *Deadspin*:

- "Spurs' Popovich continues his harsh criticism of the Trump administration"
    "Some days, I feel like we've been invaded by another power and taken over [by people] who don't feel the same. It's a strange land."
    —Gregg Popovich, head coach of the San Antonio Spurs
- "Steve Kerr Rips Donald Trump And The Whole Damn Election"

"The man who's going to lead you has routinely used racist, misogynist, insulting words. That's a tough one."
—Steve Kerr, head coach of the Golden State Warriors

The New York Times wondered in its sports section how far all this public animus from NBA figures towards Trump would go:

> *The question moving forward is whether these comments are merely a visceral reaction to the presidential election or whether they will build into something more, emboldening those around the league to speak candidly about a host of political issues.*

Notice the phrase "emboldening those around the league to speak candidly about a host of political issues." In other words, NBA stars and coaches were being not-so-subtly urged by the elites at the Old Order *Times* to dis the president—or there might be a price to pay.

When it became clear that the Warriors might be headed into another championship year, favored as they were over the Cleveland Cavaliers, star player Stephen Curry stepped forward for a political layup and made plain his feelings in *USA Today*. The headline: "Steph Curry on Warriors' possible White House visit: 'I don't want to go.'"

From the story:

> *"That we don't stand for basically what our President has – the things that he's said and the things that he hasn't said in the right times, that we won't stand for it," Curry said. "And by acting and not going, hopefully that will inspire some change when it comes to what we tolerate in this country and what is accepted and what we turn a blind eye to. It's not just the act of not going there. There are things you have to do on the back end to actually push that message into motion....*
>
> *"[Athletes are] all trying to do what we can. We're using our platforms, using our opportunities to shed light on that, so that's kind of where I stand on it. I don't think us not going to the White House is going to miraculously make everything better, but this is my opportunity to voice that."*

Since the president has repeatedly made it clear that he believes in a color-blind America where everyone is judged on merit—their character, as Martin Luther King himself used to preach—the president saw the Curry quote and, as always, punched back. The presidential tweet was crystal clear: "Going to the White House is considered a great honor for a championship team. Stephen Curry is hesitating, therefore invitation is withdrawn!"

What Curry was conveying when he said that "we don't stand for basically what our President has" could just as easily have been said—indeed was said—by anyone in the army of Old Order high priests and elites in the media, political world, academia, Hollywood, and beyond in one Swamp or another.

And it quickly became obvious that Curry and some NBA coaches weren't the only ones in the sports world carrying the torch for the idea that America should be permanently divided by race and other elitist Old Order nostrums—nostrums that have proven themselves to be as intellectually and morally bankrupt as they are un-American.

* * * * *

There are two ways for an athlete to express political views—on the field and off the field. For any prominent public figure—and any pro-sports athlete qualifies as prominent in today's media-soaked American culture—the spotlight can and will pick up his or her views and magnify them times a hundred. There is everything right in America with having a point of view and expressing it. Ordinary Americans do it all the time. In the case of the NBA coaches and Steph Curry, their views were made known off the basketball court. They went out of their way to insult the new president and his voters, and Trump being Trump, he immediately punched back. But the Swamp War was a limited one, not affecting the entire NBA.

Not so with the National Football League.

But before we get to the tale of the Swamp War that would soon consume the NFL in a fierce battle with both the president and its own fans, I'll share a tale of another football era and the politics of protest.

NEW ORLEANS, JANUARY 1965

The American Football League players are arriving at the New Orleans airport to play in the 1965 AFL All-Star game. Among the players is Buffalo

Bills quarterback Jack Kemp. Kemp is also the president of the AFL Players' Association.

It is the middle of the civil rights revolution. A year earlier, President Lyndon Johnson signed the 1964 Civil Rights Act, and in August 1965 he would sign the Voting Rights Act. But in Louisiana, the state's governor is Democrat and pro-segregationist John McKeithen, a decided reflection of his party's long support for the identity politics of segregation, the latter a legal, social, and political fact of life in the state.

Now, luggage in hand, Kemp and his teammate, the fullback and African American Cookie Gilchrist, are individually seeking out cabs. ESPN later recalled the moment:

> *Gilchrist got his ride downtown but only because the cabbie spotted a white man – Bills quarterback Jack Kemp. The driver told Gilchrist he'd let him get in so long as Kemp was the one who hired the taxi. This, apparently, resulted from a new (or perhaps temporary) Taxicab Bureau policy that gave drivers with the proper permit the option of transporting black and white passengers – but only if the party who hailed the cab was from the hack's own race.*

I didn't know Jack Kemp in 1965. I was a teenager. But decades later he would become my boss at the Bush forty-one Department of Housing and Urban Development (HUD). If I learned nothing else at HUD, it was Kemp's passionate support of civil rights. One of the joys of that experience was Secretary Kemp's "brown bag lunches" for his staff. We would gather in a conference room and hear a speaker whose expertise was anything from an arcane area of housing policy to Winston Churchill. Kemp was a huge Churchill fan, as am I. On one occasion he arranged for the late Sir Martin Gilbert, Churchill's official biographer, to regale us with Churchill stories. It was a memorable moment.

But always we heard Kemp's beliefs in Abraham Lincoln ("Mr. Lincoln") and Martin Luther King Jr.—always "Dr. King" to Kemp, beliefs that I decidedly shared. As a congressman from Buffalo, New York, it was Jack Kemp who cosponsored the legislation that would make Dr. King's birthday a national holiday, and President Ronald Reagan who signed it into law. Kemp's biographers, longtime journalists Morton Kondracke and Fred Barnes, recall this Kemp moment in their bestselling book *Jack Kemp: The Bleeding-Heart Conservative Who Changed America*. (The jacket cover of the book, not coincidentally, features Kemp in front of the towering statue of Mr. Lincoln in the Lincoln Memorial.) The two write:

> *In 1992, Kemp was asked at a journalists' breakfast where his passion [for civil rights] came from. He recalled the years he spent as a professional quarterback and the lessons of racial equality he had picked up in a locker room filled with black athletes. He added: "It is my way of redeeming my existence on this earth. I wasn't there with Rosa Parks or Dr. King or John Lewis, but I am here now and I am going to yell from the rooftops about what we need to do."*

Thus it was that when Buffalo Bills quarterback Kemp arrived in New Orleans for that fateful All-Star game, he came to a startling realization. His black teammates could not even get a cab ride to their hotel unless they took the "colored" taxis—or, as happened with his friend and teammate Cookie Gilchrist, had a white teammate ride with them. Inside the city, it was worse. As the Pro Football Hall of Fame recounts:

> *It eventually turned into a nightmare as many of the black players were left stranded at the airport for hours when they arrived in town. Once in the city, African American players were refused cab service and in some cases those who were given rides were dropped off miles from their destinations.*
>
> *Other players were refused admittance to nightspots and restaurants, while nearly all were subjected to tongue-lashings and to a hostile atmosphere on Bourbon Street in the French Quarter while sightseeing. The situation became so uncomfortable for the black players who clearly felt unwelcome that most simply returned to their hotels.*

Finally, the black players had had enough. Again from the Hall of Fame archives:

> *Later, all 21 African American players who were scheduled to suit up met at the Roosevelt Hotel, the headquarters for the*

East team. The group discussed in great detail the treatment
they had received and with a vote decided to walk out on the
All-Star game.

"The majority ruled. We felt we couldn't perform 100%
under the current circumstances," said Buffalo Bills end Ernie
Warlick. "Actually this came as a complete surprise to us. We
were led to believe that we could relax and enjoy ourselves in
New Orleans just like other citizens."

Some players were more vocal than others about the adverse
conditions and discriminatory practices experienced in New
Orleans. But, in the end Warlick and other black All-Stars,
came together. Finding the situation unacceptable, the players
decided that they would not play in the All-Star as long as it
was to be hosted in New Orleans.

Without hesitation, Jack Kemp—acting in his role as the players' union president—supported the black players. The league's president quickly stepped in. The game was moved to Houston, the players all showed up without incident, and those, like Kemp, who staunchly supported the civil rights movement used their time off the field—but never on the field—to push their cause. There is no record that anyone thought of showing up for the game and refusing to stand for the national anthem—an action that surely would have been found insulting by Americans who believed both in civil rights and the symbolism of the national anthem. Most decidedly Kemp, a fierce patriot, would have never "taken a knee" during the anthem.

Now the second story.

It was 2016.

The NFL's Swamp Warrior was the quarterback of the San Francisco 49ers, Colin Kaepernick. Kaepernick, who is both biracial and a true believer in the politics of the far left, began this Swamp War by refusing to stand as the national anthem was played at 49er games. This happened in a country that has twice elected a black man as president (and who was still in the White House as this moment unfolded), and has seen African Americans serve in the highest Cabinet positions, on the Supreme Court, and in both the Senate and House of Representatives, not to mention become Hollywood stars, professional athletes, and plenty more outside the national spotlight. Kaepernick explained his reasoning this way to NFL Media:

170

"I am not going to stand up to show pride in a flag for a country that oppresses black people and people of color," Kaepernick told NFL Media in an exclusive interview after the game. "To me, this is bigger than football and it would be selfish on my part to look the other way. There are bodies in the street and people getting paid leave and getting away with murder."

Kaepernick decided to take the field—and then ostentatiously "take a knee" during the playing of the national anthem, a gesture instantly seen by fans as insulting not just the flag but the military, a military that had produced veterans of all colors who had fought and died for what the flag represented—freedom and equality for all.

The Old Order media—but of course—leapt to Kaepernick's defense. The *Los Angeles Times* wondered editorially, "[Is it] actually possible that 240 years after the signing of the Declaration of Independence the message still hasn't sunk in that in this country, unlike some others, citizens are free to express their opinions? Even when the opinions in question are unpopular or unpatriotic or even, for that matter, wrong? And that the rest of us are free, as well, to express our agreement or disagreement?" The paper neatly skirted the fact that it wasn't that Kaepernick had an opinion about police brutality; it was that he used his professional time on the field to express it. One suspects that if a member of the *Times* editorial board insisted on opening a board meeting with a one-minute prayer opposing abortion, the *Times* would have an entirely different opinion about free expression.

GQ magazine rushed to compare Kaepernick to boxing's Muhammad Ali and baseball's Jackie Robinson—completely ignoring that neither Ali nor Robinson carried their political views into a boxing match or a baseball game.

President Obama, out of the country at a G20 summit in China, praised Kaepernick, saying, "He's exercising his constitutional right to make a statement. I think there's a long history of sports figures doing so." Curiously, neither Obama nor the media nor Kaepernick himself seemed to focus on the fact that this was the eighth year of the presidency of America's first black president. Kaepernick was in effect insisting that Obama's administration had done nothing to halt the oppression of black people. If there were bodies in the street, why hadn't Obama done anything about it—and why did Kaepernick not seem to care about the president's inaction? The question mysteriously never seemed to get asked, much less answered.

Unlike those black players and Jack Kemp in 1965 who, in the face of rampant and vivid racism infinitely worse than that of 2016 America, simply refused to take the field at all unless the venue was changed, Kaepernick went in the opposite direction. He waited to protest until he was on the field, and chose to protest in a fashion that was guaranteed to insult and anger not just millions of Americans but particularly NFL fans.

From a football perspective: the NFL became woven into the fabric of American culture long ago, and it depends not just on the players but on the fans for its very existence. And as the Kaepernick protest took off, with other players across the league joining in, incensed NFL fans saw a deliberate and repeated insult to the flag—and to themselves. They responded—and not well.

Season ticket holders tore up their once highly valued tickets. Videos flashed across the internet of angry fans burning their memorabilia, tossing team jerseys into garbage cans. Empty seats began showing up as games were played. Perhaps most significant, television ratings for NFL games plummeted.

Fast forward to the arrival of Trump in the White House. Now, President Trump took note, a very different note than President Obama—and President Trump like millions of his fellow NFL fans, was incensed. This was not, it was clear to him, a question of free expression or police brutality. This was about rich Old Order athletes abruptly giving the finger to the country and the American people who had lavished all of them with opportunity, wealth, and celebrity. The American people were not happy; the president, who is a serious football fan, was not happy. Inevitably, he spoke out.

Speaking at a September rally in Huntsville, Alabama, the president launched his own response to the kneeling players: "Wouldn't you love to see one of these NFL owners, when somebody disrespects our flag, to say, 'Get that son of a bitch off the field right now?'" The crowd in football-crazy Alabama roared its approval. For the following two weeks, Trump returned again and again to what had now become a Grade A national controversy. Voicing the anger of millions of fans, he went after the kneeling players for showing neither respect nor patriotism to their country and its flag, calling them "privileged" millionaires.

The Baltimore Ravens and the Jacksonville Jaguars played their game not in America but at London's Wembley Stadium. It came hours after Trump's

Alabama rally. The British paper *The Guardian* ran this headline: "NFL players kneel for anthem in unprecedented defiance of Trump."

Not only did they kneel, but they pointedly stood for the British anthem, "God Save the Queen."

The NFL was now in the middle of a full-fledged Swamp War, with players attacking the president. In the finest tradition of Old Order Swamp Warriors, the first card out was, but of course, the race card. Trump had said not a word about race. But suddenly these mega-rich professional athletes, in the eternal style of racial supremacists, morphed into those who judged themselves and everyone else by skin color. Identity politics—Jim Crowism—was now the coin of the realm in the NFL.

In fact, a number of players did work related to their political beliefs off the field. But doing something that was deliberately provocative on the field, understanding full well that it would insult their fans even if getting reams of adoring press from the left-leaning media, was something a fair number insisted on.

The president continued to call them out, saying, "I think it's very disrespectful to our country. I think it's very, very disrespectful to our flag."

On and on the knee-taking went. Down and down the TV ratings went. The Pittsburgh Steelers remained in their locker room while the anthem played, with a solitary player standing at attention at the end of the tunnel—an accident, he later pleaded to his teammates and fans. So too did the entire roster of the Tennessee Titans and the Seattle Seahawks stay in their locker rooms later that same Sunday. The Seattle players issued a statement, saying: "We will not stand for the injustice that has plagued people of color in this country." They said they were dedicated to "equality and justice for all." Again, there was no mention of just why this had not been achieved under the administration of America's first black president. And the new president kept ratcheting up the political heat, attacking the NFL for insulting the national anthem and the military, whether in rallies or by tweet, driving the owners and NFL commissioner Roger Goodell to distraction.

By October 2017, a mere month after Trump's first attack in the Huntsville rally, the owners, player representatives, and commissioner gathered for a secret meeting at the NFL's Park Avenue headquarters in Manhattan. In and of itself, the ritzy Park Avenue location telegraphs just how elitist and out of touch with its fans the NFL itself has become. Months later, in April 2018, someone inside the room spilled the beans of the meeting to *The New York Times*, producing a recording. What it shows is just how much of an effect the president's attacks were having on the league. The tape is a classic example of just how insular the Old Order in the sports world really is.

The *Times* reported:

> *N.F.L. owners, players and league executives, about 30 in all, convened urgently at the league's headquarters on Park Avenue in October, nearly a month after President Trump began deriding the league and its players over protests during the national anthem.*
>
> *It was an extraordinary summit; rarely do owners and players meet in this manner. But the president's remarks about players who were kneeling during the anthem had catalyzed a level of public hostility that the N.F.L. had never experienced. In the spirit of partnership at the meeting, the owners decided that they and the players should sit in alternating seats around the large table, which featured an N.F.L. logo in the middle....*
>
> *The New England Patriots owner Robert K. Kraft pointed to another "elephant in the room."*
>
> *"This kneeling," he said.*
>
> *"The problem we have is, we have a president who will use that as fodder to do his mission that I don't feel is in the best interests of America," said Kraft, who is a longtime supporter of Mr. Trump's. "It's divisive and it's horrible."*
>
> *The owners were intent on finding a way to avoid Trump's continued criticism. The president's persistent jabs on Twitter had turned many fans against the league. [Philadelphia Eagles owner Jeffrey] Lurie, who called Trump's presidency "disastrous," cautioned against players getting drawn into the president's tactics....*
>
> *The Buffalo Bills owner Terry Pegula sounded anguished over the uncertainty of when Trump would take another shot at the league. "All Donald needs to do is to start to do this again," Pegula said. "We need some kind of immediate plan because of what's going on in society. All of us now, we need to put a Band-Aid on what's going on in the country."*

The Jacksonville Jaguars owner Shahid Khan countered that the worst was behind them. "All the damage Trump's going to do is done," he said.

The owners kept returning to one bottom-line issue: Large numbers of fans and sponsors had become angry about the pro-tests. Boycotts had been threatened and jerseys burned and—most worrisome—TV ratings were declining.

Pegula complained that the league was "under assault." He unloaded a dizzying flurry of nautical metaphors to describe their predicament. "To me, this is like a glacier moving into the ocean," he said. "We're getting hit with a tsunami." He expressed his wish that the league never be "a glacier crawling into the ocean."

The Houston Texans owner Bob McNair was more direct. He urged the players to tell their colleagues to, essentially, knock off the kneeling. "You fellas need to ask your compadres, fellas, stop that other business, let's go out and do something that really produces positive results, and we'll help you."

As the meeting went on, the players voiced support for Kaepernick, with Eric Reid, a former teammate, saying his friend had been "hung out to dry" by the NFL. Reid went on: "Nobody stepped up and said we support Colin's right to do this. We all let him become Public Enemy No. 1 in this country, and he still doesn't have a job."

The meeting adjourned with nothing decided other than the need to meet again.

Trump, as the owners feared, kept pouring it on. In an interview with Fox's Sean Hannity, the president said: "I watched Colin Kaepernick and I thought it was terrible. And then it got bigger and bigger and started mush-rooming. And frankly the NFL should have suspended him for one game and he would have never done it again. They could have then suspended him for two games, and they could have suspended him again if he did it a third time, for the season, and you would never have had a problem."

And then.

On February 4, 2018, in spectacular fashion, the Philadelphia Eagles won their first Super Bowl. They defeated the Tom Brady-led New England Patriots—the Patriots being the defending champs, who had appeared in the

Super Bowl ten times and won five times. Philadelphia fans, to understate the situation, were deliriously happy. Four days later, hundreds of thousands of Eagles fans swarmed the City of Brotherly Love to give their first-time Super Bowl hometown champions a raucous "welcome home" parade.

Next up, the traditional White House visit—which, in a stunningly self-defeating Swamp War, the Eagles turned into a disaster. Eighty-one players and Eagles staff were booked to show up, according to the White House. And suddenly, the number dropped precipitously—to fewer than a dozen.

"No I'm not going to the White House. Are you kidding me?" snarked defensive end Chris Long. The prior year, when playing for the Patriots, Long had refused to go to the new Trump White House with the 2017 champions, saying to Green Stripe News in a video: "My son grows up, and I believe the legacy of our president is going to be what it is. I don't want him to say, 'Hey, Dad, why'd you go [to the White House] when you knew the right thing was to not go?'"

"I personally do not anticipate attending that," Eagles safety Malcolm Jenkins said in a tweet.

"I just don't feel welcome into that house," said running back LeGarrette Blount, who had also played for the Patriots the previous year and refused to go.

So too did Torrey Smith, the Eagles wide receiver, make clear he wasn't going because Trump was the president, quickly misinterpreting the idea that when on the field players should stick to football. "When I think of 'Stick to football,' to me it means stay out of politics, stay out of things that you don't agree with me on," he said. "People don't say 'Stick to football' that agree with the things that I talk about. It's only people that disagree that say 'Stick to football.' So for me it, it doesn't stop me. I'm not one that really looks for approval from anyone."

Clearly Smith was unfamiliar with Jack Kemp, who, retired from football, went on to be one of the most influential congressmen in history, plus a presidential candidate, Cabinet secretary, and vice presidential nominee. Kemp most assuredly did not "stick to football." But never in a thousand years would he have taken the field and deliberately insulted Buffalo fans by kneeling for the playing of the national anthem.

Smith went on CNN to talk with Don Lemon, saying:

"It's not just about politics. If I told you that I was invited to a party by an individual that I believe is sexist or has no respect for women, or I told you this individual has said offensive things toward many minority groups and I don't feel comfortable by it, this individual also called my peers and my friends SOBs, you would understand why I wouldn't go to that party."

He added in a tweet: "It goes beyond politics.... I don't think he is a good person."

Which is to say, Smith proved that it was all about politics—Old Order elitist politics, specifically. Needless to say, there are millions of Americans who disagree with Smith's decidedly left-wing description of Trump.

The turmoil continued. ESPN dug into the issue, reporting: "A large group of Eagles players had decided not to attend, including most—if not all—of the black players, a source told ESPN's Adam Schefter. In fact, five or fewer Eagles players committed to attend the White House ceremony, a source told ESPN's Don Van Natta."

Which meant, of course, that the players were continuing to play the race card—regardless of the fact that Trump had never done so with them. Now having been accused by Eagles players of everything from racism to sexism to lying to "not being a good person," and with others in the NFL refusing to stand for the national anthem, the president, sensibly, had had enough. The Eagles visit to the White House was cancelled. The Eagles fairy-tale season ended on a decidedly sour note, both for the team and the NFL itself.

By May 2018, with a new fall season looming, the NFL seemed to finally wake up. At their spring meeting, the owners voted to have all their personnel stand for the anthem. Said Goodell:

"We want people to be respectful of the national anthem. We want people to stand. That's all personnel, and to make sure they treat this moment in a respectful fashion. That's something that we think we owe. We've been very sensitive on making sure that we give players choices, but we do believe that that moment is an important moment and one that we are going to focus on."

Violations of the new policy would result in fines—for the team, not the individual players. This was done to get around dealing with the players' union on the issue. And sure enough, the NFL Players' Association quickly issued this condemnation:

> *The NFL chose not to consult the union in the development of this new "policy." NFL players have shown their patriotism through their social activism, their community service, in support of our military and law enforcement and yes, through their protests to raise awareness about the issues they care about.*
>
> *The vote by NFL club CEOs today contradicts the statements made to our player leadership by Commissioner Roger Goodell and the Chairman of the NFL's Management Council John Mara about the principles, values and patriotism of our League.*
>
> *Our union will review the new policy and challenge any aspect of it that is inconsistent with the collective bargaining agreement.*

In July the NFL Players' Association filed a grievance over the new policy.

As the September 6 season start grew nearer, with the first game being between the Eagles and the Atlanta Falcons, there was yet another gathering of team owners and players in New York. What came out of it was the kind of language heard in international diplomacy—talk of "productive dialogue," "collaboration," and "progress." All of which meant that the realization of the degree to which the players were busy insulting their own fans seemed not yet to have dawned on them. There was what was described as a "standstill agreement"—which effectively meant that the NFL would wait until after the 2018 season to return to the subject.

It would be hard to find a clearer illustration of just how entrenched the Old Order mentality is than this tale of chaos in the NFL over standing for the national anthem. What Colin Kaepernick quite unintentionally revealed was a league run by Old Order elites (the owners and the commissioner) for Old Order elites—the mega-rich players. So tone-deaf were they both to the sensibilities of their customers—the fans—that it took two seasons' worth of dithering to come to what seemed the obvious conclusion: keep politics off the field. Then the owners and some players wondered if they needed to change their minds. And the "standstill agreement" resulted.

As the fall NFL season dawned, Nike declared its Old Order colors by starting an ad campaign that featured Colin Kaepernick. In a telling response, Nike lost almost $3.75 billion dollars in market capitalization. The free market speaks.

The president, with a keen eye to an Old Order weakness, can be certain not to yield in this—or for that matter, any—Swamp War.

The NFL tale is a classic example of a Swamp War. In this one, the president—and the fans—ultimately held the winning hand.

CHAPTER EIGHT

BATTLING THE THREE
FACES OF RACE

"I have a dream that my four little children will one day live in a nation where they will not be judged by the color of their skin but by the content of their character."

—Dr. Martin Luther King, Jr.,
August 1963

Race.

It is the subject of the swampiest of Old Order Swamp Wars. And the Old Order has deployed every weapon it can think of—from the travel ban to illegal immigration to identity politics—to depict Donald Trump as a racist.

A few examples from the Old Order media:

- *The New York Times* **editorial board, November 24, 2015:** "America has just lived through another presidential campaign week dominated by Donald Trump's racist lies."
- *The New York Times* **editorial board, March 1, 2016:** Donald Trump is a "symbol of intolerance and division."
- *The New York Times* **editorial board, January 12, 2018:** "Where to begin? How about with a simple observation: The president of the United States is a racist."
- *The Washington Post* **editorial page, August 15, 2017:** "Tuesday was a great day for David Duke and racists everywhere. The president of the United States all but declared that he has their backs."
- *The Los Angeles Times* **editorial board, March 2, 2016:** "He is a racist and a bully, a demagogue."

- *The Seattle Times* **editorial board, January 12, 2018:** *"Our president is a racist."*
- Others expressed similar sentiments, such as:
    "Let's not mince words: Donald Trump is a bigot and a racist."
    —*Washington Post* columnist Dana Milbank
    "The President of the United States is racist. A lot of us already knew that."—CNN's Don Lemon

And not to be forgotten, this from Hillary Clinton on Donald Trump to the U.K. *Guardian* in 2018:

> *He does have a strong streak of racism that goes back to his early years.*
>
> *I include his anti-immigrant tirades because he character-izes immigrants in very racially derogatory ways, but he was Islamophobic, he was anti-women, he really had the whole package of bigotry that he was putting on offer to those who were intrigued and attracted to him.*

There's more of this, of course. But let's be brutally candid.

The American left is racist. Not Donald Trump. And furthermore, the left has always been racist. Say it again: always. In today's world, race was and is at the core of three Swamp Wars of the Trump era: the travel ban, illegal immigration, and identity politics.

Not every individual left-leaning soul is racist, to be sure. But to suggest that the left in general is not racist is, yes indeed, gaslighting Americans to believe the opposite of what is a provable truth and has been for over two centuries. The American left and the larger Old Order that gives it shelter need racism for their political survival—and use it regularly to try to win the latest versions of the swampiest of Swamp Wars.

First, a quick history of this obsessive leftist culture of racial supremacy.

In 2008, I took some time to study something that is strangely passed over when the Old Order mind turns to race, now notably so where Donald Trump is concerned. As the Democrats prepared to nominate Senator Barack Obama for president, I looked at the official website of the Democratic National Committee. It boasted of the party's support for civil rights but was, curiously, scrubbed clean of fifty-two years of party history. The party history section started with the first appearance of the party, in 1800, as founded by Thomas Jefferson. Then it stopped in 1848, resuming again with this sentence: "As the 19th Century came to a close, the American electorate changed more and more rapidly."

Hmmm. What exactly transpired in those missing fifty-two years—not to mention before they arrived and well afterwards? I spent some time listing the events that were not mentioned. *The American Spectator* and *The Wall Street Journal* published my findings.

- There is no reference to the number of Democratic Party platforms supporting slavery. There were six from 1840 to 1860.
- There is no reference to the number of Democratic presidents who owned slaves. There were seven from 1800 to 1861.
- There is no reference to the number of Democratic Party platforms that either supported segregation outright or were silent on the subject. There were twenty from 1868 to 1948.
- There is no reference to "Jim Crow," as in "Jim Crow laws," nor is there reference to the role Democrats played in creating them. These were the post-Civil War laws passed enthusiastically by Democrats in that pesky fifty-two-year part of the DNC's missing years. These laws segregated public schools, public transportation, restaurants, restrooms, and public places in general (everything from water coolers to beaches). The reason Civil Rights heroine Rosa Parks became famous is that she refused to yield her seat on a segregated bus to a white passenger—the bus being segregated in the first place as the direct result of Democrats' actions.
- There is no reference to the formation of the Ku Klux Klan, which, according to Columbia University historian Eric Foner, became "a military force serving the interests of the Democratic Party." Nor is there reference to University of North Carolina historian Allen Trelease's description of the Klan as the "terrorist arm of the Democratic Party."
- There is no reference to the fact Democrats opposed the Thirteenth, Fourteenth, and Fifteenth Amendments to the Constitution. The Thirteenth Amendment banned slavery. The Fourteenth Amendment effectively overturned the infamous 1857 Supreme Court Dred Scott

decision (made by Democratic pro-slavery Supreme Court justices) by guaranteeing due process and equal protection to former slaves. The Fifteenth Amendment gave black Americans the right to vote.

- There is no reference to the fact that Democrats opposed the Civil Rights Act of 1866. It was passed by the Republican Congress over the veto of Democratic president Andrew Johnson. The law was designed to provide blacks the rights to own private property, sign contracts, sue, and serve as witnesses in legal proceedings.
- There is no reference to the Democrats' opposition to the Civil Rights Act of 1875. It was passed by a Republican Congress and signed into law by President Ulysses S. Grant. The law prohibited racial discrimination in public places and public accommodations.
- There is no reference to the Democrats' 1904 platform, which devoted a section to "Sectional and Racial Agitation," claiming the GOP's protests against segregation and the denial of voting rights to blacks sought to "revive the dead and hateful race and sectional animosities in any part of our common country," which in turn "means confusion, distraction of business, and the reopening of wounds now happily healed."
- There is no reference to four Democratic platforms from 1908 to 1920 that were silent on blacks, segregation, lynching, and voting rights, as racial problems in the country mounted. By contrast, the GOP platforms of those years specifically addressed "Rights of the Negro" (1908), opposed lynchings (1912, 1920, 1924, 1928), and, as the New Deal kicked in, spoke out about the dangers of making blacks "wards of the state."
- There is no reference to the DNC-sponsored Democratic Convention of 1924, known to history as the "Klanbake." The 103-ballot convention was held in New York City's Madison Square Garden. Hundreds of delegates were members of the Ku Klux Klan, the Klan so powerful that a plank condemning Klan violence was defeated outright. To celebrate, the Klan staged a rally with 10,000 hooded Klansmen in a field in New Jersey directly across the Hudson from the site of the convention. Attended by hundreds of cheering convention delegates, the rally featured burning crosses and calls for violence against African Americans and Catholics.

- There is no reference to the fact that it was Democrats who segregated the federal government of the United States, specifically at the direction of President Woodrow Wilson upon his taking office in 1913. There *is* a reference to the fact that President Harry Truman made the military integrated after World War Two.

- There *is* a reference to the fact that the Democrats created the Federal Reserve Board, passed labor and child welfare laws, and created Social Security with Wilson's New Freedom and FDR's New Deal. There is no reference to the fact that these programs were created as the result of an agreement to ignore segregation and the lynching of blacks. Neither is there a reference to the thousands of local officials, state legislators, state governors, U.S. congressmen, and U.S. senators who were elected as supporters of slavery and then segregation between 1800 and 1965. Nor is there reference to the deal with the devil that left segregation and lynching as a way of life in return for election support for three post-Civil War Democratic presidents: Grover Cleveland, Woodrow Wilson, and Franklin D. Roosevelt.

- There is no mention that three-fourths of the opposition to the 1964 civil rights bill in the U.S. House came from Democrats, or that 80 percent of the nay vote on the bill in the Senate came from the Democrats. Certainly, there is no reference to the fact that the opposition included future Democratic Senate leader Robert Byrd of West Virginia (a former Klan member) and Tennessee senator Albert Gore Sr., father of future Vice President Al Gore.

- Last, but certainly not least, there is no reference to the fact that Birmingham, Alabama, public safety commissioner Bull Connor, who infamously unleashed dogs and fire hoses on civil rights protestors, was in fact—yes indeed—a member of both the Democratic National Committee and the Ku Klux Klan.

What was on display with all of this was obvious.

Plainly put, this is a culture of racism. Racial obsession. Racial supremacism. Race is the be-all and end-all in this particular Old Order Swamp. It is a political culture that is embodied in one political party and the broader political movement of "progressivism" or "leftism" that dominates that party, as evidenced by the party's repeated words and actions, including its on-the-record support for slavery, segregation, lynching, Jim Crowism, and using the Ku Klux Klan as a "military force." As exemplified with the New Deal-era Mississippi Senator Theodore Bilbo and others, racism was routinely used to get elected and once elected the progressive agenda of the moment was enacted. Franklin Roosevelt himself refused to support anti-lynching legislation because to do so would endanger his re-election prospects. Racism was needed for Democrats to win election - and once won, progressive programs like Social Security or the creation of the federal school lunch program could be enacted. In the Trump era, this culture of racial supremacy that is ingrained in the American left has reappeared with a vengeance as opposition to the Trump travel ban and staunch support for illegal immigration and identity politics, the latter being the son of segregation and the grandson of slavery—the original identity politics.

Let's begin with the travel ban.

DECEMBER 2, 2015

Syed Rizwan Farook and his wife, Tashfeen Malik, wearing ski masks and black tactical gear and carrying legally purchased rifles and semiautomatic pistols modified to make them more lethal, walked into the Inland Regional Center in San Bernardino, California. Farook was an American-born citizen of Pakistani descent who worked for the health department of San Bernardino County as an "environmental health specialist." His wife, Malik, was a Pakistani-born "lawful permanent resident" of the United States who had lived most of her life in Saudi Arabia. She had entered the United States on a K-1 "fiancée" visa. Both were Muslims. Over the course of minutes, they sprayed an office Christmas party with over a hundred bullets, then fled in a black SUV, leaving fourteen dead and twenty-two seriously injured. A witness identified Farook to police, the SUV was spotted, and the two were eventually chased down. They died in a gun battle with police that injured two officers.

An investigation revealed that while Malik had gone through three background checks during her immigration process, there had been no examination of her social media postings. Those postings, it was discovered after the fact, showed that before entering the United States, she had quite openly been discussing committing violent jihad once inside the U.S. Reported *The New York Times*: "Had the authorities found the messages years ago, they might have kept her out of the country. But their recent discovery exposed a significant—and perhaps inevitable—shortcoming in how foreigners are screened when they enter the United States." What the *Times* described was the very definition of an "institutionally torpid" mindset when it came to the nation's immigration system and those in the Old Order responsible for running it.

Six days after the attack, Republican presidential candidate Donald Trump spoke out. *The New York Times* headline: "Donald Trump Calls for Barring Muslims From Entering U.S."

The *Times* reported:

> *Updated, 10:42 p.m. | Donald J. Trump called on Monday for the United States to bar all Muslims from entering the country until the nation's leaders can "figure out what is going on" after the terrorist attacks in San Bernardino, Calif., an extraordinary escalation of rhetoric aimed at voters' fears about members of the Islamic faith.*
>
> *A prohibition of Muslims – an unprecedented proposal by a leading American presidential candidate, and an idea more typically associated with hate groups – reflects a progression of mistrust that is rooted in ideology as much as politics.*

The Swamp went ballistic. Trump had had the audacity to deliberately call out the Old Order's worldview of immigration policy—a policy that in operation had been careless and sloppy, and now—yet again—had had fatal consequences for American citizens. For this he was represented in the Old Order *New York Times* as calling for a policy "more typically associated with hate groups." Not to mention, to say that what Trump was proposing was "an unprecedented proposal by a leading American presidential candidate" was in fact a flat-out falsehood. It was fake news.

In a book written in 2000 (*The America We Deserve*), Trump explicitly warns in a chapter titled "Freedom from Terrorism" of what he believes "is the real possibility that somewhere, sometime" there would be an attack on "a major American city." Never does he mention the word "Muslim" or "Islam." The possible suspects he does list are the "White supremacist loser" and "a Puerto Rican terrorist gang." (There was in fact an attack in 1975 on the historic Fraunces Tavern in Manhattan by Puerto Rican terrorists. Four people were killed and forty-three were injured. Doubtless as a New Yorker himself,

Trump is well familiar with the tale.) But his main point in the book is not *who* might launch a terrorist attack in the United States. His point is that the United States is *not prepared* for such an attack no matter who launches it.

Says Trump in the book:

> *The biggest threat to our security is ourselves, because we've become arrogant. Dangerously arrogant. It's time for a realistic view of the world and our place in it. Do we truly understand the threats we face? And let me give a warning: You won't hear a lot of what follows from candidates in this [2000] campaign, because what I've got to say is definitely not happy talk. There are forces to be worried about, people and programs to take action against.*

> *Now.*

He adds, more than presciently about the elected leaders of the day: "The longer they avoid this issue, the more vulnerable they make us. We need to enlighten them now."

One year later, on September 11, 2001, Trump's prediction came horrifically true—but the attackers were not "white supremacist losers" or Puerto Rican terrorists. They were nineteen Islamic radicals, Muslim extremists—every one of them foreigners—who entered the United States via the U.S. immigration system and murdered almost 3,000 Americans in New York, Washington, and Pennsylvania. Fifteen of them were from Saudi Arabia, two were from the United Arab Emirates, and one each from Egypt and Lebanon.

In my discussion with Trump in 2014, I brought up the fact that he had predicted terrorism. Nodding, he replied:

> *"Well I actually said a long time ago—some people say I was the first to say it—that terrorism would be a big problem. I said this in my book. I predicted terrorism. To me it was inevitable. And terrorism also comes through weakness. You know, when you're weak, terrorism, you know, comes. Terrorism is a terrible thing. You don't see them; it's not an army fighting an army and everybody has a different uniform. You don't know who they are, what they are. But one thing we need is strength. The other thing, I mean this court system is so messed up that these terrorists, they*

go on trial, they are on trial for twenty-five years. And people that you know are guilty.... This isn't a question of whether or not they did it; you have trials that are going on for twenty and twenty-five years. And these guys die of natural causes before the trial is over. You have to do speedy justice, and it has to be very severe. Very severe."

Which is to say, long before he reached the White House, Trump was making it plain that the United States needed to protect itself from would-be terrorists—and that if he were president, he would set about that task. Clearly, in the aftermath of the San Bernardino shooting, he saw the travel ban as a way to make sure the country was being protected from those who would come in who, like Tashfeen Malik, were determined to commit mass murder.

In the aftermath of 9/11, no less than the government's own 9/11 Commission admitted that the nation's immigration system was out of control. Its review included this:

The September 11 Travel Operation

The success of the September 11 plot depended on the ability of the hijackers to obtain visas and pass an immigration and customs inspection in order to enter the United States. It also depended on their ability to remain here undetected while they worked out the operational details of the attack. If they had failed on either count—entering and becoming embedded—the plot could not have been executed.

In other words, the Old Order's immigration system had failed—miserably. Again, almost 3,000 people were killed in the 9/11 attacks. To a person, the killers were radical Islamists. Radical Muslims. As were Syed Rizwan Farook and Tashfeen Malik, the murderers in San Bernardino. In fact, the San Bernardino attack was the third by radical Islamists in the United States in 2015 alone. Earlier in the year, there had been attacks on a cultural center in Garland, Texas (the three radical Muslim extremist perpetrators had been born in the United States), and on both an Armed Forces Career Center and a U.S. Navy Reserve center in Chattanooga, Tennessee (the radical Muslim perpetrator had been born in Kuwait; his parents described themselves as "natives of the State of Palestine").

The month before the murders in San Bernardino, radical Islamists had attacked in Paris, leaving 129 dead. As reported in *The Guardian*, the Paris attack was led by one Abdelhamid Abaaoud who "was initially thought to have been in Syria – where he had boasted of planning attacks on the West— and his presence in France has raised questions about how one of Europe's most wanted men could travel freely around the continent." Which is to say, Europeans were raising the same concerns about their own immigration system that Trump was raising about America's.

In the fourteen years between the 9/11 attacks and Trump's statement in December 2015, there were attacks by radical Islamists in forty-three countries around the world; seven of those attacks were in America. To say the least, the idea that the United States should take a hard look at who was coming into the country, as well as who was already here, and why, would seem to be plain common sense.

Not in the Old Order.

In addition to the *Times'* assailing Trump's proposal "as more typically associated with hate groups" (strangely it said no such thing when he had earlier focused his concern on potential attacks from white supremacists or Puerto Rican terrorists), some of Trump's Republican opponents for the 2016 presidential nomination, defenders of the Old Order status quo, jumped in with some variation of the *Times* response.

In true Swamp War style, Trump's proposal was instantly and roundly denounced by Republican opponents New Jersey governor Chris Christie and Ohio governor John Kasich. Christie called Trump's proposal "ridiculous," while Kasich labeled it "outrageous." Senator Lindsey Graham said that Trump was a "xenophobe, racist, and a bigot," and Jeb Bush, the former Florida governor, settled for saying Trump was "unhinged." And that was before the Old Order media reacted, repeatedly describing Trump's idea, as the *Times* had, as being racist and discriminatory.

Collectively it was an appalling performance, with candidates and the media utterly unaware that what Trump was proposing was perfectly in line with both American history and the law. There was nothing in the least racist about it. In fact, there was and is plenty of precedent for what Trump was proposing. As it happened, I was invited on CNN shortly after the candidate had made his proposal—and pointed out there was nothing unusual in American history about the government of the United States putting restrictions on foreigners coming into the United States, much less restricting them inside the country.

Presidents from John Adams to James Madison, Woodrow Wilson, Franklin D. Roosevelt, and Jimmy Carter had done a version of what Trump was proposing, targeting over time French, British, German, Japanese, Italian, and Iranian "aliens." The last in that list, targeted by Carter during the Iranian hostage crisis, were aliens from a country that is 98 percent Muslim, while the targeted French, British, Germans, and Italians were from white majority countries.

In my CNN *New Day* appearance shortly after then-candidate Trump's call for the travel ban, I noted some of the facts that all of Trump's critics seemed to be either unaware of or were ignoring—and I suspected that it was in fact the first, not the second. I had already written about these facts in a column in *The American Spectator* titled "FDR Was Trump on Steroids," dated December 8, 2015—seventy-four years to the day after Roosevelt used what was called the Alien Enemies Act to issue three presidential proclamations on the day after Pearl Harbor. The Alien Enemies Act was passed in 1798 and signed into law by President John Adams - and it was very much still on the books in 2015. I wrote:

> *For those who read history, and alas, perhaps lots of people who should do not, there was FDR in the aftermath of Pearl Harbor and the entrance of the U.S. into war with Germany, Italy, and Japan doing the following things that would make Donald Trump look like a nerdy weakling....*
>
> *Germany, Italy and the Japanese were the Muslims of the day in December, 1941. And FDR responded as follows, first with the Germans in presidential proclamation 2526 that was titled as being targeted to...this is a direct quote—"Aliens: Germans."*

The Roosevelt German proclamation was accompanied by two others that day, proclamation 2525 on "Aliens: Japanese" and 2527 on "Aliens: Italians." And to be clear, the "Aliens: Japanese" proclamation was decidedly not the same as a later FDR executive order—a decidedly racist not to mention unconstitutional Executive Order 9066 issued over two months later in February 1942—that ordered Americans of Japanese descent to be sent to internment camps for the duration of the war.

Once elected and sworn in, the now-President Trump quickly moved to execute his promise of a travel ban. The legal branch of the Old Order instantly responded, with lawsuits quickly piling up within days of its announcement. The American Civil Liberties Union, of course, promptly played the race card, appealing for funds to stop what it racialized as a "Muslim ban." The group's fundraising shot up, bringing in more Trump "Resistance" cash to the tune of over $140 million. The group was joined in lawsuits by various Old Order state attorneys general, with prominent business leaders from Amazon, Expedia, and Lyft joining in.

It took until June 2018, but finally the United States Supreme Court made a decision—for the president.

From *The New York Times*:

Trump's Travel Ban Is Upheld
by Supreme Court

WASHINGTON—The Supreme Court upheld President Trump's ban on travel from several predominantly Muslim countries, delivering to the president on Tuesday a political victory and an endorsement of his power to control immigration at a time of political upheaval about the treatment of migrants at the Mexican border.

In a 5-to-4 vote, the court's conservatives said that the president's power to secure the country's borders, delegated by Congress over decades of immigration lawmaking, was not undermined by Mr. Trump's history of incendiary statements about the dangers he said Muslims pose to the United States.

Writing for the majority, Chief Justice John G. Roberts Jr. said that Mr. Trump had ample statutory authority to make national security judgments in the realm of immigration. And the chief justice rejected a constitutional challenge to Mr. Trump's third executive order on the matter, issued in September as a proclamation.

The court's liberals denounced the decision. In a passionate and searing dissent from the bench, Justice Sonia Sotomayor said the decision was no better than Korematsu v. United States, *the 1944 decision that endorsed the detention of Japanese-Americans during World War II.*

In this first race-based Swamp War of the Trump era, the racial supremacists lost. Next up for the racial supremacists? Illegal immigration.

2008

Stanford had called. Rutgers had called.

Both universities were very much interested in seventeen-year-old Jamiel Andre Shaw II. With good reason.

Shaw's high school football coach, Hardy Williams, said the African American "Jas" was a "special kid," adding that he was "a Houdini on the football field." The *Los Angeles Times* noted of the rising star athlete with the big smile whose "solid GPA" (grade point average) also made him an academic star that as "a junior, Jamiel rushed for more than 1,000 yards last year, averaging just over 14 yards per carry. An invitational All-City first-team selection, he scored 11 touchdowns, returned punts and kickoffs, and played defensive back. He also competed in track." His teammates called him the "spirit of the team," said Williams. A role model to his younger brother, Thomas, he never missed church.

Shaw's mom, Army sergeant Anita Shaw, was stationed in Baghdad, Iraq. It was her second tour of duty. Her son, reported the *Times*, was "the apple of his father and mother's eye," determined to pursue a career as a sports agent.

Pedro Espinoza had no universities interested in him. Born in Mexico, brought to America when he was three years old by his illegal immigrant parents, Pedro "Darky" Espinoza had what was said to be an "abusive home life" that made him "groomed for violence." In fact, instead of going to a university, Espinoza had joined the 18th Street gang—as a killer. If Jamiel Shaw had an ambition to be a sports agent, Espinoza had a different ambition altogether. It was his goal, he had told his parole officer, to so prove his allegiance to the 18th Street gang that he would land on death row.

In October 2006, Robert B. Loosle, the special agent in charge of the criminal division in the FBI's Los Angeles field office, testified on the 18th Street gang before the Subcommittee on Criminal Justice, Drug Policy and Human Resources of the House Committee on Oversight and Government Reform. Said Loosle of the gang: it had "gained notoriety for their extreme level of violence, their flexibility, their high level of organization, and their willingness to participate in a wide variety of criminal activities. Although the level of sophistication in their criminal activities may vary, these gangs remain consistently violent."

And there was another trait of the Hispanic gang of illegals. Writer and gang expert Tony Rafael, author of the 2009 book *The Mexican Mafia*, is blunt, saying of Hispanic gangs that "they don't want their neighborhoods infested with blacks, as if it's an infestation…. It's pure racial animosity that manifests itself in a policy of a major criminal organization." Rafael takes time in the book to elaborate in a conversation with the left-leaning Southern Poverty Law Center. The latter, in 2007, had written a report with the headline "Latino Gang Members in Southern California Are Terrorizing and Killing Blacks."

The report says, among other very disturbing things, that the Mexican Mafia had been playing a serious role in killing African Americans in Los Angeles. The report quotes former Los Angeles County attorney Michael Camacho on the subject of the targeted black victims by Hispanic gangs from over the border: "There's absolutely no motive absent the color of their skin."

At 8:40 p.m. on Sunday, March 2, 2008, young Jamiel Shaw was walking home from the mall with two friends. He had returned from football camp at Pasadena City College only hours ago. He had on a red Spiderman backpack. Red is the color associated with a rival gang of the 18th Street gang.

He was three doors away from home when a white car suddenly pulled to a stop. Inside were 18th Street gang members Joel "Killer" Rodriguez and Ysenia Sanchez, who waited in the car with engine idling as Pedro "Darky" Espinoza jumped out and approached Shaw. Only the day before, on March 1, Espinoza had been released from prison, where he had been serving time for assault with a deadly weapon. Now, freshly out to roam the streets again, he had already obtained another gun. The acquisition had been made in California, the state that boasts of having the toughest gun control laws in the country.

On his cell phone with girlfriend Chrystale Miles, Shaw suddenly stopped talking. Miles could hear a voice demand of Shaw: "Where you from?" Before Shaw could respond, Espinoza pulled his gun and shot Shaw in the stomach. As the seventeen-year-old lay on the sidewalk writhing in pain, Espinoza stood over him, pointed the gun at Shaw's head execution style, and pulled the trigger. Getting back in the car, Espinoza is said to have boasted: "I'm a killer."

Three doors away, at the Shaw home, Jamiel Shaw Sr. heard the gunshots—and with a sickening rush of instinct raced out the door. The local NBC affiliate would later report of the scene:

> *The first law enforcement officer on the scene, a veteran LAPD sergeant, said the scene of Shaw's murder was "the most sorrow and despair I've ever seen," describing the sight of Jamiel Shaw Sr. screaming in agony at the sight of his son's body.*

From Iraq, hastily retrieved by the United States Army, Anita Shaw called home, crying. Sobbing over the boy she still called "my baby," she pleaded: "Tell me it's not my son."

Six days later, Pedro "Darky" Espinoza, an illegal immigrant who is the son of illegal immigrants, a Mexican gang member newly out of prison, was arrested and charged with the murder of Jamiel Andre Shaw II.

In an interview with *Sports Illustrated* conducted shortly before the 2016 election, Jamiel Shaw's father was explicit about his decision to support Donald Trump for president (emphasis mine):

> *"I hate illegal immigration. I don't hate illegal aliens, per se, because I understand that I can't say, Oh it's your fault my son is dead. I just tell them, Your practice of coming here illegally is why my son is dead.... By you perpetrating it over and over...it's kind of desensitizing [us to] it and, you know, now my son is dead. And no one cares about the avoidable way it happened. "*

"No one cares," said this father. No one cared that his son's death was avoidable. He was correct.

In 2019, in yet another of an endless series of crimes by illegals, Newman, California police officer Ronil Singh was shot to death. One Gustavo Perez Arriaga, a member of the Mexican-American Sureno street gang and an illegal immigrant, was charged with the murder. As with the attack on young Jamiel Shaw, this murder by an illegal was hardly a stand alone act. The Department of Homeland Security has an entire section of its web site listing in specific detail the crimes committed by illegals in America—and Trump's opponents simply do not care. The real question here is, why? And the answer is stark: because the Old Order's immigration lobbies have had a chokehold on American immigration policy, not to mention on enforcement of immigration laws.

In one Swamp—San Francisco—the Old Order held sway in the jury box. Thirty-two-year-old Kate Steinle, walking with her father on a city wharf, was shot in the back by five-time deported Mexican illegal immigrant Jose Ines Garcia Zarate. He was charged with, and was tried for, murder. In came the verdict from the citizens of the Swamp that is San Francisco. Garcia Zarate was, reported CNN, "acquitted of murder and involuntary manslaughter charges, as well as assault with a deadly weapon. Jurors convicted the Mexican citizen of being a felon in possession of a firearm, which could bring a three-year sentence."

Amazingly, his lawyer had the chops to say: "Nothing about Mr. Garcia Zarate's ethnicity, nothing about his immigration status, nothing about the fact that he is born in Mexico had any relevance as to what happened on July 1, 2015." Clearly, Garcia Zarate's mere presence in the country he had been deported from five times had everything to do with Kate Steinle's death. Had he not been in San Francisco in the first place, Steinle would not have been shot.

The fact is that in the argument about plain, old-fashioned border security, the left wing of the Old Order is, but of course, playing the race card. It sees the illegals sneaking or surging—depending on the day—across the border not in terms of legal and illegal process but in terms of race. There are endless examples, but one will suffice: a pre-midterm election headline of an article by Michael Tomasky in *The Daily Beast* in October 2018. It reads: "Trump's Closing Argument: The Brown People Are Coming!"

Well, no. Trump has said zero about the skin color of illegal immigrants. He has talked constantly about the need for border security, about building a wall with a "door" for those wishing to come into America legally. Shutting down the government in December 2018 over the lack of funding for a border wall, in January 2019 he would address the nation on the "National Emergency" that had resulted from the flood of illegal immigrants across the southern border. He mentioned race but once, saying the sadly obvious: "America proudly welcomes millions of lawful immigrants who enrich our society and contribute to our nation. But all Americans are hurt by uncontrolled, illegal migration. It strains public resources and drives down jobs and wages. Among those hardest hit are African Americans and Hispanic Americans."

It is his opponents who see and divide by race, not Trump. And they see and divide by race, of course, because they are mired in the culture of racial supremacy—as they and their political ancestors have been for two centuries. Why? It gets them votes.

* * * * *

In another example of challenging the left's need to use race to divide Americans for political purposes, I was asked by CNN to discuss an article in *The Wall Street Journal* that reported on President Trump's threat to cut off the federal government's payments to insurance companies for Obamacare. The move was widely covered, and it was crystal clear that Trump was issuing the threat to bring Democrats to the negotiating table—a standard tactic from the legendary *Art of the Deal* negotiator.

Easy, right? Who knew I was about to wade into a seriously deep Swamp War? Appearing the next morning on CNN's *New Day*, I made a comparison that seemed pretty obvious to anyone who has read history. I said that Trump was the Martin Luther King of health care. Specifically, I said:

> *"When I was a kid, President Kennedy did not want to intro-
> duce the civil rights bill because he said it wasn't popular, he
> didn't have the votes for it, et cetera. Dr. King kept putting
> people in the streets in harm's way to put the pressure on so that
> the bill would be introduced. That's what finally worked."*

Smelling salts all around. "Ohhhhhhh, Jeffrey" chastised my sparring partner, the progressive Symone Sanders. There was an uproar in the liberal media, not least at CNN. A CNN public relations staffer came to me and asked if I would write an article for the CNN opinion website explaining myself. I did. The piece had this headline: "Why I compared Trump to MLK."

I wrote, in part (emphasis added):

> I compared the President's words to Dr. King's strategy in
> the early 1960s. What was that strategy? King described it

in his letter from a Birmingham jail. *The letter was written by Dr. King as he sat in a Birmingham jail, arrested for leading a civil rights march. He was responding to eight fellow clergymen who had taken out an ad in the local newspaper calling Dr. King and his fellow demonstrators "extremists" and worse, calling instead for negotiation. Sitting in jail, King wrote his now-famous response.*

The reference I had in mind as I spoke on CNN was this section:

"You may well ask: 'Why direct action? Why sit-ins, marches and so forth? Isn't negotiation a better path?' You are quite right in calling for negotiation. Indeed, this is the very purpose of direct action. Nonviolent direct action seeks to create such a crisis and foster such a tension that a community which has constantly refused to negotiate is forced to confront the issue. It seeks to so dramatize the issue that it can no longer be ignored."

King continued: "So must we see the need for nonviolent gadflies to create the kind of tension in society that will help men rise from the dark depths of prejudice and racism to the majestic heights of understanding and brotherhood. The purpose of our direct-action program is to create a situation so crisis-packed that it will inevitably open the door to negotiation. I therefore concur with you in your call for negotiation."…

In other words, whether he knows it or not (and I suspect not) President Trump is using Dr. King's strategy—in Dr. King's own words—"to create a situation so crisis-packed that it will inevitably open the door to negotiation."

This is simple, basic American history. In fact, Dr. King had gotten his strategy from his own hero, India's Mahatma Gandhi, who had used exactly the same strategy of forcing a crisis to bring India to a standstill—and thus get the British to the negotiating table to grant India's independence. In my case, I was old enough in 1963 to remember the history clearly. I remember Dr. King from real time. Along with President Kennedy and Robert Kennedy, he was indeed a hero—and to the point, all three were my serious heroes. The early 1960s was a rare moment when the Democrats could finally drop racism once and for all. Indeed, I had long since memorized various JFK speeches in the day, and my favorite line comes from his June 11, 1963, address to the nation on civil rights. The line, which I quoted from memory in that earlier, quite impromptu and constructive on-air conversation about race with my friend Van Jones, was: "Race has no place in American life or law." It didn't—and doesn't. JFK was right, and so was his brother Bobby Kennedy when he gave a speech as attorney general honoring Kentucky's centennial of the Emancipation Proclamation. RFK approvingly quoted a Kentuckian, the late Justice John Marshall Harlan, as saying: "Our Constitution is colorblind, and neither knows nor tolerates classes among citizens."

But almost immediately in the Trump era, the systemic racism that runs deep in the Old Order and the American left was now once again in play in twenty-first-century America. JFK, Bobby Kennedy, and Dr. King were long gone. Once again, the Old Order leftists had reverted to form and played the race card, this time with Trump. And now it wasn't just Trump who was being accused of racism—it was me.

First that night I had to appear on Anderson Cooper's show with Bakari Sellers. Sellers proceeded to say that "what we saw him [me] do was pervert" the King legacy. He said that "I hope you are empathetic enough to see how disrespectful this is." He went on to bring Robert Kennedy into the discussion. To which I replied: "By the way, I stood in line for six hours to pass Robert Kennedy's casket and touch the flag when I was seventeen years old." Where was Sellers, I asked? Not born. Right.

The conversation on Don Lemon's CNN show went this way:

> *Lemon: You have three people you work with, right? You work with Bakari [Sellers], you work with me, you work with Symone [Sanders]. Three people of color.*
>
> *Lord: No no no.*
>
> *Lemon: No, let me get the point out. Let me get the point out.*
>
> *We are telling you that that comparison was insulting, and you're ignoring it. Don't you think you should take that into consideration whether or not you're trying to make a point or not, even if it's to the point of, "If I offended you, I'm sorry"?*

Lord: Don, Don. Don, Don. When I lived as a teenager in the South and my dad lost his job standing up for a black waitress—

Lemon: You're not answering my question now. You're not answering my question in the moment.

Lord: I am answering your question, Don. [I repeated this at least three times, to no avail.]

Lemon: Don't take me back to some before-the-war crap. I want to hear what you're saying to the coworkers you work with now, Jeffrey. Answer the question now! I don't want to hear about something from fifty dong-damn years ago!

The very first line from Don, not to mention the last line, ignited a fire for me.

The idea that I was supposed to treat him, Bakari Sellers, and Symone Sanders not as equals, not as professional colleagues and fellow Americans, but rather take the patronizing view that they were "people of color" and therefore needed to be patronized because of their skin color, was as insulting to them as it was to me. This was pure identity politics. Segregation on steroids, twenty-first-century Jim Crowism. Hell would freeze over before I endorsed racism. Period. I replied that Lemon sounded like Bull Connor— that judging people by color was not moral. He replied, astoundingly to me, that I was "crazy" if I didn't judge by race. To my ears he sounded like someone else from my youth—George Wallace, the hard-line segregationist governor of Alabama. It was Wallace who pushed identity politics in his infamous inaugural address as governor in 1963 with this line: "Segregation today, segregation tomorrow, segregation forever."

What I heard that night on CNN in so many words was "identity politics today, identity politics tomorrow, identity politics forever." As mentioned, I view identity politics as the son of segregation. Hell will freeze over before I accede to identity politics—what I consider to be outright racism. And in terms of Dr. King, I could only imagine that he would not be happy to realize that he had literally given his life to guarantee that Americans would judge their fellow citizens not by the color of their skin but by the content of their character—and now three prominent Americans, who happened to be black, were hotly demanding—whether they knew it or not, and I certainly believed they did not—that I treat them as segregationists once treated Dr. King. It was dragging America backward on race, and using CNN to do it. I flatly refused. To be as blunt as I can, I will refuse through eternity.

And Lemon's other line, "Don't take me back to some before-the-war crap"? He had no way of knowing what my personal history on civil rights was—and as he made clear in his zeal to push identity politics on me, he didn't care. I did. Passionately so—and with reason.

As a Baby Boomer who had come of age in the 1960s, I was then and am now a serious admirer of Dr. King's. The civil rights movement was a big deal for me. And it was personal. When I was growing up in Massachusetts, my father held Calvin Coolidge's seat on the Northampton City Council. Coolidge, who began his political career in Northampton with that council seat, had run for president in 1924 on a platform that specifically said: "We urge the Congress to enact at the earliest possible date a federal anti-lynching law so that the full influence of the federal government may be wielded to exterminate this hideous crime."

Which is to say, while the Democrats that year were letting the Ku Klux Klan literally run their convention, Coolidge was standing up for the civil rights inherent in opposing lynching.

Dad was also a Republican city committee chairman who was an out-front supporter of Edward Brooke, the Republican Massachusetts attorney general who would become the first black person to sit in the United States Senate in the twentieth century with his 1966 election. Dad had first supported Brooke for secretary of state in 1960, an election Brooke lost. Two years later Brooke was elected Massachusetts state attorney general. In 1966 he won the seat in the U.S. Senate. By then we had moved to Staunton, Virginia, where my father had taken a job as the manager of a Holiday Inn franchise. But Ed Brooke remembered my dad's lonely support for him, and my parents were invited to Brooke's Senate swearing-in in January 1967. Both Dad and Mom were working and unable to attend, so they sent me, at age sixteen, to fly to Washington solo for the ceremonies. Meeting with Senator Brooke in his new Senate offices—and seeing my hero Bobby Kennedy to boot—made it the most memorable political moment of my young life.

But back in our new home in Staunton, the moment in time that would turn out to make a lasting impression on me in terms of race and civil rights was in progress. I wrote about it several years before the appearance on Lemon's show, in *The American Spectator*:

I attended school at a thoroughly modern high school, grades 8-12. There was a duplicate a bare six miles away—for the black kids. Except that this was 1965 and integration was arriving. There was one black girl in our school—one among about a thousand white kids. Maxine was her name. She was in my French class and rode my school bus, since we both lived on the same route. While she was actually closer to the "black" school her parents wanted her to go to the allegedly better "white school"—and thanks to the 1954 Supreme Court decision Brown v. Board of Education, *she could and did exercise that right. Now that the law was slowly—very slowly—taking effect, she was literally the first black child in the area to do so. Shy but friendly, I made friends with Maxine because, it finally struck me, I was one of the few kids who would speak with her. We were both outsiders, something that her blackness and my new face and New England accent only emphasized. ("He talks like one of them damn Kinidy boys" was a comment I overheard.)*

After about two weeks, I began to realize that when Maxine boarded the school bus coming and going every day, something odd happened. School buses have seats for two, and as such the safety rules require only two kids can sit in the same seat. Curiously, I realized the other kids were scrunching three and sometimes four in a seat with the silent assent of the bus driver—because no one would sit with Maxine. I talked with my parents. I knew who Rosa Parks was, and I certainly knew of Dr. King. But there was no pretension to leading some sort of teen-age crusade. I was just mad. Maxine was being deliberately, quite publicly humiliated because of her race. Since she was picked up in the morning well after I was, my chance would only come in the afternoon when everyone boarded the bus at the same time. That next afternoon, as school ended and we all clambered noisily aboard the bus, I took a determined breath and sat down with Maxine.

You could hear the proverbial pin drop. For the entire ride to her home no one said a word—except Maxine and me as we shyly chatted about French class. When she got off the bus, the silence gave way to taunts. "Whoeee, Jeff has got himself a girl-friend!" Friendly kid that I was, I just grinned. And sat next to Maxine the next day, and the next and the next. Friends were eventually made, and after a very long time—almost the rest of the school year—Maxine got other seatmates than me. But it was abundantly clear that racism, as thick as it could be cut, was in the air.

Meanwhile, Dad had a bigger problem. As was his custom-ary practice, he would always leave the house after dinner and go tour the hotel one last time for the night. Checking to see that all is well in the disparate parts of one of these operations, he said, was a managerial must. That particular night he walked into the hotel coffee shop, stumbling into an incident that would change his—and our—lives. The hotel owner, perhaps intoxi-cated, was in the process of publicly berating a frightened wait-ress. She was black. The owner, white. Dad said racial epithets filled the air. Loud. Abusive. Humiliating. Very, very public. In an instant my father physically positioned himself between the terrified, tearful black waitress and the white owner, telling the owner that whatever the young woman had done or not done (it was something of a trivial nature), this behavior towards an employee was unacceptable. Whereupon the owner promptly fired both the waitress and my father. On the spot.

Now what? Dad had moved our family hundreds of miles from familiar turf. Civil rights—racism—was no longer an abstract. This wasn't grainy gray images of Walter Cronkite from the old Zenith. This was real life, vividly so. Shaken but determined, Dad decided to try again. Taking the family sav-ings he bought an old diner in the middle of town, turning it into one of the new fashionables of the day—a pancake house. There was a glistening new grill in the window so passersby could see the product being made. He interviewed for cooks.

Now came "mistake" number two. The best qualified cook was a black woman. He gave her the job. A job that meant she had supervisory authority over others—who were white. Word spread like wildfire that Dad had made a black woman a boss over whites—men and women both. Only months ago as the manager of the brand new hotel in town he was a part of the town gentry, a regular attendee at Rotary meetings and the like. Now, his restaurant was boycotted and he was the subject of scorn, fighting for his—and our—economic survival. I will never forget the sight of my dad, the collar of his old World War II jacket up to protect against the cold (a jacket that bore the insignia of a Captain of army artillery) walking the streets to hand out fliers advertising his pancakes, all too frequently to be brusquely ignored. Sometimes, after school or on weekends, I went with him.

It was no use. Phone calls were coming into the house now. Ugly, whispering anonymous calls to my mother. The "n... lover" phrase snarled through the phone line. The water was cut off, requiring a special trip to the water department to verify that yes, the bill had already been paid. Did Mom wish to regis-ter to vote as a Republican? Sorry, said the registrar—the books were in the attic. Get them, Mom said with a smile. I'll wait.

There's more here, but you get the idea. After two years of this Dad simply had to yield to common sense and our family retreated across the Mason-Dixon line to Pennsylvania, which is the family home today. He passed away just shy of 90 not long ago. I mentioned this story in his eulogy, startling his friends who had never heard it. Mom, I assure you, has never forgotten.

As a lesson in racism, this was, for me, a "defining moment."

Suffice it to say that in the family turmoil that resulted, I became even more passionately supportive of Dr. King's and the JFK/RFK view of a col-orblind America. The Abraham Lincoln view—a view that Dr. King himself had correctly traced to the founding of the country with the Declaration of Independence and the Constitution. To be specific, these were Dr. King's lines in his famous 1963 "I Have a Dream" speech:

In a sense we have come to our nation's capital to cash a check. When the architects of our republic wrote the magnificent words of the Constitution and the Declaration of Independence, they were signing a promissory note to which every American was to fall heir. This note was a promise that all men, yes, black men as well as white men, would be guaranteed the unalienable rights of life, liberty, and the pursuit of happiness....

Now is the time to make real the promises of democracy. Now is the time to rise from the dark and desolate valley of segregation to the sunlit path of racial justice. Now is the time to lift our nation from the quicksands of racial injustice to the solid rock of brotherhood. Now is the time to make justice a reality for all of God's children.

Dismissing my parents, as Don Lemon did, or dismissing anybody else famous or unknown who had stood up for civil rights in the day and paid a price for it—not to mention in a day before my colleagues in this debate had even been born or had just been born—was flatly unacceptable to me. In my parents' case, this was one small, unpublicized skirmish in the war for civil rights—but for our small family, it was a major battle. Having my parents' courage—and that of so many who stood up for civil rights, known and unknown, some with their lives on the line—dismissed as "before-the-war crap" when it had a direct relevance to today's battles was something I simply would not be quiet about.

Indeed, in closing out my on-air, much earlier conversation with Van Jones in 2016, I said:

We have to be passionate about making sure that this country is colorblind. We have to, as Robert Kennedy used to say, [make sure] that this country is colorblind. We have to, as President Kennedy used to say, [make sure] that race has no place in American life or law. That's what we have to do, and we have lost that totally because the Democratic Party insists on dividing people by race, and it's wrong, it's morally wrong.

I meant every word of it. And I was absolutely unwilling to let those on the left whitewash their mind-blowing history of racism that had fueled—

and still fuels—their politics under the guise of "identity politics." As long as I had a voice, Jim Crow was not coming back. Most assuredly I wasn't going to sign on to this garbage live on CNN.

The central question in this racial Swamp War against Trump is, why? Why is there a felt need to play the race card—yet again—this time against Trump, as had been done before with every single Republican nominee since at least Nixon?

There is an answer, a simple if disgraceful one. The left needs and uses racism—slavery, segregation, Jim Crow-style identity politics—to win elections and carry out its progressive agenda of the moment. As I have written in the *Spectator*:

> *This is the age old formula of the American Left. From slavery to segregation, lynching, the Ku Klux Klan and on to racial quotas, attacking Korean grocers (as done by then Washington D.C. Mayor Marion Barry) or suing Arizona (over its illegal immigration policies)—the Left uses race to gin up a racial base and repays with big government.*

Case in point: Carter Glass, the man the Federal Reserve honors with a memorial in the main lobby of its headquarters, the Eccles Building, in Washington. As I have noted in the pages of the *Spectator*:

> *Glass's entire political career as state senator, congressman, Secretary of the Treasury and U.S. Senator was based on playing the race card. As the author of the Virginia state constitution in 1902, it was Glass who insisted on both a poll tax and literacy tax being in the revamped constitution. Said Glass, when queried as to if this wasn't designed to deliberately discriminate against African-Americans:*
>
> *"Discrimination! Why that is exactly what we propose. To remove every Negro voter who can be gotten rid of, legally, without materially impairing the numerical strength of the white electorate."*

Glass succeeded in using racism to get elected—and once elected, he pushed his non-racist progressive agenda that created the Federal Reserve and, later, when in the Senate, the Glass-Steagall Act that separated the interests of commercial and investment banking. Racism was the fuel that Glass needed to win elections—and as a rising progressive star, he used it.

Today, the looming issue is illegal immigration—once again, a legitimate issue that has nothing to do with race. Yet the orderly admission of those who wish to immigrate to a country where 100 percent of the population is descended from immigrants is infused by the Old Order as part of the Swamp War over race. The issue of illegal entrance is quickly swept aside to focus on race—exactly what the political ancestors of these people have been doing for two centuries. But since the left uses race to fuel its political agenda, of course it has to describe Trump's opposition to illegal immigration as racist.

Again, note what Hillary Clinton said of Trump in 2018: "I include his anti-immigrant tirades because he characterizes immigrants in very racially derogatory ways." As Clinton well knows, Trump has never denounced legal immigration beyond saying that America needs to know who is coming into the country and needs to get the people who can contribute. His objection is to illegal immigration, not immigration. He is, himself, the son and grandson of legal immigrants, not to mention being married to a legal immigrant. Clinton knows this—but goes straight to the race card anyway. Why? Because, as Carter Glass did at the turn of the twentieth century, using the racism of Jim Crow style identity politics is the political fuel that the left depends on to win elections.

Indeed, no less than *The New York Times* acknowledged Clinton's use of racial politics to win in 2016, featuring a front-page article on her election strategy that specifically said Clinton was seeking to turn "black" and "brown" voters into "a durable presidential coalition." Which is to say, Hillary Clinton, like George Wallace before her, was about "segregation today, segregation tomorrow, segregation forever," eternally dividing Americans using the racism of identity politics to try to win elections and permanently run the country.

And the suggestion that Trump is a racist because of this part of his announcement speech?

> *"When Mexico sends its people, they're not sending their best. They're not sending you. They're not sending you. They're sending people that have lots of problems, and they're bringing those*

problems with us. They're bringing drugs. They're bringing crime. They're rapists. And some, I assume, are good people."

The hard fact that illegal immigrants have indeed brought crime and drugs into the United States is easily documented through a simple check with the U.S. Department of Homeland Security's U.S. Customs and Border Protection office. And one headline and story after another read like this one:

Agents Arrest Another Illegal Alien Convicted of Rape

TUCSON, Ariz. – For the second time in less than a week, Border Patrol agents assigned to the Nogales Station arrested an illegal alien previously deported following a rape conviction in the United States.

In the most recent incident, agents patrolling west of Nogales Wednesday evening arrested Samuel Nungaray-Cons, a 35-year-old Mexican man, for being illegally present in the country. During processing, agents conducted a records check on Nungaray and learned he was previously deported following a rape conviction and incarceration in 2005 in Bonneville County, Idaho.

In other words, Trump was right and there is nothing remotely racist about pointing out a serious fact in the ongoing debate over illegal immigration—a debate that Trump's critics, not Trump, have racialized.

What about the case of Trump's concern over a federal judge's presiding over a lawsuit involving Trump? First, no less than Supreme Court justice Sonia Sotomayor—when she was an appeals court judge—delivered a speech titled "A Latina Judge's Voice," in which she plainly stated: "I intend tonight to touch upon the themes that this conference will be discussing this weekend and to talk to you about my Latina identity, where it came from, and the influence I perceive it has on my presence on the bench."

Judge Gonzalo Curiel in fact belonged to the San Diego La Raza Lawyers Association, which is affiliated with the Hispanic National Bar Association. And the HNBA issued a statement in 2015 with the headline "The Hispanic National Bar Association Rejects Trump's Racist Assertions."

The statement, hardly a model of judicial neutrality, says, among other things:

> *The HNBA calls for a boycott of all of Trump business ventures, including golf courses, hotels, and restaurants. We salute NBC/ Universal, Univision and Macy's for ending their association with Trump, and we join them in standing up against bigotry and racist rhetoric. Other businesses and corporations should follow the lead of NBC/Universal, Univision and Macy's and take similar actions against Donald Trump's business interests. We can and will make a difference.*

Which is to say a race-based lawyers association tied to the judge was calling for a boycott of Trump's various businesses. One can see why Trump would be wary of getting a fair trial from the judge.

After the dust-up over Dr. King, I gave Don Lemon a copy of historian David McCullough's book *The American Spirit: Who We Are and What We Stand For.* The book is a collection of McCullough's speeches over the years that focus on what he calls "core American values to which we all subscribe, regardless of which region we live in, which political party we identify with, or our ethnic background." McCullough makes the point that I kept trying to make in those discussions, but certainly far more eloquently.

Many months later, Lemon's beloved older sister died tragically in a drowning accident. He was, I was told, understandably devastated. What was heartening was that people of all political stripes—including Sean Hannity—reached out to him, as Lemon would later emotionally recount when he returned to his show from the needed funeral obligations. I wrote a column about him for the *Spectator* as a reminder to one and all that, as he himself had said, political differences on these media shows are just that—and that there is far more to life that can and should be celebrated in common. I have enormous respect for Don Lemon. And I hope that in our discussion that night, as in my earlier conversations with my friend Van Jones and Bakari Sellers and Symone Sanders, all of whom I greatly respect, we contributed to a better and honest understanding of the issue of race. I certainly hope the issue will soon be banished to what Ronald Reagan called the "ash heap of history." Until then, we have to respectfully agree to disagree.

What I saw in these conversations on race—both my own and in the accusations that were and are hurled repeatedly at President Trump—was the disturbing reality of the Old Order's fiercest Swamp War. The American left conflates skin color with progressive ideology.

Over at Fox, Tucker Carlson has fearlessly attacked the phony-baloney "diversity" BS, taking on the so-called diversity issue for what it has really become. The word "diversity" once was accurately defined as being truly inclusive of all. But today the left has, in typical style, redefined it in racist terms. Americans, according to the left, must now be judged by skin color—identity politics. This was the very essence at the heart of slavery and segregation. This is standard, not to mention ancient, left-wing practice. And if, heaven forbid, you dare to depart from the approved left-wing orthodoxy, then you are, but of course, a racist. Taking the topic head-on, Tucker zeroed in on those social media giants who were busy banning diverse voices on their sites, saying correctly: "And if diversity is our strength, why is it okay for the rest of us to surrender to one of our central rights, freedom of speech, to just a handful of tech monopolies?"

Bingo. And in a blink, Tucker Carlson was attacked for standing up for a colorblind, truly diverse America. Ex-CNNer Soledad O'Brien, a true believer in the Jim Crowism that is identity politics, tweeted: "I really would like all the US companies that support Fox news and this dude to recognize how racist (and against many of these organizations' stated missions) what he's saying is."

This kind of racial garbage never ceases to amaze.

Like Soledad O'Brien, the American left has conflated race with progressivism for decades. It began with white Southerners, telling them that unless they believed in slavery or segregation, they were not good Democrats or progressives or whatever. Hello, Woodrow Wilson. Today, using the exact same principle of "race equals progressivism," leftists insist that to be black—or Hispanic or a woman or, in today's world, gay—means one has to be on the left, and in today's world most especially that means anti-Trump.

And if you, as the conservative saying goes, are a minority and walk off the progressive political plantation, woe betide you and your fortunes. Black Americans from rapper and mogul Kanye West to political activists and media figures Deneen Borelli (of CRTV), Candace Owens (of Turning Point

USA), and Paris Dennard (CNN contributor), and oh so many more have found out about this directly.

Those who are both black and Trump supporters in particular are targets of the Old Order's serious racial intolerance. Again, as Justice Clarence Thomas noted years ago in his confirmation hearing, this is what happens when a minority departs from the Old Order script and is "diverse" in thinking that departs from that of the Old Order:

> *"And from my standpoint as a black American, as far as I'm concerned, it is a high-tech lynching for uppity blacks who in any way deign to think for themselves, to do for themselves, to have different ideas, and it is a message that unless you kowtow to an old order, this is what will happen to you. You will be lynched, destroyed, caricatured by a committee of the U.S. Senate, rather than hung from a tree."*

After the 2018 midterms, which featured a governor's race in Georgia between Republican Brian Kemp, who is white, and Democrat Stacey Abrams, a black woman, *The Washington Post* ran a story that exemplified how the Old Order leftist media plays the race card. Abrams had lost in a close race to Kemp. The *Post* story's headline: "What's up with all those black men who voted for the Republican in the Georgia governor's race?"

Got that? In the eyes of the *Post* Georgia voters are not individual human beings. They are not Americans. No, they are supposed to belong to racial and gender categories. And those racial and gender categories are arbitrarily assumed to be synonymous with progressivism. If you are a black man, you must vote your race. If you are a white woman, you must vote your gender. And, of course, that means if you are black or female, you must be a progressive. It is the same-old, same-old culture of racism, racial supremacy and racial stereotyping that has politically fueled the left for over two centuries—on vivid display in the Old Order *Washington Post* in 2018, the twenty-first century.

The good news about President Trump is that in the area of race, as with everything else, he is willing not just to stand up for a colorblind America, but to dish it right back to his racist Old Order critics who are saying the same thing of Trump today that their predecessors, as Old Order racial supremacists, said of Nixon, Reagan, the Bushes, McCain, and Romney. (When *The Washington*

Post's Jonathan Capehart accused Trump in a column of being a racist, Trump sent this reply: "Jonathan – You are the racist, not I. Get rid of your 'hate.' Best wishes …")

When it comes to race, the Old Order and its Swamp War are finally, at long last, being called out. It is the left that is now and has always been a serious opponent of real racial diversity. Trump and his supporters are fighting back in the name of a colorblind America, taking the racial supremacists head-on.

And thank God for that.

CHAPTER NINE

ROCKET MAN, THE MULLAHS, AND THE WORLD

"He won the Cold War, not only without firing a shot, but also by inviting enemies out of their fortress and turning them into friends."

—former British prime minister Margaret Thatcher, in her eulogy for President Ronald Reagan

mergency Alert

Ballistic missile threat inbound to Hawaii. Seek immediate shelter. This is not a drill.

It was 8:07 on a Saturday morning in January 2018. An emergency alert from Hawaii's Civil Defense Emergency System was spreading rapidly. Hawaiians were in an abrupt panic.

Drivers on the busy H-3 main highway stopped their cars and fled on foot into a nearby tunnel. In Honolulu for a USA PGA tournament, golfers dropped their clubs and ran. One tweeted: "Under mattresses in bathtub with my wife, baby and in-laws. Please Lord let this bomb threat not be real." Local television and radio stations urgently informed their audiences: "If you are outdoors, seek immediate shelter in a building. Remain indoors well away from windows. If you are driving, pull safely to the side of the road and seek shelter." Families raced to their garage—if they had one. Early-morning beachgoers were suddenly in full flight to their hotel rooms.

On and on this went—for a full thirty-eight minutes. Then came the correction from the Hawaii Civil Defense Agency:

No missile is headed toward the State of Hawaii. Repeat...No missile is headed toward the State of Hawaii

Finally, CNN reported that Hawaii governor David Ige said, "It was a mistake made during a standard procedure at the changeover of a shift, and an employee pushed the wrong button."

But what are facts in the land of Old Order movie stars when it comes to resisting Donald Trump?

Actor Jim Carrey, who was in Hawaii, tweeted a warning:

> *I woke up this morning in Hawaii with ten minutes to live. It was a false alarm, but a real psychic warning. If we allow this one-man Gomorrah and his corrupt Republican congress to continue alienating the world we are headed for suffering beyond all imagination.*

Actress Jamie Lee Curtis was in high anti-Trump dudgeon herself, tweeting:

> *This Hawaii missle (sic) scare is on YOU Mr. Trump. The real FEAR that mothers & fathers & children felt is on YOU. It is on YOUR ARROGANCE. HUBRIS. NARCISSISM. RAGE. EGO. IMMATURITY and your UNSTABLE IDIOCY. Shame on your hate filled self. YOU DID THIS!*

It wasn't just anti-Trump movie stars who got in on this, either. Hawaii Democratic congresswoman Tulsi Gabbard took time to speak to CNN and knew exactly who to blame for the false alarm. After quickly passing over the actual culprit, who was an employee of her fellow Democrat, the governor, with a brusque "Yes, this false alarm went out, and we have to fix that in Hawaii," the congresswoman zeroed in on the person she saw as the real culprit, saying, "We've got to get to the underlying issue here, of why are the people of Hawaii and the US facing a nuclear threat coming from North Korea? And what is this president doing, urgently, to eliminate that threat?"

Call all of this a tale of the Old Order—foreign policy version.

If ever there were a vivid example of Old Order incompetence, duplicity, and hypocrisy, its reaction to President Donald Trump's handling of North Korea is it.

The very first questions would seem obvious, and Gabbard had unwittingly touched on them. How in the world did North Korea get nukes in the first place? What has been the Old Order way of dealing with North Korea?

On October 18, 1994, President Bill Clinton stepped in front of the television cameras to say:

> *"Good afternoon. I am pleased that the United States and North Korea yesterday reached agreement on the text of a framework document on North Korea's nuclear program. This agreement will help to achieve a longstanding and vital American objective: an end to the threat of nuclear proliferation on the Korean Peninsula.*
>
> *This agreement is good for the United States, good for our allies, and good for the safety of the entire world. It reduces the danger of the threat of nuclear spreading in the region. It's a crucial step toward drawing North Korea into the global community....*
>
> *Today, after 16 months of intense and difficult negotiations with North Korea, we have completed an agreement that will make the United States, the Korean Peninsula, and the world safer. Under the agreement, North Korea has agreed to freeze its existing nuclear program and to accept international inspection of all existing facilities.*
>
> *This agreement represents the first step on the road to a nuclear-free Korean Peninsula."*

As Trump prepared to meet with North Korean supreme leader Kim Jong Un twenty-four years later, ABC News was reporting that "North Korea has a small arsenal of small nuclear weapons as proven by its six nuclear tests. As of last summer, U.S. intelligence believes that North Korea has enough nuclear fissile material for as many as 60 nuclear weapons based on the amount of enriched uranium and separated plutonium it possesses."

Said Trump to former Arkansas governor Mike Huckabee in an interview for Huckabee's TBN television show: "This should have been handled 10 years ago. It should have been handled during the Obama administration. The truth is, Mike, I was handed a mess. Not only there. I was handed a mess in the Middle East. Just a total mess."

Which is to say the agreement that President Clinton announced in 1994, constructed by a bevy of Old Order politicians and diplomats, had failed utterly. The Old Order establishment was, in plain colloquial American

English, taken to the cleaners. Hoodwinked. And notably, in the day, Donald Trump got it.

In December 2017, as President Trump took heat from the various provinces of the Old Order over his tough policy towards North Korea, the president—what else?—tweeted out a 1999 video of himself on NBC's *Meet the Press* with host Tim Russert. The video had been shot a mere five years after President Clinton had announced his agreement with North Korea—and Trump didn't believe a word of what Clinton had said. In the video, Russert asks Trump about North Korea, to which Trump (then still a private citizen) responded:

> *"They're going to have those weapons pointed all over the world, and specifically at the United States. Wouldn't you be better off solving this really, potentially, unbelievable.... The biggest problem this world has is nuclear proliferation, and we have a country out there, North Korea, which is sort of wacko, which is not a bunch of dummies...and they are going out and they are developing nuclear weapons. And they're not doing it because they're having fun doing it. They're doing it for a reason. And they're continuing to do what they are doing, and they're laughing at us; they think we're a bunch of dummies. I'm saying we have to do something to stop it. You want to do it [stop them] in five years when they have warheads all over the place? Every one of them pointing to New York City, to Washington?... Is that when you want to do it? You better do something now. You better do it now."*

At one point, Russert brought forth the thinking of the Old Order of the day and started to say: "If the military told you, 'Mr. Trump you can't do that...'" Trump brushed the idea off and kept going.

Predictably, Trump was a voice in the wilderness. Certainly nothing he said was going to deter the Old Order from continuing in its Old Order ways regarding North Korea. Clinton was succeeded for eight years by Republican George W. Bush, who in turn was followed by Democrat Barack Obama for eight years. Both presidents, while different in tone, relied on the Old Order diplomatic mechanisms ("Six-Party Talks") to prevent North Korea from getting nukes. They failed. And along the way, the Old Order wise men and women also failed to stop the North Koreans from getting the long-range missiles that could deliver those nukes.

Now president himself, true to the viewpoint on North Korea he had expressed in 1999 on *Meet the Press*, Trump was determined to take an entirely different approach. Predictably, his Old Order critics were immediately wringing their hands. Here, for example, is the alarmed *New York Times* headline from August 2017: "Drop the Bluster on North Korea."

Wrote the editorial board:

> *As President Trump has implicitly conceded, his approach to the North Korean nuclear threat is failing.... Mr. Trump needs to face the reality that he cannot solve this crisis by proxy, that he must intervene directly and that he should do so soon.... Talks should begin without preconditions; what's most urgent is to halt the program's progress.*

A week later, the president issued a sharp statement on North Korea. The *Times* headline: "Trump Threatens 'Fire and Fury' Against North Korea if It Endangers U.S."

The story was written in tones that verged on the apocalyptic:

> *BRIDGEWATER, N.J.—President Trump threatened on Tuesday to unleash "fire and fury" against North Korea if it endangered the United States, as tensions with the isolated and impoverished nuclear-armed state escalated into perhaps the most serious foreign policy challenge yet of his administration.*
>
> *In chilling language that evoked the horror of a nuclear exchange, Mr. Trump sought to deter North Korea from any actions that would put Americans at risk.*

HuffPost sought out the usual Old Order suspects to make the case against Trump after the "fire and fury" statement. They complied. "That is about the stupidest and most dangerous statement I have ever heard an American president make," John Mecklin, editor in chief of *Bulletin of the Atomic Scientists* told *HuffPost*. He added: "It's exactly wrong. It increases the likelihood of nuclear war. And those kind of threats are just not something an American president should make."

Then there was the query to perpetual Old Order leftist Noam Chomsky, described by *HuffPost* as the "MIT linguistics professor emeritus and renowned foreign policy critic." Unsurprisingly, it was noted that Chomsky "agreed with Mecklin's assessment. 'Trump's statement is extremely dangerous.'"

Yet a third Old Order thinker was summoned to trash Trump. *HuffPost* described him as "Bruce Blair, a nuclear safety expert at Princeton University," adding that Blair was worried about Trump's leadership style. The article linked, but of course, to another in *Politico*, in which Blair fretted about the weapons at Trump's disposal as president. Trump was described as a "maniac," and Blair feared that the risk of escalation to nuclear conflict "is growing by the day.... Trump has unchecked authority to order the use of conventional or nuclear weapons against North Korea." Blair went on to say, "I believe that both options are being prepared right now and that these preparations reflect the military's acceptance of Trump's authority to exercise either of them." Blair described America as a "nuclear monarchy."

Point still not made, a fourth "expert" was brought in to slam the president and close out the evidence that Trump's departure from the Old Order norms was horrific. "'Trump's statement is incredibly reckless and foolish,' Kingston Reif, director of disarmament and threat reduction policy for the Arms Control Association," told the left-leaning website. Note well that not one of these Old Order experts addressed the hard fact of just how America and the world had gotten to this place to begin with.

In September 2017, with the "fire and fury" statement having been made only weeks earlier, the president went to the traditional fall opening session of the United Nations. Standing at the General Assembly podium, he said (emphasis added):

> *"No one has shown more contempt for other nations and for the wellbeing of their own people than the depraved regime in North Korea. It is responsible for the starvation deaths of millions of North Koreans, and for the imprisonment, torture, killing, and oppression of countless more.*
>
> *"We were all witness to the regime's deadly abuse when an innocent American college student, Otto Warmbier, was returned to America only to die a few days later. We saw it in the assassination of the dictator's brother using banned nerve agents in an international airport. We know it kidnapped a*

*sweet 13-year-old Japanese girl from a beach in her own coun-
try to enslave her as a language tutor for North Korea's spies.*

*"If this is not twisted enough, now North Korea's reckless
pursuit of nuclear weapons and ballistic missiles threatens the
entire world with unthinkable loss of human life.*

*"It is an outrage that some nations would not only trade
with such a regime, but would arm, supply, and financially
support a country that imperils the world with nuclear conflict.
No nation on earth has an interest in seeing this band of crimi-
nals arm itself with nuclear weapons and missiles.*

"The United States has great strength and patience, but
if it is forced to defend itself or its allies, we will have no
choice but to totally destroy North Korea. Rocket Man is on
a suicide mission for himself and for his regime. *The United
States is ready, willing and able, but hopefully this will not be
necessary. That's what the United Nations is all about; that's
what the United Nations is for. Let's see how they do."*

Predictably the Old Order foreign policy gurus were now terrified. In one
speech Trump had violated just about every Old Order norm that exists. He
threatened to "totally destroy North Korea." He mocked the North Korean
Communist dictator as "Rocket Man"—and later "Little Rocket Man." (He
borrowed the "Rocket Man" label from an Elton John song.)

In the style of "Tinker to Evers to Chance," the ball was tossed from the
Trump policy critics to the Old Order media, which promptly swung into
action. A *Los Angeles Times* headline: "Will Trump's 'Rocket Man' speech lead
us to war?"

Fretted the paper:

*Never mind grand strategy. Trump made sure the media's favor-
ite soundbite would be a schoolboy taunt and a threat of mass
annihilation....*

*The problem with Trump's threat wasn't only the juvenile
language he chose, or that it inevitably distracted attention
from the rest of his message. His taunt, far from serving an
underlying strategy, was probably counterproductive.*

CNN White House correspondent Jim Acosta tweeted: "UN speech was a lot of Trump tweets strung together. Saber-rattling. But no clear doctrine. Threats of confrontation around the world." And Gail Collins of *The New York Times* shook her head in frightened disbelief: "I believe I am not alone in feeling that the best plan for dealing with a deranged dictator holding nuclear weapons is not threatening to blow him up." In fact, Collins was hardly alone. The Old Order foreign policy wing was apoplectic, giving the president blistering reviews.

Dr. Daniel A. Pinkston, a lecturer in international relations with Troy University who has considerable experience on the subject of North Korea, sniffed that "Trump continues to demonstrate that he really knows practically nothing about foreign policy and international security policy. And he doesn't seem too interested in public policy. This pandering and bluster essentially will have zero effect on Sŏn'gun Korea's strategic preferences and the regime's plans to achieve them."

Politico caught up with Joel Wit, a Korea expert at Columbia University and Johns Hopkins University's School of Advanced International Studies. Wit was appalled with Trump's "Rocket Man" label: "The relationship is already so bad that I'm not sure how much worse it could get. But if there's something guaranteed to make it worse, it's hurling personal insults at their leader." Then there was this from one Sung-Yoon Lee, a North Korea specialist at the Fletcher School of Law and Diplomacy at Tufts University: "This kind of bluster will not only not deter North Korea, but Kim will call Trump's bluff and conduct more weapons tests…. For the U.S. to descend to North Korea's level is demeaning."

In February 2018—a month after the Hawaii scare—the increasingly frantic *Times* ran the headline "Playing With Fire and Fury on North Korea."

Pleaded the *Times* (emphasis mine):

> *It's hard to come away from the State of the Union address* without a heightened sense of foreboding about President Trump's intentions toward North Korea. The signs increasingly point to unilateral American military action. To which we say: Don't.
>
> The references to North Korea in the address were worrying enough. Mr. Trump called the country's leadership "depraved." He trumpeted his "campaign of maximum

pressure" to ensure that the North does not succeed in perfecting a nuclear-tipped missile that could strike the continental United States. He asserted that "past experience has taught us that complacency and concessions only invite aggression and provocation." He pledged, "I will not repeat the mistakes of past administrations that got us into this dangerous position."

Mr. Trump seemed to be building a case for war on emotional grounds, *invoking the case of Otto Warmbier, a University of Virginia student who died last year after being detained by North Korea...*

And then.

Mere months later the president accomplished the astonishing feat of meeting Kim Jong Un in a summit in Singapore. None of his predecessors of either party had managed to meet with a North Korean leader since the armistice that ended the Korean War in 1953—a full sixty-eight years earlier. Arguably it was the most ballyhooed summit in the Far East since Nixon had gone to China forty-six years earlier in 1972, shaken Mao Tse-tung's hand, and toasted with Chou En-lai. Television screens around the globe were filled with images of Trump and Kim smiling, laughing, with Trump at one point courteously gesturing for the Korean leader to go in a certain direction on a walkway.

Yet as the summit loomed, the Trump critics who had earlier demanded that the president must immediately begin talks with North Korea, as the *Times* editorialized, without preconditions, now took the opposite stance.

"There is no way that President Trump can be ready by May to have a high-stakes negotiation on denuclearization on the Korean Peninsula. It's just impossible," Samantha Vinograd, a former official at the Obama administration's National Security Council, told the *New York Daily News*. The president, you see, was being played; Kim was "playing to the President's ego and the President's weaknesses by flattering him." (This from an advisor to a president who had eight years to solve the North Korean nuke problem and failed.) U.S. Naval War College professor Tom Nichols added, "This trap is so obvious even Wile E. Coyote wouldn't walk into it."

Again, recall that the *Times* was demanding in 2017 that "Mr. Trump needs to face the reality that he cannot solve this crisis by proxy, that he must intervene directly and that he should do so soon.... Talks should begin without preconditions; what's most urgent is to halt the program's progress."

Mission accomplished. But suddenly, the summit ended with the first signs of success, and the *Times* was not happy. The editorial board was at it again with this:

> *Mr. Trump's chumminess with one of the globe's most notorious despots would have been noteworthy under any circumstances....*
>
> *Mr. Trump has a deep and abiding fondness for strongmen. The more ruthlessly they have had to act to hold on to power, the more he respects them....*
>
> *It's not that Mr. Trump doesn't grasp the depths of Mr. Kim's butchery—he just thinks such cruelty shouldn't get in the way of a good deal.*

Of all the Old Order media sniping about "Mr. Trump's chumminess with one of the globe's most notorious despots," *The New York Times* had less than zero credibility. This is the paper whose 1930s-era Moscow bureau chief was later revealed to be a public relations agent for Stalin. As the facts of the Stalin-induced famine in 1930s Russia began to surface, Walter Duranty notoriously went out of his way to hide the fact from *Times* readers. Said the *Times* chief when he was asked by a colleague what he was going to report in the *Times* for Americans to learn of the brutal horrors:

> *Nothing. What are a few million dead Russians in a situation like this? Quite unimportant. This is just an incident in the sweeping historical changes here. I think the entire matter is exaggerated.*

Decades later, yet another *Times* reporter was accused of covering for yet another brutal Communist leader in the fashion of Duranty and Stalin. This time it was the paper's Herbert L. Matthews, who staunchly admired Cuba's Fidel Castro. As Castro was leading his guerrilla campaign against the island's dictator, Matthews was convincing the U.S. State Department that Castro wasn't a Communist at all. Reported Matthews in the *Times* on July 5, 1959:

> *There are no Reds in the Cabinet and none in high positions in the Government or army in the sense of being able to control*

either governmental or defense policies. The only power worth considering in Cuba is in the hands of the Premier Castro, who is not only not Communist but decidedly anti-Communist...

The Black Book of Communism notes of the regime run by brothers Fidel and Raúl Castro:

From 1959 through the late 1990's more than 100,000 Cubans experienced life in one of the camps, prisons, or open-regime sites. Between 15,000 and 17,000 people [dissenters] were shot.

Not only was Matthews tolerating this in the pages of the *Times* but by the time President Obama moved to open relations with the murderous Castros, here was *The New York Times* gushing as follows:

Mr. Obama's Historic Move on Cuba

Following months of secret negotiations with the Cuban government, President Obama on Wednesday announced sweeping changes to normalize relations with Cuba, a bold move that ends one of the most misguided chapters in American foreign policy.

The administration's decision to restore full diplomatic relations, take steps to remove Cuba from the State Department list of countries that sponsor terrorism and roll back restrictions on travel and trade is a change in direction that has been strongly supported by this page. The Obama administration is ushering in a transformational era for millions of Cubans who have suffered as a result of more than 50 years of hostility between the two nations....

[T]his move will inevitably inform the debate about the merits of engagement. In all likelihood, history will prove Mr. Obama right.

When Obama then went to Cuba himself, the paper ran the headline "Mr. Obama's Honest Message in Cuba."

The editorial page showered praise on Obama's meeting with Raúl Castro:

President Obama began his speech to the Cuban people on Tuesday with humility and grace. "Cultivo una rosa blanca," he said, reciting the opening line of one of the most famous poems by José Martí, the island's national hero. "I plant a white rose."

It was an inspired way of extending an olive branch to a neighboring nation with which America has feuded for more than half a century. Mr. Obama made a compelling case that the ties that bind Cuba and the United States are more power- ful than their differences.

"I have come here to bury the last remnant of the Cold War in the Americas," Mr. Obama said Tuesday morning at the Grand Theater of Havana, drawing applause.

Suffice it to say, this *Times* sympathy for brutal Communist dictators during the twentieth and early twenty-first centuries was hardly new by the time Trump became president.

Yet all of a sudden, with Trump doing in North Korea exactly what the paper—and other liberal media outlets—had demanded, the story now was that Trump was cozying up to "Mr. Kim's butchery" because the president "just thinks such cruelty shouldn't get in the way of a good deal."

The website MarketWatch took its turn rounding up Trump-scorning Old Order foreign policy experts to weigh in on Trump's historic summit. Jeffrey Lewis, the director of the East Asia Nonproliferation Program at the Middlebury Institute of International Studies at Monterey, wasted no time mocking both Trump and his advisors in tweets, such as:

I wonder if Trump's "aides" have explained that to him. Or, if in their toddler-handling, they have led him to believe that this offer is something unusual. Or perhaps he imagines that only he can go Pyongyang.

Robert E. Kelly, a professor of political science at Busan National University in South Korea, tweeted:

Trump's chaotic management style, erratic, moody personality, and chronic staffing problems, especially regarding East Asia. I just don't see it. We can always hope, but it is just as reasonable to fear that Trump, the reality TV star who somehow stumbled into the presidency for which he is woefully unfit, will wander from decades of joint US-South Korea policy, about which he naturally knows nothing, and make some kind of deal for a "win" that no other US official would endorse.

Is it any wonder that post-summit, Trump took to Twitter as he arrived back home on Air Force One and responded this way in a series of tweets?

- Just landed—a long trip, but everybody can now feel much safer than the day I took office. There is no longer a Nuclear Threat from North Korea. Meeting with Kim Jong Un was an interesting and very positive experience. North Korea has great potential for the future!
- Before taking office people were assuming that we were going to War with North Korea. President Obama said that North Korea was our biggest and most dangerous problem. No longer—sleep well tonight!
- A year ago the pundits & talking heads, people that couldn't do the job before, were begging for conciliation and peace—"please meet, don't go to war." Now that we meet and have a great relationship with Kim Jong Un, the same haters shout out, "you shouldn't meet, do not meet!"
- The World has taken a big step back from potential Nuclear catastrophe! No more rocket launches, nuclear testing or research! The hostages are back home with their families. Thank you to Chairman Kim, our day together was historic!
- I want to thank Chairman Kim for taking the first bold step toward a bright new future for his people. Our unprecedented meeting – the first between an American President and a leader of North Korea – proves that real change is possible!

Strip away the specifics of the Trump-Kim summit and relationship and what is laid bare is Trump's new populism taking on the Old Order view of the world. Indeed, the blatant hypocrisy of both the Old Order media and Old Order foreign policy "experts" on Trump and North Korea is emblematic of exactly how the Old Order has been forced to deal with Trump and his legions. The essence of the Old Order cry is the age-old bleat, "But that's not the way we do things."

Indeed.

* * * * *

Let's look at another example that is "not the way we do things" that turns out not to work.

JANUARY 2016

The cash was stacked on wooden pallets. Swiss francs, euros, and other currencies, to the tune of a down payment of $400 million on a total transaction of $1.7 billion, arrived in the dark of night in Tehran, unloaded from the belly of an unmarked cargo plane.

The recipients: the mullahs of Iran. The money: payment and interest from an arms deal with Iran that were frozen by the United States when the shah was toppled from power in 1979 and the new Islamist government was holding American diplomats hostage.

By a strange "coincidence," *The New York Times* reported that the "secretly organized" payment "was announced on the same day that the nuclear deal with Iran was completed and Tehran released four detained Americans."

All political hell immediately broke loose.

Arkansas Republican senator Tom Cotton called the payment "a $1.7 billion ransom to the ayatollahs for U.S. hostages." Cotton was the exact opposite of a Swamp creature and an Old Order high priest. He grew up on a farm in rural Arkansas, went to public high school, then went on to Harvard, Harvard Law, and a clerkship with the U.S. Court of Appeals before settling into a private law practice in Arkansas. Then came 9/11. Cotton abruptly left his practice and signed up for the U.S. Army, where he went on to serve as an infantry officer. He did two combat tours in Iraq, winning a Bronze Star along the way. All of which is to say, Cotton had zero patience for the usual Old Order elitism.

Not so President Obama. In July, *The Washington Post* opened a story on the aftermath of the deal by noting that President Obama, shortly after the deal was clinched, had "swung by the State Department to personally thank the negotiators." But even the *Post* was making a grudging acknowledgment in its story:

> *The legacy-making deal, completed a year ago Thursday, is still a work in progress. And by virtually all accounts, Iran has done everything it is required to do under the agreement.*

But the best-case scenario, that the deal would exert a moderating influence on Iran's behavior, has yet to be realized. Human rights abuses have piled up and Tehran has conducted missile tests that U.N. chief Ban Ki-moon has called inconsistent with "the constructive spirit" of the deal.

Which is to say, the Obama Old Order deal with Iran was the same as the Bill Clinton Old Order deal with North Korea. The trusting, arrogant Old Order politicians and diplomats had fecklessly negotiated a deal that resulted in the United States' being taken to the cleaners—again.

By August 2016, as the newly minted Republican nominee, Trump pounced on the inevitable target: "Our incompetent Secretary of State, Hillary Clinton, was the one who started talks to give 400 million dollars, in cash, to Iran. Scandal!"

As a classic of Old Order foreign policy thinking, other than Bill Clinton's North Korea debacle, it would be hard to find a better example than the atrocious deal crafted with the Iranian ayatollahs. *The Wall Street Journal* began to unravel the story, reporting:

The settlement, which resolved claims before an international tribunal in The Hague, also coincided with the formal implementation that same weekend of the landmark nuclear agreement reached between Tehran, the U.S. and other global powers the summer before.

"With the nuclear deal done, prisoners released, the time was right to resolve this dispute as well," President Barack Obama said at the White House on Jan. 17—without disclosing the $400 million cash payment.

Senior U.S. officials denied any link between the payment and the prisoner exchange.

But of course they did.

The attitude so vividly on display in the Obama administration's dealings with Iran was a classic example of Old Order thinking, with the attitude of "we're smarter and more sophisticated than everybody else" foremost in evidence. If nothing else, it was a stark reminder of the attitude evidenced in the making of America's disastrous Vietnam policy in the 1960s. The late *New*

York Times reporter David Halberstam vividly captures the thinking in his Pulitzer Prize-winning book *The Best and the Brightest.*

The policymakers involved in Vietnam, Halberstam writes, were the "modern, contemporary men—the best and the brightest—who came to Washington to build us a Camelot and left behind them a country divided by war, torn by dissent." One of the key characteristics of these architects of disaster was what Halberstam called their "phenomenal hubris."

That had nothing on the "phenomenal hubris" of today's Old Order. And the hubris is not limited to the Obama diplomats who negotiated the treaty.

The chairman of the United States Senate's Foreign Relations Committee was not an Obama Democrat. He was Tennessee Republican Bob Corker. With the treaty negotiated and in final form, the expectation among its critics was as obvious as it was constitutional. Article Two, Section Two of the United States Constitution explicitly says of the president's and Senate's joint responsibilities in dealing with treaties: "He [the President] shall have Power, by and with the Advice and Consent of the Senate, to make Treaties, provided two thirds of the Senators present concur."

But Obama and Senator Corker had a different view. And in the style of "Tinker to Evers to Chance," with the Iran treaty now negotiated, Obama threw the ball in Old Order bipartisan fashion to Senator Corker. What happened next was duly noted in the *Washington Times* by Jed Babbin, a deputy undersecretary of defense in the George H. W. Bush administration who was serving as a senior fellow of the London Center for Policy Research.

Wrote Babbin, clearly astounded:

> *Mr. Obama refused to submit his Iran deal to the Senate for ratification under Article 2, Section 2 of the Constitution, which is the only way such agreements can become treaties binding on the United States.*
>
> *Enter Mr. Corker. He sponsored a measure that required the president to submit the agreement to the Senate but turned the Constitution upside down.*
>
> *Under Article 2, Section 2 the president must get a two-thirds vote in favor of any treaty to make it a part of the law of the land. Instead, Mr. Corker's provision required opponents of the deal to muster a two-thirds vote—66 senators—to*

vote against it. It was a pretense to conceal another Republican cave-in to Mr. Obama.

Mr. Corker's provision passed the Senate by a vote of 98-1, Sen. Tom Cotton, Arkansas Republican, being the only negative vote. In an entirely predictable result, when the time came for a disapproval vote, Republicans couldn't even overcome the Democrats' filibuster to get a final vote on disapproval.

After that, it was a small matter for the president to take the Iran deal to the U.N. Security Council, which eagerly approved it. What Mr. Corker had done was to enable Mr. Obama to claim Senate approval of his deal even though the Senate hadn't done anything of the sort.

It was one of the more brazen displays of bipartisan Old Order arrogance. It was a Swamp War in which the Constitution itself was simply deep-sixed, with bipartisan agreement. What Obama would do instead is submit the treaty to the United Nations Security Council. And Corker would handle the rest.

One could go on endlessly here, but you get the picture. Always there is the Old Order insisting that things have always been done a certain way, repeatedly ignoring the results, no matter how bad. The topic at hand can change—North Korea becomes Iran becomes the G7 Summit becomes trade with China—but no matter. The dynamic of a calcified Old Order, the global version of the American domestic Old Order, is still ever present, with the accompanying pressure to preserve the status quo regardless of the results.

Founded in the 1970s to focus on economic policy, the G7 (Group of Seven) is composed of the seven countries with the most advanced economies in the world, as ranked by the International Monetary Fund. In alphabetical order the members of the G7 are: Canada, France, Germany, Italy, Japan, the United Kingdom, and the United States. In early June 2018, with Canada as that year's host, they gathered in the Charlevoix region of Quebec for their annual meeting.

The New York Times, in classic Old Order style as its Trump hatred permeated its news columns, provided "Tinker to Evers to Chance"-style coverage before the group gathered:

Seven nations are getting together to discuss gender equality with a leader who once bragged about grabbing women's genitals, pluralism and tolerance with politicians who have promised to turn away refugees, and economic cooperation with a country severing ties with its neighbors.

What could go wrong?

Can one imagine the *Times* beginning a story on President Bill Clinton's attending a G7 summit or any other world gathering with: "Seven nations are getting together to discuss gender equality with a leader who once was accused of raping a woman, and groped and harassed several others..."?

Of course not. The Old Order protects its own.

In other words, the problem at the 2018 summit would be the American president and his policies—not any of the other leaders or their policies. And high on the agenda: trade.

From the editorial pages of *The Wall Street Journal* ("Trump's Tariff Folly") to *The New York Times* warning that tariffs "are blunt tools that are far less effective than Mr. Trump realizes" to the conservative corner of *National Review* ("Against the Tariffs") and oh so much more, Trump was repeatedly lectured about the need for free trade. Frequently left out of the lectures was the reality that Trump himself had long been on record as being a free trader—but someone who believed in fair trade. In the words of the president's chairman of the Council of Economic Advisors, "President Trump is very, very serious when he says that he's a free trader and that he's pursuing symmetry and reciprocity." Not hard to understand. Unless...

Canadian prime minister Justin Trudeau was well out there suggesting that he and the other Western allies were standing up against Trump—in favor of free trade. Trump, went the line, was supporting tariffs, which would, the president was endlessly lectured, lead to trade wars.

When Trudeau had visited China in December 2017, a Bloomberg headline was "World at 'pivot point,' needs to embrace free trade: Trudeau."

But there was predictably more here than meets the eye—and Trump had not the slightest hesitation in pointing out that America's G7 allies were in fact guilty of massive hypocrisy on the issue.

Thus it was that when the G7 gathered in Canada, the president of the United States had the audacity to confront the G7 leaders on the issue of free trade. Said the president in a tweet as he headed to Canada for the summit in

June 2018: "Canada charges the U.S. a 270% tariff on Dairy Products! They didn't tell you that, did they? Not fair to our farmers!"

In fact, no. Trudeau had not talked about this sky-high Canadian tariff on the product of U.S. dairy farmers. As Trudeau well knew, trade between Canada and the United States had been anything but free, much less fair. J.J. McCullough, a Canadian columnist and commentator, took to the pages of—amazingly—*The Washington Post* to admit that Trump had in fact caught Trudeau dead to rights. Wrote McCullough:

> One of President Trump's darkest talents is his ability to identify an opponent's delicate spot and stab it remorselessly. From his knack for condescending nicknames (Low Energy Jeb, Little Rocket Man) to inviting Bill Clinton's various accusers to the second presidential debate, there's no denying the man has a skill for knifing sensitive areas.
>
> And now he has found Canada's vulnerable flank: dairy tariffs.
>
> Though Canada enjoys broadly free trade with the United States through the North American Free Trade Agreement, it has never been absolute, and the deal makes several concessions to Canadian protectionism and politics. Chief among them are Canada's extraordinarily high tariffs on American dairy products, which at last week's Group of Seven summit in Quebec, Trump correctly identified as a 270% tariff. As the CBC reminded, "Canada levies a tariff of 270 percent on milk, 245 percent on cheese and 298 percent on butter in an effort to keep U.S. and other foreign dairy imports out." These tariffs exist almost exclusively for the benefit of the agriculture sector of Quebec, a province with a unique stranglehold on Canadian politics.

Suddenly, the facade of Old Order game playing cracked.

As reported by Bloomberg, the president "also repeated an earlier proposal that U.S. trading partners should drop all trade barriers, including tariffs and subsidies to industries and producers in their own countries. 'We're the piggy bank that everybody is robbing. And that ends,' Trump said."

Contrary to Trudeau's assertions, Charles Payne, a Fox Business Network anchor and commentator, set the record straight in a tweet of his own:

> *I know tariffs don't work but why does Canada have these tariffs?*
> *270% dairy*
> *69.9% Sausage*
> *57.8% Barley Seed*
> *49% Durum Wheat*
> *26.5% Bovine/Meat*
> *18% Table Linen*
> *Why did Canada create an "ingredient strategy" tariff in 2015?*
> *To protect those important industries and curb US imports.*

In a snapshot, here was the global wing of the Old Order in action.

For anyone who had observed the Trump campaign and the anger of the American people who so strongly supported his candidacy, it was crystal clear that Trump, indeed, was "making an overdue stand against an expiring global order." The Paris climate accord and the Iran nuclear deal were nothing if not vivid symbols of an Old Order that had come to symbolize an arrogant, corrupt elitism overflowing with both weakness and political correctness—an Old Order that was very much worth standing up against.

Then there was China. For years Donald Trump the private citizen had been warning America's Old Order elites that they were leading the country into disaster through their trade policy with China. That day in May 2014 when he spoke to me, he was literally shaking his head at their conduct. In words that signaled exactly what he would do as president, he said:

> *"They don't understand the challenge, and the challenge is only going to get worse. China's two years ahead of schedule. Our leaders are impotent. They have no idea what's going on with respect to China. I can also say with respect to Russia and virtually every other place on the planet, China, with what they have done economically, is incredible. They have taken our jobs; they make our product. They have done so brilliantly for themselves, and it's hard to believe that we allow it to happen. And we have all the cards. We built China. We have made China. Because the money they have sucked out of this country has gone to build*

bridges, schools, and roadways and everything, things that we don't have, that we can't build.

"On top of it they then loan us money. So China is a huge problem, and it's only gotten worse; it hasn't gotten better. It's inconceivable that people don't see the China problem in this country. That people—our leaders—don't see the China problem."

By the fall of 2018, President Trump had indeed followed through on his promise to deal with China. One Trump tariff on Chinese goods had followed another. There were tariffs on everything from solar panels to washing machines to, as reported by *The New York Times*, "Chinese products like flat-screen televisions, medical devices, aircraft parts and batteries—some 1300 imported goods in all."

The Old Order blowback was instantaneous. A CNBC headline: "Largest US business group attacks Trump on tariffs."

If Trump had tried, he could not have gotten a more perfect example of an Old Order vested interest that would quickly jump to protect itself with a Swamp War. The CNBC story began:

The U. S. Chamber of Commerce, the nation's largest business group and customarily a close ally of President Donald Trump's Republican Party, is launching a campaign on Monday to oppose Trump's trade tariff policies.

With some of America's tightest trading partners imposing retaliatory measures, Trump's approach to tariffs has unsettled financial markets and strained relations between the White House and the Chamber.

The new campaign, detailed first to Reuters, is an aggressive effort by the business lobbying giant. Using a state-by-state analysis, it argues that Trump is risking a global trade war that will hit the wallets of U.S. consumers.

"The administration is threatening to undermine the economic progress it worked so hard to achieve," said Chamber President Tom Donohue in a statement to Reuters. "We should seek free and fair trade, but this is just not the way to do it."

And then came December 2018 and this headline in Reuters: "Automakers rise on report of China moving to cut U.S. car tariffs."

The story said: "China is moving to cut import tariffs on American-made cars to 15 percent from the current 40 percent, Bloomberg reported on Tuesday citing people familiar with the matter."

In other words, Trump's tough negotiating tactics with the Chinese worked.

Never asked or even wondered is the question of just how the United States got into such a disadvantageous trade relationship with China and its own G7 trading partners in the first place. And politically speaking, millions of Americans who suffered from the globalism policies of Old Order institutions like the Chamber of Commerce and so many others were not happy with the results.

In fact, precisely this type of negative reaction to globalism and Old Order elites had earlier appeared in Britain during the Brexit campaign. Led by ex-Tory Nigel Farage, the successful underdog campaign to take Britain out of the elitist, bureaucratic clutches of the European Union wildly upset the British Old Order elites. And the battle over Brexit and Prime Minister Theresa May's plans to do what the British people voted for still rages as this is written.

What is it that keeps Old Order elites not just in America but around the world from understanding that millions of their respective fellow country-men are done with this Old Order elitism that strangely benefits Old Order elites—and no one else?

As I walked offstage at a Trump campaign event being covered by CNN in 2016, I met a man who was certain—against all the odds as presented in the American Old Order media—of a Trump victory. That man was Nigel Farage, the selfsame leader of the Brexit campaign. Farage spent some time with me discussing the American presidential campaign, Brexit, and the polling during the Brexit election. The Old Order pollsters of Britain had been wrong then—insisting the Leave campaign would lose. And the American Old Order pollsters were wrong now, he told me confidently, telling me flatly he believed Trump would win.

Farage was right.

When it comes to dealing with the world outside of America, Donald Trump—in the style of his predecessors who likewise had more control over foreign policy than they did domestic policy (thanks to the role of Congress and the courts in the latter)—is in fact bringing radical change. And it is crystal clear that his millions of supporters are cheering him on—even as the Old Order is determined to resist.

In this Swamp War, to the teeth-gritting exasperation of his opponents, Trump is winning.

THE AMERICAN DIVIDE

"They love him most for the enemies he has made."

*—General Edward Stuyvesant Bragg, in a presidential
nominating speech for New York governor Grover Cleveland
at the Democratic Convention of 1884. Cleveland was
elected the nation's twenty-second president that November.*

SEPTEMBER 9, 2018

A Sunday afternoon at a brewery/restaurant in Central Pennsylvania. The place is filled with Americans wearing red baseball hats that read "Keep America Great."

These are the men and women who are at the core of Donald Trump's support. They are business owners, real estate developers, lawyers and more. Well educated, they are hardly the stereotype of toothless, racist rubes that Never Trumpers and left wingers so condescendingly paint Trump supporters as being. Prior to 2016, many had never been involved in a political campaign in their life. In fact, many met for the very first time through social media for Trump supporters. But as they talk to me, they make it plain. They were inspired to come together with a whole lot of people they had never met before because they see their country as being in trouble. I spend the afternoon talking to them, and it is crystal clear they are intensely pleased with the man whose candidacy for president has brought them together. Trump is praised for sticking with his promises. The tax cuts and the nominations of Neil Gorsuch and Brett Kavanaugh to the Supreme Court are emphatically supported. Yes, so too is building the wall along the southern border decidedly favored.

But there's more to it than just policy. They make it plain that they have had more than enough of being treated by self-anointed Old Order elites, as one woman tells me, like "the little people"—elites that they see whether on cable news or in their own lives. The point is made that the more Trump is attacked by what I call the Old Order defenders in various Swamp Wars, the more they intend to stand by their man.

In the end, Swamp Wars are wars for the soul of America.

Do Americans really believe in freedom? Liberty? The Constitution? Do we believe in a country ruled not by an aristocracy of Old Order self-selected elites who see themselves as morally and intellectually superior, but rather ruled by Americans ourselves?

Recall this statement by the FBI's Peter Strzok: "I can smell the Trump supporters at Walmart."

To Strzok, non-Old Order Americans "smell." To Hillary Clinton they are a "basket of deplorables. Right? The racist, sexist, homophobic, xenophobic, Islamophobic—you name it." To Never Trump Republican consultant Rick Wilson the Trump supporters I spent time with that September afternoon - successful professionals one and all - were Trump's "credulous rube ten-toothed base." And to former President Obama they are "bitter, they cling to guns or religion or antipathy to people who aren't like them."

Robert Bork described this as a war for the general culture. Rush Limbaugh described the Old Order problem of elites to the audience on his May 17, 2018 show this way:

> You have to understand the arrogance of these people. These people…it's hard to describe. I've tried I don't know how many different ways to describe the establishment, the elites, the people in this club, how they think, what they think of themselves, their arrogance and their hubris, their exclusionary existence. The fact that people who make the country work are nothing more than cogs of dirt to them.
>
> You people, all of us, we're just plebes. We're nameless faces. We're interchangeable. We're not in their league. We can't stop what they do. We'll never even know what they do. The whole game is to prevent us from ever really knowing what they do anyway. They think they run the world, and they have counterparts in the European Union who think the same thing. They have counterparts in Asia. This club of elites is worldwide, and they all have common beliefs.

Whether the story is Old Order high priests demanding a right to security clearances after they leave government, or the one-sided prosecutorial games of Special Counsel Robert Mueller and his staff of Hillary Clinton supporters, or the politicization of the Department of Justice, or for that matter any number of other, seemingly unrelated stories, like the conduct of the National Football League or the inner workings of a cable news network, the real story is always the same.

On one side are Old Order elites determined—make that obsessed—with holding on to their power and privilege. On the other side of this American divide are hard-working rank-and-file Americans who get up and make the country work every single day—and who, in 2016, elected Donald Trump precisely because he promised to come to Washington and "drain the Swamp."

The Wall Street Journal's Kimberley Strassel captured the Department of Justice's Old Order problem succinctly as news arrived of the verdict against momentary Trump aide and longtime lobbyist Paul Manafort and the charges against onetime Trump lawyer Michael Cohen. Her column's headlined: "When Justice Is Partial: Mueller is determined to sniff out any wrongdoing he can find—on one side."

Wrote Strassel:

> *The country has watched the FBI treat one presidential campaign with kid gloves, the other with informants, warrants and eavesdropping. They've seen the Justice Department resist all efforts at accountability, even as it fails to hold its own accountable. And don't get them started on the one-sided media.*
>
> *And they are now witnessing unequal treatment in special counsel Robert Mueller's probe. Yes, the former FBI director deserves credit for smoking out the Russian trolls who interfered in 2016. And one can argue he is obliged to pursue any evidence of criminal acts, even those unrelated to Russia. But what cannot be justified is the one-sided nature of his probe....*
>
> *If there is only "one set of rules," where is Mr. Mueller's referral of a case against Hillary for America? Federal law requires campaigns to disclose the recipient and purpose of any payments. The Clinton campaign paid Fusion GPS to compile a dossier against Mr. Trump, a document that became the basis*

*of the Russia narrative Mr. Mueller now investigates. But the
campaign funneled the money to law firm Perkins Coie, which
in turn paid Fusion. The campaign falsely described the money
as payment for "legal services." The Democratic National
Committee did the same. A Perkins Coie spokesperson has
claimed that neither the Clinton campaign nor the DNC was
aware that Fusion GPS had been hired to conduct the research,
and maybe so. But a lot of lawyers here seemed to have been
ignoring a clear statute, presumably with the intent of influenc-
ing an election.*

As it happens, courtesy of California Democratic senator Dianne
Feinstein, yet another perfect illustration of the Old Order game has come
to light. It seems Feinstein, unawares, had a staff member who was a spy for
the Chinese government. The FBI learned of this—and went straight to the
senator with the news. She promptly fired the staffer.

Here is South Carolina senator Lindsey Graham, writing directly to FBI
director Christopher Wray, highlighting this story of an Old Order double
standard:

*Although I appreciate the FBI's diligence in identifying the
staffer with potential ties to the Chinese government and providing Senator Feinstein with a defensive briefing, I am deeply
troubled that the Trump Campaign was not afforded the same
treatment when the FBI began to suspect that campaign staffers
George Papadopoulos, Carter Page, Michael Flynn, and Paul
Manafort had improper ties to the Russian government.*

*It appears that rather than provide then-candidate Donald
Trump or Trump Campaign officials with a defensive briefing
to inform them of the FBI's concerns, the Bureau opted to use a
confidential informant and a dossier funded by the Democratic
National Committee to launch an unprecedented counterintelligence investigation into the Trump Campaign.*

What Graham was spotlighting is exactly the Old Order mindset at
work. Feinstein has served in the United States Senate for over a quarter of a
century. She is the very embodiment of the Old Order. So, of course, the FBI

went straight to her to let her know they think she has a problem. But Trump? No briefing for him about possible Russian moves to infiltrate his campaign. None. Instead the FBI leadership did the opposite. Instead they looked for ways to sabotage, undermine, and deceive Trump's campaign—working with the Clinton campaign to do it.

Why? Rush Limbaugh said it well the week of the Manafort-Cohen news. The target from the get-go was Donald Trump, solely because he was an outsider who posed a serious threat to the Old Order elites who rule the Swamp. Said Limbaugh of the targeting of Trump:

> "But they're gonna stop at nothing to get the guy. And they'll stop at nothing at ruining him, folks.
>
> "I think this is what people need to understand. We're up against people, Donald Trump represents [the] clearest, gravest threat to their way of life that they have ever seen, including the Soviets, including the Chicoms, including 9/11. These people feel frightened, more frightened and more on edge with Donald Trump being elected to president than they ever felt during or after 9/11.
>
> "And I am not making this up.
>
> "Donald Trump represents the gravest threat to their lifestyle, to their careers, to their standing, to their daily contentment and happiness, the greatest threat they've ever faced. He is specifically what they despise. He is specifically what they have arranged. I mean, these people in the Washington establishment thought they had it all taken care of, that Trump could not happen, that an outsider knowing so little about how Washington works and using so few people and resources from inside the Beltway, no way could anybody ever beat them. They thought that they had a closed system that nobody could infiltrate, that nobody could come in and win.
>
> "It's just like the NFL owners. The NFL owners and the people that financed them and all this, they've got a system, and there's no way somebody they don't want is gonna end up in the NFL. It's the same thing with any highfalutin club. One of the first things they do is to take steps to make sure that people they

do not want in do not get in. And they try to handle every quirk they can imagine.

"They never dreamed Donald Trump would run for president. Well, they might have dreamed it, but they never thought it'd be real. They always thought it'd be a publicity stunt. They never thought he would win. The fact that he did and upended somebody they think could not lose.... They haven't been normal since. They haven't been of sound mind since. They have been singularly focused on taking care of this threat.

"This is no different than having something that can literally destroy you find its way into your house. You would stop everything to get it out. I don't care what it is. If it was a sand flea, if a giant bear found its way into your house, you would. And if you can't leave—I mean, these people can't leave the establishment. They've got to stay there. They have got to get rid of whatever gets in there. And that's what's going on.

"And if they have to destroy his business, if they have to destroy his family, individually, if they have to destroy him, they will do it, and they will not give it a second thought. Self-preservation, number one. Number two, making sure that nobody else ever tries it."

Limbaugh was spot-on. From one Swamp War to another, the topics can and do change. But the constant is that the Old Order way of doing business is under assault by Trump and his new populist supporters. "This is the way it has always been done" is now a completely unsatisfactory way of running the government in the Trump era—not to mention in American society at large.

* * * * *

Call it the blue trickle.

In spite of repeated predictions that a "blue wave" of anti-Trumpism was going to sweep away the Republican House and Senate in the 2018 midterm elections, in the end the blue wave never materialized. To understand how badly the anti-Trumpers and Never Trumpers failed, one only need look at the first midterm performance of Democratic presidents Obama and Clinton. Obama lost over sixty seats in the House, Clinton over fifty. Trump lost forty-one House seats. Yes, for sure the Trump loss was enough to swing control of the House to the Democrats, but not with a huge margin. Both Obama and Clinton lost Senate seats (six and eight, respectively) while under Trump, four Senate seats flipped from Democrat to Republican, and the Republicans held on to Senate control, something that has happened only four times in the seventy-three years since World War Two.

As Americans prepared to vote, south of the U.S. southern border, a caravan of thousands of migrants mysteriously formed and began marching towards the U.S.-Mexico border. Images of the constantly swelling crowd played out on television. At one point a group of young males was seen tearing down the gates that separated Guatemala from Mexico, with the crowd barging into Mexico past Mexican authorities. These images also energized the Trump base, with the president once again emphasizing illegal immigration as he relentlessly campaigned for one Senate Republican candidate after another.

The drama heightened when, out of the blue, mail bombs began appearing in the offices of Trump opponents, ranging from former presidents Obama and Clinton to various Democratic senators, members of Congress, and even CNN staffers. The sender, quickly identified, turned out to be a Trump supporter named Cesar Sayoc, a troubled man with a lengthy arrest record.

That incident was no sooner in the rearview mirror when a gun-toting, Trump-hating anti-Semite named Robert Bowers burst into a filled Pittsburgh synagogue and slaughtered eleven people, injuring others.

What was stunning if not surprising was that Swamp dwellers in the media and elsewhere instantly deflected blame from the alleged perpetrators to the president. CNN's president, Jeff Zucker, issued a statement in the wake of the mail bomb that showed up at the network's New York bureau. It included this:

> *There is a total and complete lack of understanding at the White House about the seriousness of their continued attacks on the media. The President, and especially the White House Press Secretary, should understand their words matter. Thus far, they have shown no comprehension of that.*

As I would write in a column for *NewsBusters*, effectively Zucker was saying that the shooting a year earlier of Trump-supporting Republican congressman Steve Scalise by a self-admitted fan of MSNBC's virulently anti-Trump host Rachel Maddow somehow had been a result of both Maddow's and her network's daily vitriolic attacks on the president. Not to mention that the shooter, James Hodgkinson, was also a staunch supporter of Vermont senator Bernie Sanders. Clearly only Hodgkinson was responsible for his actions, not the harsh anti-Trump words from Sanders, Maddow, and MSNBC. If, God forbid, some nut attacked the president or another Trump supporter like Congressman Scalise, should the anti-Trump CNN be blamed? Should Jeff Zucker be blamed? Of course not.

Interestingly, after the election CNN got itself into a free press spat with the White House after its White House correspondent Jim Acosta refused to yield the microphone at a presidential press conference. The White House was so irked that Acosta, having asked several questions, had appeared to push a young White House intern's hand away as she was trying to reclaim the microphone and give it to another reporter, that it promptly lifted Acosta's White House pass.

CNN, which had closed its eyes and looked the other way at all those Media Matters campaigns to take away the free press rights of conservatives on Fox and in talk radio, was now angrily demanding—in the name of the First Amendment—that Acosta get his pass back. No less than Fox News came to CNN's defense, issuing a statement that said:

"FOX News supports CNN in its legal effort to regain its White House reporter's press credential. We intend to file an amicus brief with the U.S. District Court. Secret Service passes for working White House journalists should never be weaponized. While we don't condone the growing antagonistic tone by both the President and the press at recent media avails, we do support a free press, access and open exchanges for the American people."

As interesting as this was, still later Media Matters launched another anti-free press campaign, this one targeting Tucker Carlson at Fox. In direct contrast with Fox, which had stood up for CNN's free press rights, CNN quickly abandoned Fox when the reverse was happening. CNN made a point of joining the anti-free press mob targeting Fox and Carlson. Anchors Don Lemon and Chris Cuomo took to the airwaves to attack not Media Matters—but Carlson. With Lemon saying that while he didn't believe people should be taken off the air for a "'one-off' comment" but it's different "when it's how you use your platform comprehensively, how you use it on an overall basis, on a general basis every single day." Which is another way of saying that if a conservative dares to disagree with the liberal agenda - not to mention do it effectively - they should be removed from the air. In a blink CNN was back to supporting the idea of selective press censorship—as long as the attack was not on CNN.

Donald Trump does not accept either the Old Order or its rules about what can and cannot be discussed in an open society. And for that, the Old Order and the denizens of its various Swamps cannot abide him. As this is being written, *The Washington Post* is reporting that a Swamp War has broken out at Lehigh University. The university gave Donald Trump an honorary degree in 1988. Now there is a move by faculty members to take back the degree. Reports the *Post*, "Nearly two-thirds of the university's faculty members on Tuesday approved a motion to revoke the president's honorary degree, saying statements he has made are 'inconsistent with the character and high standards expected of honorees.'"

Liberal sensibilities thus offended, authoritarian-style censorship is but of course the reflexive order of the day. Another Swamp War is launched.

But there is one bright light in the Swamp Wars—my old CNN friend Van Jones. He is a liberal's liberal, and we had become known for our televised sparring as 2016 unfolded. Off camera we had become fast friends. Notably, both of us were struggling with beloved aging moms suffering the ravages of dementia. The two moms passed away within months of each other in 2018, and we commiserated on a phone call. But when it came to waging a Swamp War on the president he opposed, Jones did something entirely different than most. He looked for an area of agreement—of common ground. And he found it, amazingly enough, in the issue of prison reform.

An issue that had ironically gone nowhere in the Obama years, it was described by no less than President Trump's son-in-law and senior White House aide Jared Kushner as "very close to my heart." As noted, Jared's dad, Charles Kushner, had served prison time for tax evasion. The personal experience had been searing, and now in the White House the new president himself made the issue of simple fairness in the criminal justice system a cause. There was a "summit" on the issue at the White House—and there was Van Jones sitting side by side with Jared Kushner as the president whom Jones had spent so much time opposing in 2016 joked: "He constantly says such nice things about me." The audience laughed.

Yet this was typical of both the president and Van, not to mention Jared Kushner. Focused on a real problem, they made solving it a common cause. Said Van on a panel he co-moderated with Kushner: "If we can't get together for liberty and justice for all, something's wrong with this country. We'll do something on this issue; we'll fight about everything else, but on this issue let's get together." They did, and in December Trump signed the bill—passed overwhelmingly by both the Republican House and Senate—into law. It was a bright moment of hope smack in the middle of the Swamp.

So where do the Swamp Wars stand at the start of the president's last two years of what he promises will be the first of two terms? The Swamp and its dwellers long ago declared war on this president—and those millions of Americans who support him. A caller to the Limbaugh show summed up exactly something that he thought the president should say on the stump:

> *"You sent me here to expose this corruption. I'm doing it. You sent me here to change the way Washington has normally been run. I'm doing it. They don't like it. They're attacking me, but I'm just the person that's here. They're not really attacking me; they're attacking you."*

The Limbaugh caller was right on the money. These Swamp Wars target the president—but they are in fact really about the middle class and working Americans who support him. They are truly seen inside the Swamp as being just as Hillary Clinton labeled them—"deplorables."

It is more than safe to say that the 2020 election will be the Swamp War of all Swamp Wars, a battle royal over exactly who will run America— Americans or the Swamp dwellers in Washington and around the country and the world who are fanatically devoted to keeping their power, privilege, and control over American culture and politics.

I asked the future president in 2014 what a leader was. He responded: "A leader is someone people follow, and the reason they follow is respect… and the primary way I have found over the years, and the easiest way, to get respect is to win."

Thus far, to the Swamp's Old Order fury and, safe to say, to the delight of his supporters—as evidenced in 2018 by the turnout in those now famous Trump rallies attended by tens of thousands of enthusiastic Americans— Donald Trump is winning the Swamp Wars.

Stay tuned.

* * * * *

Let's end by going back to this description of the French *ancien régime* from the British historian Simon Schama.

> *Virtually as soon as the term was coined, "old regime" was automatically freighted with associations of both traditionalism and senescence. It conjured up a society so encrusted with anachronisms that only a shock of great violence could free the living organism within. Institutionally torpid, economically immobile, culturally atrophied and socially stratified, this "old regime" was incapable of self-modernization.*

What America and the rest of the world are witnessing in the Trump election and the Trump presidency is nothing less than a revolt against the American *ancien régime*—an American Old Order. President Donald Trump is the elected "shock of great violence" whose task is to "free the living organism" of the American constitutional republic that has been trapped—encrusted—in a smothering, institutionally hostile American Old Order run by an arrogant elite that is "culturally atrophied and socially stratified" in a Swamp of special privilege. And these Swamps are located throughout the country and around the globe. Swamp Wars are the vividly visible evidence of just how deep and widespread this Old Order has become in American society across the board.

There is no length to which the Old Order's generals, lieutenants, and privates won't go to destroy this characteristically American revolution against Old Order tyranny until its targets, to quote Justice Thomas, "kowtow to an old order."

In the style of authoritarians throughout history, they will actively seek to stifle free speech and selectively silence their most potent opposition in a free press—while gaslighting Americans that it is the president and his supporters who are doing what they themselves are all about. They will demand special privileges—like the "right" to keep a security clearance after leaving government. They will use the legal system—beginning with a hyperpoliticized Department of Justice—to try to personally destroy not only the president, his family, and his famous business empire but his lawfully executed policies as president. And woe betide the Trump supporter in or out of the media who has the audacity to stand up and object to Old Order Swamp Wars. You can even be targeted for simply going out to dinner or a movie—as Trump-connected folks such as Senator Ted Cruz, Senator Mitch McConnell, Department of Homeland Security secretary Kirstjen Nielsen, and Florida Republican attorney general Pam Bondi have all discovered. Or, in my case, you can get knocked off CNN for mocking and condemning the anti-Semitism of the American left when it has been illustrated repeatedly.

To paraphrase, hell hath no fury like an Old Order scorned.

One verdict—but only one verdict—on the progress on the battlefields of the Swamp Wars will come in November 2020.

Buckle in.

And God bless America.

ACKNOWLEDGMENTS

Many thanks to my redoubtable agent, Alex Hoyt, whose persistence was essential. To David Bernstein and Heather King of Bombardier Books and Post Hill Press, your patience with a necessary delay was deeply appreciated. To Sean Hannity, Lynda McLaughlin, Mark Levin, and my American Spectator bosses and friends, R. Emmett Tyrrell, Jr. and Wlady Pleszczynski, for your encouragement and kindness in a difficult moment that will always be appreciated. And as always, to my wonderful extended family for your patience and understanding.